JUSTICE BEYOND OUR BORDERS

Judicial Reforms for Latin America and the Caribbean

Christina Biebesheimer
Francisco Mejía

Editors

Distributed by the Johns Hopkins University Press
for the Inter-American Development Bank

Washington, D.C.
2000

©2000 Inter-American Development Bank
1300 New York Avenue, N.W.
Washington, D.C. 20577

Produced by the IDB Publications Section

Distributed by the Johns Hopkins University Press
2715 North Charles Street
Baltimore, Maryland 21218-4319

To order this book, contact:

IDB Bookstore
Tel: (202) 623-1753
Fax: (202) 623-1709
E-mail: idb-books@iadb.org
www.iadb.org/pub

The views and opinions expressed in this publication are those of the authors and do not necessarily reflect the official positions of the Inter-American Development Bank.

**Cataloging-in-Publication data provided by the
Inter-American Development Bank
Felipe Herrera Library**

> Justice beyond our borders : judicial reforms for Latin America and the Caribbean / Christina Biebesheimer, Francisco Mejía, editors.
>
> p. cm.
> Includes bibliographical references.
> ISBN:1886938806
>
> 1. Justice, Administration of. 2. Justice, Administration of—Case studies. 3. Due process of law. 4. Legal aid. 5. Public defenders. I. Biebesheimer, Christina. II. Mejía, Francisco. III. Inter-American Development Bank.
>
> 347 J867—dc21   00-134612

Table of Contents

Chapter Three
Judicial Reform in the Basque Country: A Case Study 117
Juan Enrique Vargas Viancos

About the Authors

Christina Biebesheimer is Attorney and Senior Officer in the State and Civil Society Division of the Sustainable Development Department of the Inter-American Development Bank. She focuses on Bank policy, project formulation and training initiatives related to justice system reform and strengthening civil society and democratic institutions. Prior to joining the Bank, she worked in international corporate and banking law.

Carolyn Herzog is a corporate transactional attorney, managing contracts, export and intellectual property for AXENT Technologies, Inc., a multinational, publicly traded, information security software company. Prior to joining AXENT, Ms. Herzog worked as a Staff Attorney for the International Law Institute (ILI) where she developed and administered legal and economic reform training programs for participants from countries with transitioning economies. She was first introduced to the ILI while working for the World Bank.

John Linarelli is a Lecturer in Law at the University of Wales, Aberystwyth, in the United Kingdom. His research interests include the role of law and institutions in developing and transitioning economies. Mr. Linarelli has served as Senior Fellow of the International Law Institute (ILI) in Washington, D.C. He has also been an Adjunct Professor of Law at Georgetown University Law Center, a Lecturer at the Catholic University of America Columbus School of Law, and a Visiting Researcher at the Department of Economics of the University of California, Irvine.

Francisco Mejía is an Economist and Senior Officer in the State and Civil Society Programs Division of Regional Department 1 of the Inter-American Development Bank. His primary focus is on public sector reform projects involving the executive, judicial and legislative branches in Argentina, Brazil, Bolivia, Chile, Paraguay and Uruguay. Prior to joining the IDB, Mr. Mejia worked for over 12 years in research, public service and as a consultant for various governments and international agencies in Latin America and the Caribbean.

Robert J. Rhudy is Executive Director of the Legal Services Society of Maryland, which provides legal assistance to low-income people in civil cases. Mr. Rhudy is the founder and former president of the National Association of Interest on Lawyer Account Programs, Inc., which includes foundations that finance legal assistance and administration of justice projects. He has also consulted on the development of legal services by the American Bar Association, the National Legal Aid and Defender Association, the U.S. Legal Services Corporation, the Ford Foundation and the Micronesian Legal Services Corporation.

Juan Enrique Vargas Viancos is the Director of the Center of Juridical Investigations and professor of oral litigation at the undergraduate and post-graduate levels at the Diego Portales University in Chile. He has served as Director of the Center of Juridical Development, which supports judicial reform projects in Latin America, and as an advisor on judicial reform to the Chilean Ministry of Justice

Introduction

This book has its origin in the commitment of the Inter-American Development Bank to work with the countries of Latin America and the Caribbean to strengthen justice systems and the rule of law. The Bank has provided numerous grants and loans to support judicial reform and modernization. The projects are designed to address each country's specific conditions. The aim is to confront such challenges as fragile judicial independence; court congestion and delays; barriers to access to justice; weak human rights protection; out-of-date organizational and institutional frameworks; lack of modern information and managerial systems; poor human resource management and judicial training; and spiraling violence and concerns for public safety.

The consolidation of democracy and the efficient and equitable functioning of a market economy require establishing the rule of law—that is, modern and transparent laws and a strong, impartial, independent, efficient and easily accessible justice system to enforce those laws. Nearly all of the countries of Latin America are engaged in the process of reforming and modernizing their justice systems.

In 1997, the IDB joined the U. S. Agency for International Development and the National Center for State Courts to sponsor a Second Judicial Reform Roundtable to examine best practices in justice reform in Latin America and the Caribbean. Roundtable participants—many of them judges, prosecutors, ministers of justice and academics from the region—noted that although information-sharing within the region has increased, those working on justice reform in Latin America have relatively little information regarding what is happening in that field in other parts of the world. To enrich the options for the Latin American countries working on justice reform, the Bank then hired experts to study reform processes around the world. Their findings are presented in this publication.

The objective, then, is to examine justice reform efforts that have been successful outside of Latin America and the Caribbean—that is, *Beyond Our Borders*. The aim is to look not only at what is working in other places, but also at what may be appropriate for the reform process in the region. We believe that this expands our understanding of what can be useful, sensible and successful in justice reform, and educates us as to what might be necessary to adapt solutions that have worked in other countries to the Latin American context.

In Chapter One, authors John Linarelli and Carolyn Herzog of the International Law Institute (ILI) review model practices in judicial reform from around the world in areas as diverse as case tracking and judicial management, procedural reform in civil and criminal matters, and court and non-court based alternative dispute resolution systems. Many of these practices may be particularly attractive for implementation in Latin America because they do not require significant financial resources or the enactment of difficult new legislation. Some in fact require only the willingness and determination of judges to implement the changes, as in the example of case management practices in the U.S. District Court for the Eastern District of Virginia.

Chapter One shows that whether in the United States or as far away as Egypt or Singapore, reforming the administration of justice is a great challenge, regardless of the type of justice system that is used. The chapter also points out that effective judicial reform and court management can bridge what has traditionally been viewed as a divide between civil and common law systems—that is, lessons learned under one system can be very usefully applied in the other. For example, the general trend to give judges and the courts more control in case processing, as illustrated in Lord Woolfe's recommendations for the United Kingdom's common law system, owes its origin in part to practices of judges in the civil law system. These in turn borrow increasingly from lessons from the common law systems in terms of modernizing civil law case management.

In Chapter Two, Robert J. Rhudy of the Maryland Legal Services Corporation analyzes a broad range of models for structuring and financing legal aid and access to justice programs. He then discusses the conditions under which these models could be applied in Latin America. In addition to laying out the strengths and weaknesses of a variety of service delivery and financing models, Rhudy shows how mixes of these models are actually functioning. Four case studies are presented: two in Canada (Quebec and Ontario), one in the Netherlands, and one in Arizona in the United States. Rhudy emphasizes the conditions and requirements needed for successful implementation of legal aid and access to justice programs, as well as the necessity for clear and transparent performance evaluation systems.

Chapter Three presents an in-depth case study of a comprehensive judicial reform effort undertaken over the last decade by the Basque government in the north of Spain. The author, Juan Enrique Vargas Viancos, provides a detailed account of this complex process, the nature of the changes enacted and implemented, the conditions under which they were undertaken, and the outcomes and results of the process. Vargas concludes that the reform process in the Basque Country could be adapted to Latin America. In many cases, this could bring about complex changes, improve service, and achieve significant reforms without changing laws.

Vargas points out that the key to successful reform, at least in the Basque experience, rests more on the strategic direction of the reform effort than on the specific content of individual initiatives. He emphasizes the importance of maintaining a long-term vision; having clear leadership committed to change; creating a broad based and multidisciplinary team capable of implementing change; generating short-term wins; being flexible without losing sight of the goals; involving critical stakeholders such as judges and lawyers in the reform process; and effectively managing incentives for change.

The case studies and other examples presented in the book do not constitute a recipe for change that can be literally transplanted without proper consideration for distinct regional, national and local circumstances. Nevertheless, we expect and hope that the cases will provide useful references, expand the universe of opportunities for change, and increase knowledge about the challenges of justice reform in diverse environments.

This book does not argue the case for investing in the rule of law. It is written for those already persuaded that development of the rule of law is important in the short term and critical for long-term development of Latin America. The book is intended for the practitioner and written for those working on justice reform and in need of better tools with which to do it. The hope is that describing successful justice reforms from around the world will shed additional light on how to achieve similar success in Latin America.

**Christina Biebesheimer and
Francisco Mejía, Editors**

CHAPTER ONE

MODEL PRACTICES IN JUDICIAL REFORM: A REPORT ON EXPERIENCES OUTSIDE THE REGION

*John Linarelli and Carolyn Herzog**

This chapter presents an overview of judicial reforms outside of Latin America and the Caribbean that have potential application to courts and judicial systems in the region. While the countries within Latin America have shared information on judicial reform, experiences worldwide are not as well known to those working in the field in the region. The objective is, then, to support the development and expansion of reform initiatives for justice systems in the region by identifying model practices in key areas of judicial reform. The chapter reviews reform efforts that have been successful and examines which reforms could best be incorporated into project design in Latin America.

The International Law Institute (ILI) has identified the following for consideration as model practices:

1) Differentiated case tracking as a form of case management, as developed by Lord Woolf in the United Kingdom and as used in other jurisdictions. This reform plan was designed to wrest control of the resources of the judiciary from litigation counsel and reallocate control to the courts. Case tracking provides courts with the ability to control the pace and scope of civil proceedings.

2) Case management tools other than tracking, such as the use of preliminary and pre-trial hearings and protocols, scheduling orders, active case management by judges, use of case managers and judicially-based mediation, and the use of summary procedures. These tools are in use or are being considered in many jurisdictions, including Australia, Egypt, Finland, Singapore, Japan and the United States.

---

* The authors prepared this chapter as staff members of the International Law Institute.

3) Development of public interest litigation, as has been done in India. This recommendation is made with some reservation, however, because of its potential disadvantages and deleterious effects.

4) The streamlining of appeals and the implementation of review on appeal rather than an entire rehearing of the case. Spain has passed legislation to limit appeals in this manner.

5) Alternative forms of dispute resolution, in particular the use of the mini-trial, and the potential use of judges in the facilitation of settlement.

6) Criminal procedure reforms in Italy that have promoted a model of procedural justice, including improved preliminary hearings, the requirement that attorneys take the lead in presenting both oral and written evidence in criminal trials, expedited procedures for certain crimes, limited forms of plea bargaining, and the use of summary trials. Italy initiated this major reform in order to alleviate significant case backlogs and delays that were plaguing its system of criminal justice.

7) The use of a conflict resolution board to provide community treatment for minor juvenile offenses in Norway. Diversion of certain types of juvenile offenses from the formal criminal justice system to informal methods of justice appears to be a global trend.

8) The improvement of victim participation rights in criminal justice, as practiced in Germany and Belgium.

9) The specialization of courts and procedures to handle the growing complexity of cases. The use of commercial courts, for example, is a prevalent trend that may improve the environment for foreign investment. Other specialized courts may cover non-commercial issues such as civil and criminal matters involving children.

10) Models for the funding of legal aid in order to improve access to justice, particularly for persons of limited financial means. There are various options to fund legal aid for both civil and criminal cases.[1]

11) Reform of the judicial appointment system in Spain in order to open and diversify the career track for judges, among other improvements. The reforms include recruitment of practicing attorneys.

While this chapter aims to help Latin American countries looking outside the region for ideas for judicial reform, it is intended neither to provide models to be transplanted wholesale nor to impose any "recipes" for judicial reform. The practices described here are recommended only for further study. Their actual use would require adaptation to the realities of the legal system and professional legal culture of the country looking to undertake reforms (Linarelli, 1996).

---

[1] See Chapter Two for a detailed discussion and evaluation of options for funding and structuring legal aid programs.

In addition to extensive bibliographical and documentary research, this chapter is based on interviews with experts on judicial reform working in development institutions, embassies and research centers. It also uses data gathered from questionnaires sent to constitutional courts, ministries of justice, attorney generals and other justice system institutions in 43 countries.

We have conducted this study based on the assumptions that Latin America judiciaries may have scarce resources and would prefer to optimize the use of existing resources. Therefore, the focus is not on hardware innovations or informatics solutions. For example, we do not cover electronic data issues, although many judicial systems have planned or implemented reforms in this area. Some computerization would be prudent, however, to measure court performance before and after reform, particularly when case management techniques are adopted. It may be that existing computer equipment could be optimized to meet the increased needs that come from caseflow management.

MODEL PRACTICES IN CIVIL JUSTICE

Differentiated Case Tracking

A prevalent practice and growing trend is the development and implementation by courts of case management systems. Under these systems, the court takes an active role in the scheduling and timing of important events in the case. This case management system is different from the traditional method of judicial involvement in fact-finding generally found in civil systems. The concept of case management can include a number of features, most prominent among them identification by the court of the issues in the case, summary disposition of some issues, scheduling of important steps in the case, issuance of scheduling orders, setting of conferences between the parties and sometimes the court, and the delimitation of disclosures to one another by the disputing parties.

A particularly popular practice in case management is the scheduling and control of cases through case tracking. Armstrong (1995) states that "tracking is based on the idea that different cases should be treated differently," while Zuckerman (1995) adds that "Cadillac-style procedures are not needed to process bicycle-size lawsuits."

Tracking promotes the efficient use of scarce resources in a judicial system. Parties to litigation do not internalize the costs of the court in their consumption of judicial resources, and parties to court proceedings do not (at least directly) bear the costs of the judiciary and its administration. The result is that parties have no incentive to use court resources efficiently. Tracking in essence makes the court a "party" to the litigation so that its scarce resources will not be demanded as free goods by the litigants.

Tracking also promotes settlement of cases. Its primary focus is in moving cases along toward disposition by either court decision or settlement. As explained by Lord Woolf (1996) in his report on the British judicial system:

> Case management for the purposes of this report involves the court taking the ultimate responsibility for progressing litigation along a chosen track for a predetermined period during which it is subjected to selected procedures which culminate in an appropriate form of resolution before a suitably experienced judge. Its overall purpose is to encourage settlement of disputes at the earliest appropriate stage; and, where trial is unavoidable, to ensure that cases proceed as quickly as possible to a final hearing which is itself of strictly limited duration.

Tracking should be distinguished from the legislation of deadlines or waiting periods. Legislated deadlines may be a necessary but not sufficient condition for court reform. Procedures that are proposed and implemented by the courts themselves may be more effective in mitigating judicial delay (How, 1996).

The sections that follow are descriptions of two case tracking systems. One is found in judicial reform in the United Kingdom, as reflected in the Woolf Report recommendations to improve that nation's judiciary. The second is the system of case tracking used in Australia. Other variations of the case management system can be found in Singapore and in various jurisdictions of the United States.

The nature of case management is the introduction of the judge and the court into the management of the litigation and control of the pace of the proceedings. This concept is not new to civil law systems. It is new, however, to common law systems, and this is the likely reason why innovations in case management systems are principally found there. There are notable differences, moreover, in the case tracking method and the traditional concept of controlling proceedings that exists in civilian systems. Case tracking may be transplantable to civil law courts, where, in some jurisdictions, actors in the judicial process (judges, lawyers and parties) complain of case backlog and delay. Case tracking can be viewed both as a contemporary practice in judicial control of proceedings and as evidence of a convergence in styles of judicial decisionmaking (Lindblom and Watson, 1992).

Case Tracking in the United Kingdom

One of the most important recommendations in the Woolf Report is that there be "a fundamental transfer in the responsibility for management of civil litigation from litigants and their legal advisors to the courts." Lord Woolf proposed a three-tier system: first, an increased small claim jurisdiction; second, a fast track for simple cases and those seeking relatively modest recoveries; and third, a multi-track system for remaining cases. A more detailed review of the tracking system proposed by Lord Woolf follows below.

The Use of a Procedural Judge

A procedural judge would examine all cases in which there has been a response by the defendant. This judge then assigns the case to the appropriate track. The procedural judge cannot subsequently be assigned to the case once it is placed in a track. All cases would be examined by a master or district judge after a defense is filed with the court.

For the fast track, the work of the parties and the court for allocation of a case to tracking can be done in writing, with no need for a hearing. The parties provide information to the court by completing questionnaires provided by the court. A trial date would be set during the tracking procedure. In placing a case on the fast track, the procedural judge would designate a week for the trial, establish a timetable for the case, and otherwise provide directions for the case.

For the multi-track, the judge can schedule a case management conference, issue written orders for case management, fix a trial date, and engage in other case management functions. Case management is usually carried out during a minimum of two interlocutory management hearings. The first hearing is a case management conference, usually conducted by the procedural judge and held soon after the defendant files his or her statement of defense. The second hearing is a pre-trial hearing, usually conducted by the trial judge.

With respect to the case management conference:

> The objective…is to set the agenda for the case before significant costs have been incurred and too much time has elapsed. At a case management conference the procedural judge will narrow the issues, decide on the appropriate future work and case management required, and set a trial date and a timetable for the case and consider ADR [alternative dispute resolution] and the question of costs. (Woolf, 1996)

The Fast Track

A fast track is established for cases with a value not exceeding £ 10,000. It has a timetable of 20 to 30 weeks, limited discovery, a trial of not more than three hours, and no expert testimony. Costs for these cases will be fixed.

The fast track proposal in the United Kingdom is based on practices in place in Canada and the United States. The features peculiar to common law procedure, such as discovery, can be modified or eliminated to suit civil law systems.

The fast track will not be used for a case otherwise qualified for it if the case

1) raises issues of public importance; 2) is a test case; 3) requires oral testimony from experts; 4) requires significant oral argument or evidence; or 5) requires substantial documentary evidence.

One of the remarkable features of the practices advocated by Lord Woolf is the establishment of fixed costs for fast track cases. In the United Kingdom, the losing party in a civil proceeding pays his or her opponent's costs. In the fast track system, there is a standard system of fixed costs so that each party will know their cost exposure at the initiation of the proceeding. The maximum legal costs for a fast track case is estimated at £ 2,500, excluding VAT and disbursements. A num ber of detailed guidelines apply to the fixing of costs in fast track cases.

The Multi-Track

The procedural judge determines whether a case belongs in the multi-track system. As explained by Lord Woolf:

> The multi-track will include a wide range of cases, from straightforward cases just above the fast track limit to the most complex and weighty matters involving claims for millions of pounds and multi-party actions with many claimants. Case management will reflect this. The central principle is that the court will manage every case, but the type of management will vary according to the needs of the case. In broad terms, this means that simpler cases will need less of a hands-on approach by the courts and more complex cases will require greater judicial involvement. (Woolf, 1996)

Two requirements of the case management conference and pre-trial review in the multi-track are that the parties:

1) Provide estimates of the amount of costs they have incurred and expect to incur in connection with the case; and

2) State whether they have discussed alternative dispute resolution (ADR), and, if not, explain their reasons for not having done so. Moreover, in deciding on the future conduct of the case, the judge may take into account unreasonable refusals to attempt ADR. "Where a party has refused unreasonably a proposal by the court that ADR should be attempted, or has acted uncooperatively in the course of ADR, the court should be able to take that into account in deciding what order to make as to costs" (Woolf, 1996). The promotion of ADR is clear and unmistakable in the Woolf Report.

Cases in the multi-track system must adhere to a timetable fixed by the court. The parties are unable to change the major hearing dates without court permission.

The Woolf Report recommends streamlined procedures for all cases, particu-

larly for small medical negligence claims, Crown Office cases, and intellectual property cases where there is a substantial disparity in the financial means of the parties.
Some cases will be decided on the basis of written statements, without the need for
oral hearings.

Sanctions

The Woolf Report recommends an elaborate system of sanctions to ensure that the
bar complies with case management procedures. Some of the more notable features are:

1) Orders that require the parties to take actions within certain deadlines
should include an automatic sanction for noncompliance, although the sanctioned
party can apply for relief. "The onus should be on the party in default to seek relief
from a sanction, not on the other party to apply to enforce the sanction" (Woolf,
1996).[2]

2) "The court should intervene and impose sanctions on parties who conduct
litigation in an unreasonable or oppressive manner even if they have not breached
specific rules, orders or directions" (Woolf, 1996).

Assessment

The Woolf Report proposes important reforms that will significantly change the
conduct of civil proceedings in the United Kingdom. Many appear to have been
transplanted from other legal systems. For example, a successful differentiated case
tracking system can be found in the Fairfax County Circuit Court, a major metropolitan trial court of general jurisdiction in Virginia in the United States. Other U.S.
courts practice tracking with varying levels of success. Tracking is also used in Canadian and Australian courts.

The Woolf Report sharply criticizes the adversarial system, and particularly
the ability of the parties to control the pace of litigation. It thus supports management of litigation by courts, recommending a "fundamental shift in the responsibility for the management of civil litigation" and a "radical change of culture for all
concerned" (Woolf, 1996). Some British legal professionals have expressed concern that Lord Woolf's recommendations promote a civil law "inquisitorial" system
(Jolowicz, 1996). Lord Woolf's response is that "the legal profession will...be performing its traditional adversarial role in a managed environment governed by the
courts and by the rules which will focus effort on the key issues rather than on
allowing every issue to be pursued regardless of expense and time..." (Woolf, 1996).

---

[2] It would be instructive for this approach to be compared to Rule 37 of the U.S. Federal Rules of Civil
Procedure, which is widely perceived to have failed in controlling abuse of discovery procedures.

The labels "inquisitorial" or "adversarial" in our view are not helpful. The nature of case management in the tracking system advocated by Lord Woolf is very different from traditional case management by civil judges. The actual character of proceedings in civil law countries is often highly adversarial. The focus here is on the actual functions of courts in proceedings, rather than on shorthand descriptions. There is no fundamental change in the adversarial character of common law (or any other) litigation in the use of tracking as a means of case management.

Moreover, we are not convinced that tracking in all cases controls excessive adversarial tactics. The lawyers may simply be adversarial within the deadlines of the case tracking system. In fact, a case tracking system that pushes cases too fast could deter settlement, in that the court's expedited deadlines may increase the range of settlement values as the parties focus their attention on the proceeding rather than on negotiated resolution of their dispute (Williams and Williams, 1994). Parties may harden their positions when they are aware that the court will render a quick decision.

Australia

Australia has developed various ways to deal with case flow management, including two models identified by Justice David Ipp of the Supreme Court of Western Australia:

1) Management involving continuous control by a judge, who personally monitors each case ad hoc. A judge is assigned at the beginning of the case and remains with it until its conclusion. This is referred to as the "individual list" method of case management.

2) Management through routine and structured control by the court, in which the court receives information through required reporting by the parties to the court at fixed deadlines. Cases are managed by being assigned to procedural judges or other judicial personnel at different times and stages of the litigation. This "master list" method of case management is the most prevalent in Australia, although the federal judiciary is considering adoption of an individual list system.

The tracking practices used in Australia are described below.

Differentiated Case Tracking in Family Courts

The Family Court in Australia has been an innovator in case management practices since it instituted its first set of procedures in 1985. The court takes responsibility for the pace of its proceedings through a differentiated case management system that assigns cases to tracks or to a summary hearing procedure.

A judge administrator in each region of the Family Court is responsible for maintaining listing systems and appointing a case management judge. That judge in turn appoints on a rotating basis specific list judges who take on the actual supervision of cases. The case management judge also serves as or appoints a complex case judge to manage the tracking of difficult cases.

Each case in which a defense has been filed is assigned to a track at what is called a directions hearing, usually before a registrar. A directions hearing is to be held not later than six weeks after commencement of the action. During the assignment of tracking, the court assesses whether conciliation would be appropriate, and whether a pre-hearing conference is necessary.

The tracking scheme in the Family Court is as follows:

1) *The direct track* is for matters involving narrow and simple issues, and where the hearing on the merits should last no more than one day. Matters involving property issues require careful attention to determine whether they can be resolved in the direct track. The court determines whether requirements for conciliation or pre-hearing conferences could be eliminated in order to determine a hearing date. The court issues orders concerning presentation of evidence by the parties.

2) *The standard track* is the residual track for matters that cannot be disposed of summarily or that should not be placed on the direct or complex tracks. The cases tend to be those that involve property or children and that will take more than one day but no more than five days of hearing time. There may be special cases that can fit within the standard track but which nevertheless warrant individual case management by the same judge. These cases tend to involve multiple hearings, complex issues or social dynamics. Courts have the discretion to deal with these cases differently but keep them in the standard track.

3) *The complex track* is for difficult matters that will require six or more days of hearing time. These cases are subject to individual case management by a judge assigned for the duration of the case.

The Family Court encourages conciliation and ADR, where appropriate. ADR is integrated into the track system. Pursuant to legislation governing the court's proceedings, the court encourages ADR at fixed points in the tracking process.

Case Management Other than Tracking

While countries such as the United Kingdom have developed tracking systems, judiciaries in several other countries have implemented procedures and practices that do not rely on tracking as a principal means of case management. This reflects a growing trend in response to greater complexity in litigation, improved understanding of the economics of judiciaries and litigation, technological advances in courts, and increases in the amount of litigation (or demand for judiciary services).

The various practices and procedures examined here are designed to dismiss clearly nonmeritorious or ineligible cases, resolve cases in a manner appropriate to its nature (simple cases, for example, can be disposed of more rapidly with less procedure), push the parties toward disposition of the case by a certain date, evaluate whether other methods of dispute resolution would better serve the parties, and schedule various stages of the proceeding that will involve judicial resources. These procedures may be combined with an approach to adjudicating cases that brings together different styles. In common law systems, "litigation is moving towards the non-adversarial practice of discontinuous trials" (Australian Law Reform Commission, 1996). In civil law systems, there is significant movement toward a concentrated trial with greater emphasis on oral presentation of evidence.

The law and economics literature on sequential versus unitary trials does not reflect a consensus on the economic efficiency of procedures that reveal information in stages. An influential work by Landes (1993) states:

> In a variety of instances, a sequential trial lowers the expected cost of litigation compared to a unitary trial for both the plaintiff and defendant because it holds out the prospect of avoiding litigation on subsequent issues if the defendant wins the current issue or the parties settle the remaining issues after the current one is decided. Consequently, a sequential trial (a) increases the plaintiff's incentive to sue, (b) increases the number of lawsuits, and (c) reduces the likelihood that the parties will settle out of court by narrowing the range of mutually acceptable settlements. Hence, sequential decision-making may increase the aggregate cost of litigation even though it lowers the expected cost of litigating (as opposed to settling) a particular dispute.[3]

Others have challenged Landes' approach on the basis of information economics and game theory models (Chen et al., 1997). The Landes approach, moreover, does not appear to take into account the social costs of the court system itself that are incurred in any court proceeding, perhaps because the parties do not internalize these costs. The costs borne by the judiciary do not enter into the incentives that apply to the parties. Landes' approach, although not expressly applied to civil law systems, has rich implications for their reform, but there is no one economic model that can be used to assess judicial reform.

---

[3] Landes uses the term "sequential" to refer to "separate trials on two or more dispositive issues" and "unitary" to refer to "a trial in which all issues are presented before deciding the case."

The Australian Federal Courts

The federal courts in Australia do not practice any systematic or general form of tracking that applies to all of the courts. There are a number of judicial events, however, that form the basis for managed litigation. The federal courts use a "directions hearing" as the primary vehicle for supervising civil cases. As explained in the Federal Court of Australia's Annual Report for 1994-95:

> When an initiating document is filed, matters...are given a return date for directions before a single judge. At directions hearings the judge gives whatever directions are necessary to assist the parties to identify the relevant issues. The judge also makes the necessary orders for the progress of a case to trial, such as orders for particulars and discovery. A case is adjourned to a fixed date by which parties are expected to have completed any interlocutory steps, which have been ordered. When a judge is satisfied the case is ready for trial, a trial date is fixed according to the availability of the parties, counsel and witnesses.

Directions hearings are addressed in Order 10 of the Federal Court Rules of Australia, which provides the courts with broad powers to manage litigation (see Appendix 1.1). An example of how federal courts use the order is set forth in *TPC v. Rank Commercial Ltd.,* 53 F.C.R. 303 (1994). In *Rank Commercial,* the defendants argued on appeal that the trial court was in error in making an expedited timetable for the preparation of evidence so that the court could decide the case within about two months. The case involved a petition for an injunction of a takeover bid, a matter of urgency. The trial judge issued directions to accomplish a quick trial within the time period of an injunction. The directions included dispensing with discovery and exchanging witness statements and expert reports. On appeal, the appellants argued "that there was no basis for a finding that the proceeding could be finally disposed of within two months, that the expedited timetable allowed insufficient time for the preparation of the case for trial and that the expedited timetable created a risk that the determination by the trial judge would be founded on insufficient and inadequate evidence."[4]

The appellate court upheld the trial court's rulings, explaining that "experience shows...that the time taken for the resolution of civil proceedings can be substantially reduced by proper case management," and that "without compromising the rights of the parties to a fair hearing of their case, much saving of time can be achieved through case management, especially if, as is to be expected, counsel

---

[4] *Rank Commercial,* 53 F.C.R.: 315.

and solicitors for the parties co-operate fully in the process."[5] *Rank Commercial* provides a signal to the bar as to the approach that the Australian federal judiciary will take towards case management.

In addition to directions hearings, the Australian federal courts use listing and pre-trial settlement conferences. These conferences are intended to satisfy the court that the parties have paid attention to the possibility of settlement and to streamline the issues to be decided by the court. Case management conferences are also used to determine the most efficient way to bring a case to trial.[6]

The "Rocket Docket" in the United States

As measured by the number and complexity of civil cases, the U.S. District Court for the Eastern District of Virginia has a heavier caseload than the national average for federal courts. The court is also "one of the most efficient and effective federal courts in the nation" (Dayton, 1992). Although the court has a substantial caseload, case management statistics show that it has significantly shorter disposition rates for civil cases that the national average. On average, civil cases brought before it are set for trial no later than six months after the filing of the case, and most cases are tried approximately four to five months after filing. Decisions in civil cases before the Alexandria Division of the court are often rendered within about three months of the joining of issue in a case (which, in the U.S. system, would occur with the filing of an answer by the defendant).

The court's success in case management is not due to tracking, alternative methods of dispute resolution or other new methods of case management. Rather, the court and its judges are committed to active case management, and the bar respects the rules and orders laid down by the court. The court controls its docket through the use of a standard scheduling order and through local rules that supplement the U.S. Federal Rules of Civil Procedure. The court's power to use such locally based tools is found in Rule 16 of the Federal Rules of Civil Procedure (see Appendix 1.2).

The Alexandria Division uses a master docket system, which means that cases are not assigned to particular judges, but that different judges handle matters within a case on a rotational basis. The principal features of the procedures that control civil cases are:

1) In the U.S. federal courts, a case is commenced with the filing of a complaint. Upon the filing of a complaint, the case is placed on the master docket of the division. The clerk's office reviews the docket monthly. The clerk monitors

---

[5] Ibid.: 316-17.
[6] Various other reforms are being considered in Australia, including the use of individual case management and some changes to conferences used by the courts.

cases to identify when the pleading stages have concluded and issue is joined (Dayton, 1992).

2) Once all pleadings have been filed, the chief judge enters a scheduling order (see Appendix 1.3). The order sets pretrial conference dates and a deadline for the completion of discovery and pretrial conference dates. It requires that motions be filed in sufficient time for their hearing before the final pretrial conference. All motions must be heard to obtain a ruling and must be scheduled no later than the Friday before the pretrial conference. The final pretrial conference is usually set two to three months after the filing of the suit, and the discovery cutoff is set for the Friday before the pre-trial conference. The order advises parties that the judge presiding at the pretrial conference will set a trial date for three to eight weeks after the conference. Counsel thus must be in a position to go to trial as early as three weeks after the pretrial conference.

3) Fridays are reserved for motions scheduled by the clerk of the court upon request of parties. The requirement that all motions be heard no later than the Friday before the pretrial conference is significant. In U.S. federal litigation, there are a variety of motions that can be filed after the parties have joined issue, such as summary judgment motions and motions concerning discovery. The court will not hear untimely motions.

Local Rule 11 of the court requires that motions be in writing, and prohibits the use of form motions unless irrelevant material is deleted. Pursuant to Local Rule 11, an attorney filing a motion must certify that "he or she has carefully reviewed the remaining portions of the motion and in good faith believes that the contents are pertinent to the case." The local rules provide for tight briefing schedules for motions. To promote settlement of disputes, Local Rule 11 provides that "before endeavoring to secure an appointment for a hearing on any motion, it shall be incumbent upon the party desiring such hearing to meet and confer in person or by telephone with his or her adversary in a good-faith effort to narrow the area of disagreement."

The court pushes counsel hard to avoid delay. Local Rule 11 (J) explicitly provides that "any requests for an extension of time relating to motions must be in writing and, in general, will be looked upon with disfavor." The court and counsel take case efficiency very seriously and lawyers rarely seek extensions. The environment of the court is such that extensions are considered inappropriate except in rare cases.

4) The court's approach to managing the discovery process illustrates its management approach and has been influential in controlling delay and expense in litigation before the court. Local rules limit interrogatories in a civil case to 30 for each party, including subparts, and limit the number of non-party depositions to five. Even some administrative boards within the executive branch of the U.S. government allow more liberal discovery. In addition, local rules require that any objections to requests for discovery be filled within 15 days after service of the discov-

ery request. Court rulings on discovery must be complied with within 11 days. Parties may not extend the time limits for discovery, as set forth in the local rules and the scheduling order, without the court's express permission, which is rarely given. As a condition for the court considering a motion, counsel must provide a statement accompanying the motion that it has complied with the meet-and-confer requirement. The court has not hesitated to impose sanctions on lawyers who fail to comply with its rules and orders.

5) Attorneys are required to meet prior to the pretrial conference to attempt to draft a stipulation of uncontested facts. Furthermore, attorneys must bring to the conference witness and exhibit lists, exhibits marked and ready for filing, and a written stipulation of uncontested facts. All evidentiary objections to exhibits must be made at the pretrial conference. The court will rule on these objections at trial. Trials are scheduled randomly with the judges in the division. In non-jury trials, lawyers are required to file written proposed findings of fact and conclusions of law in advance of the trial.

6) The roles of magistrate judges are probably as broad as permitted under federal law. Their civil duties include deciding discovery motions, handling pro se prisoner-related matters, hearing matters designated by the chief judge, and, in some instances, handling all matters in civil cases if so stipulated by the parties.

The Eastern District of Virginia provides an example of how a court can accomplish reform on its own initiative, without a legislative mandate and on the basis of existing powers granted by the legislature in federal statutes and existing rules of procedure. In the case of the Eastern District of Virginia, no new case management techniques were used. Rather, the court relied on existing resources to impose extensive judicial control over the points in civil proceedings that the court perceived as the causes of inefficiency and needless expense. As explained by Dayton (1992), "the district judges' firm commitment to fair and efficient case management and the bar's cooperation in this endeavor are the principal reasons that the Eastern District of Virginia has consistently maintained its status as the most efficient and effectively-managed federal district court in the nation…The clerk's offices in each division have worked to ensure that cases do not languish due to noncompliance with time deadlines imposed by statutes, court rules, or orders. The court will not tolerate dilatory tactics; attorneys who practice in the district understand this and comply with rule- and court-imposed deadlines. Judges and magistrate judges generally rule promptly on nondispositive and dispositive motions."

Finland

A growing trend is the adaptation of case management in civil law systems, but with more concentrated hearings and orality borrowed from common law systems. Germany undertook such a reform in 1977 to reduce its backlog of cases (Von

Mehren, 1988), while Finland legislated procedural reforms for its lower courts in 1993. Under these reforms, the Finnish system divides civil cases into two hearings: a preliminary hearing and a main "on-the-merits" hearing.

Ervo (1994) describes Finland's system prior to the reforms as follows:

> The main problem was the lack of preparation which litigants and lawyers perpetrated on the courts. Very frequently neither the facts nor the disputed points of law were known to anyone before the first court hearing. This, of course, was the cause of many adjournments. There tended to be many sessions before the court could render its judgement and it was also possible that the membership of the court might change in the meantime. Clearly, this was neither very rational nor any sort of guarantee of a fair judicial hearing.

In contrast, under the current Finnish system:

1) The plaintiff files a written summons with the court, which reviews it and, if it is allowed, sends it to the defendant for a response within a given time limit. The defendant is required to respond to the summons and set forth any counterclaims in his or her response. Under the previous system, summons and responses could be very general in nature. Also as a result of the reforms, litigants are required to make detailed proffers of evidence in the initial stages of the proceeding.

2) The preliminary hearing occurs after the filing of the summons. The possible alternatives for disposition are settlement, summary judgment, or a decision to hold a main hearing. The judge takes an activist role and can pressure litigants to settle or conciliate.

3) If the case is not disposed of in the preliminary hearing, the main hearing is to occur no later than 14 days later. Since the same official presides over both the preliminary and the main hearing, there is no need to present evidence that was already brought forth. The main hearing may be conducted in a separate session with two additional judges or with a jury. Jurors decide questions of law as well as questions of fact—a change from the previous system. The main hearing looks much like a trial, with opening arguments, presentation of evidence and closing arguments. The new policy allows for adjournments only in exceptional circumstances and for a limited time. Cases that go on for more than one day are to continue on the next day or very shortly thereafter. The emphasis is on creating an environment of immediacy and orality. The main hearing is oral and witnesses are called. Before the reforms, attorneys could simply read from written statements at the hearing. Judges are required to apply preclusionary principles, similar to rules of evidence, in order to prevent parties from presenting evidence not previously identified in the preliminary hearings. Consistent with the civilian base of the Finnish system, judges examine witnesses, but the parties also maintain the right to do so (Ervo, 1994).

The new system requires parties to be well prepared prior to going to court. Although the Finnish system has not been radically altered, some of the reforms are worth further study. The state of Finland's civil proceedings before and after reform suggests that there may be significant benefits from even small changes if reforms are needed.

Egypt

The judiciary in Egypt has adopted two types of procedural reform: the use of case managers, and judicial mediation.[7] Although these reforms were influenced by U.S. reforms, they reflect Egyptian practices and are more than just copies (Chodosh et al., 1996).

Egypt is a civil law country, so on paper judges have the ability to exercise control over cases. However, because of large caseloads and resource constraints on the Egyptian judiciary, judges have not been able, in practice, to exercise control. "Judges are reluctant to impose upon the advocates the requirement of more timely submissions of evidence and legal argument. Because of the large caseload, they perceive themselves to lack the necessary time to review the submissions" (Chodosh et al., 1996). In Egypt, an estimated 10 to 15 appearances are required on average to address solely evidentiary matters in first instance civil litigation. Only about 15 to 20 percent of the cases heard in civil courts on a given day are prepared with sufficient evidence for the judge to issue a decision. The incentive within the judicial system is for judges to address each case in each court session, even on very limited points. This causes postponement of numerous deadlines. Chodosh et al. (1996) report that "many judges perceive the enforcement of deadlines to be futile, because even if deadlines could be enforced, the judges would not have time to respond adequately to cases ready for adjudication." Traditionally, extensions have been routinely granted as a matter of course. The preparation phases of civil cases were found to take an average of two years in Egypt, and the adjudicatory phases an average of two months. About 75 percent of an Egyptian judge's court time is consumed by administrative tasks (Chodosh et al., 1996).

The interaction of lawyers with the courts in Egypt has been described as follows:

> Given the practical inability of judges to fulfill their duties expeditiously, lawyers are able to prolong the litigation process by utilizing the procedural tools at their disposal, thereby earning additional fees with each

---

[7] Mediation is discussed in further detail later this section. Egypt's judicial mediation is covered here together with case management because the two reforms are related.

substantial procedural turn of the case. The practical inability of the judiciary to keep track of these procedural developments adds considerably to backlog and delay. Moreover, procedural rights that ensure fairness are subject to excessive use by attorneys and those litigants (usually defendants) who are interested in delaying the adjudication of a dispute as long as possible. (Chodosh et al., 1996)

Given this unfortunate state of affairs, the Egyptian reformers have developed a two-pronged approach to judicial reform. First, Egypt has adopted a case management technique that seeks to restore the judge's control over the pace and conduct of civil proceedings through the specialization of the case management function in case managers. Case managers can be described as having somewhat less power than a magistrate has in a U.S. federal district court. Under the Egyptian reforms:

The case manager is not vested with any power to issue findings on the merits of the case; however, the case manager has the power to (i) dismiss complaints that do not satisfy pleading requirements; (ii) provide the parties with a pre-established calendar for evidentiary and legal submissions; (iii) meet with the parties to ensure that the evidence and legal authorities are submitted within the established deadlines; (iv) recommend to the judicial panel sanctions for non-compliance, including dismissal, default judgment, claim, issue and evidentiary preclusion, and civil penalties; (v) order the parties to confer on whether they wish to pursue judicial mediation with a retired judge or normal litigation according to the case management schedule established by the case manager; (vi) implement the parties' choice of the judicial mediation option; and (vii) streamline the issues of outstanding dispute between them and schedule dispositive hearings before a judicial panel. The case manager has the power to bind the parties subsequently to any agreement they happen to reach. (Chodosh et al., 1996)

In addition, court administrators with responsibilities for docketing and service will come under the direct control of the office of the case manager.

One of the potential disadvantages of this system is that some of the functions of the case manager may already be performed by judicial clerks, with no positive effects on backlogs and court congestion. The Egyptian approach, however, formalizes the role, and when combined with the case management procedures described below, the institution of the case manager has the potential to streamline cases by permitting judges to concentrate on judicial functions.

Under the reformed Egyptian system, parties have the option of confidential court-based mediation conducted by a retired judge. The judicial mediator is trained and certified as a professional neutral. The mediation process does not differ significantly from the current widely accepted concept of mediation. Egyptian judicial mediation occurs very early in the lifespan of a case, and no additional written presentations are required of the parties. A potential disadvantage is that only retired judges may be certified as neutrals, which restricts the potential supply of such mediators.

Under the reforms, the civil process in Egypt works as follows:

1) A plaintiff files a complaint with the clerk of the court. The clerk sends the complaint to the office of the case manager, where it is docketed, copied and sent to the defendant(s).

2) The case manager determines whether the complaint meets the requirements of the Egyptian Code of Civil Procedure. If the complaint is deficient, the plaintiff is notified through the use of a standard form.

3) The clerk of the court sends to the parties a standardized notice identifying (i) the date of the first meeting with the case manager; (ii) a standardized schedule of procedural events and the responsibilities of the parties at each stage, including the obligation of the parties to gather and bring to the first meeting with the case manager evidence in support of claims and defenses; and (iii) a description of sanctions that the case manager may recommend for failure of the parties to comply with the notice.

4) The first meeting between the case manager and the parties occurs within 30 days of the date of service of the complaint on the defendant(s). In this first meeting, the case manager issues a standard form to the parties that sets forth a schedule for the proceedings, including deadlines for evidentiary submissions and court hearing dates. The case manager will issue a standard "order to confer" to the parties so that they will consider judicial mediation.

5) If the parties do not choose mediation within 10 days, the case manager will assume they have not opted for mediation. The litigation will then progress in accordance with the schedule mandated by the case manager in the first meeting. If they choose mediation, the case manager issues a standard order outlining the schedule for the mediation and the responsibilities of the parties. Mediation shall be no more than 60 days in duration, as set forth in the scheduling order. The order authorizes at least one appearance before the mediator. The mediator is assigned by the case manager. Subsequent meetings are permitted only if the mediator certifies that they will be productive. The mediation order also has an appendix with a list of questions to be asked by the mediator that will assist the parties in preparing for the mediation. The order establishes the mediation as part of the judicial process and provides the parties with disincentives to attempt to abuse the process through court-ordered sanctions.

6) The parties and the mediator execute a standard confidentiality agreement

that includes provisions on the sanctions that can be imposed by the court for noncompliance with the agreement. The mediator reviews a standard questionnaire with the parties and takes down verbal answers from the parties. His notes are for his use only. The mediator then meets with each party privately "to discuss the party's settlement position and then decides whether to pursue settlement negotiations in private caucuses with the parties or to provide an early evaluation of the merits and expected outcome of the claims" (Chodosh et al., 1996). If settlement discussions fail, the mediator provides neutral evaluation.

After the first mediation session, the mediator provides certified answers to a questionnaire to the case manager. The mediator certifies either that the case has settled, and provides a settlement agreement for court approval; that the case is likely to settle in additional sessions and that he may need at most 30 days beyond the initial 60 day authorization; or that the case is unsuitable for continued mediation. Based on the mediator's questionnaire, the case manager issues the appropriate order.

7) If mediation is unsuccessful or is not elected by the parties, the case manager meets with the parties within 30 days of the first meeting or the most recent order, whichever is later, for purposes of evaluating the gathering of evidence. The case manager uses the same questions posed by the mediator, but this time they are not confidential. The case manager orders the parties to submit to the court all evidence in support of their claims and defenses. The case manager may take oral testimony if the parties consent. This second meeting is the cutoff for evidence to be submitted to the court. The case manager has the authority to grant one extension only, and his decision is not reviewable. The case manager organizes the evidence in the file for the judicial panel that will hear the case. Case preparation is finalized in this second meeting. Judges presiding over the case may request evidence not gathered by the case manager and may reject the case manager's recommendations.

Singapore Civil Procedure

A growing trend in several court systems is the use of summary procedures to dispose of cases that do not require full consideration on the merits. The tracking systems outlined above provide for some form of summary disposition of cases.

Singapore has an efficient judiciary that receives very high ratings from various organizations that evaluate judicial systems. Among the numerous innovations Singapore has incorporated into its civil proceedings are the following:

1) The addition by the Supreme Court of Order 14A to Singapore's Rules of Civil Procedure. Order 14A supplements the typical motions found in common law procedure, such as the summary judgment motion, by empowering courts to summarily determine any question of law or construction of a document at any stage of a proceeding. Upon making such a determination, the court may dismiss

the case or take such action as it deems just. Although Order 14A is not revolutionary in its approach, it is indicative of an emerging trend in judicial systems. Lord Woolf (1996) has recommended a similar approach for the United Kingdom. As reported by Ho (1996), Order 14A sets forth the following requirements:

- The question must be one of law or interpretation of a tax and it must be suitable for determination without a full trial of the action;
- The determination must finally resolve (subject to any possible appeal) the entire cause or matter or any claim or issue therein; and
- The parties must have had an opportunity to be heard on the question or have consented to an order or judgment on determination of the question.

The standard for determining whether a case or issue can be decided under Order 14A is "whether all the necessary and material facts relating to the subject matter of the question have been duly proved or admitted" (Ho, 1996).

2) Pre-trial conferences for the purpose of increasing judicial efficiency. Since April 1992, these conferences have been extended to most civil cases and are used in the High Court, which has original as well as appellate jurisdiction. The objectives of the pre-trial conference are to i) promote settlement; ii) narrow issues in dispute; iii) assess the readiness of the parties for trial; iv) issue directions as necessary to get the parties ready for trial; and v) determine the amount of time each party needs for the trial. Pre-trial conferences are intended to reduce the amount of time needed for trial, lessen the likelihood of adjournment after trial dates have been set and court resources allocated to the parties, and fix cases for definite trial dates.

3) Singapore's Subordinate Courts, the lowest level of courts, conduct settlement conferences known as court dispute resolutions (CDRs) in all civil cases prior to trial. Similar to pre-trial conferences, CDRs are conducted "without prejudice," with the presiding judge or magistrate providing an evaluation of the case and discussing the likelihood of success. CDR is court-based and not merely court-annexed. Judges serve as mediators. It is similar to the Egyptian judicial mediation model, but uses actual judges rather than retired judges. The courts in Singapore do not charge extra for CDR. The goal of the Singapore judiciary is "to develop and institutionalize within our justice system a Singapore model of mediation which can serve as a model for other court jurisdictions with similar ethnic and cultural diversities" (Ho, 1996). Cases amenable to CDR are identified early in the proceedings, facilitated by differentiated case management.[8]

---

[8] Singapore has experimented with differentiated case management, which was first introduced in the Subordinate Courts in 1995 on a pilot basis.

The Singapore judiciary operates a Court Mediation Center outside of CDR, which handles a variety of civil matters. The center was established in 1995, and a year later the judiciary piloted its use for the mediation of certain types of criminal matters, particularly those in which "the dispute concerns inter-personal relationships, such as those involving relatives, friends, or what is called relational disputes" (Ho, 1996).

Changes to Civil Procedure in Japan

In 1996, the Japanese Diet passed significant revisions to the Japanese Code of Civil Procedure covering nine principal areas: 1) preparatory procedures to clarify issues and streamline civil litigation; 2) production of documents; 3) limited discovery; 4) protection of secrets; 5) special provisions on small claims; 6) appeals to the Supreme Court; 7) suspension of provisional enforcement of judgments; 8) standing to sue requirements; and 9) transnational litigation (Davis 1996). Of particular interest are the four reforms discussed below.

Preparatory Procedures. Articles 249-56 of the Japanese Code of Civil Procedure cover preparatory procedures under which the court and the parties have traditionally held in camera meetings in order to determine contested issues of fact and law prior to formal open court sessions. The reforms have opened up the procedure to third parties with an interest in the proceedings. The court can now require the parties to submit briefs and documentary evidence in the preparatory procedure. In addition, the courts no longer require the consent of the parties for the use of the procedure. Safeguards have been enacted to ensure that this informal procedure does not turn the subsequent formal court hearing into a mere formality, and to preserve the openness of the court system.

The issues to be decided in the subsequent hearing stage are identified at the conclusion of the informal procedure. The reforms restrict but do not prohibit the introduction of new evidence and issues at a later stage. The introducing party is under an obligation to explain to the opposite party and the court the reasons why such matters were not disclosed previously. Under the prior version of the code, the parties could present new evidence and raise new issues up to the time of closing of the formal hearing. The changes require that evidence and issues be raised at appropriate times in the proceedings, and mandate sanctions for noncompliance. Article 139 of the Code of Civil Procedure has always provided for sanctions in the event of untimely production of evidence in an intentional or grossly negligent fashion. This provision may come into greater use with the revisions of the code.

Production of Documents. Article 312 of the code permits courts to order the production of documents under the following limited circumstances: i) where a party references the document in his or her court submissions; ii) where substantive law permits the party with the burden of proof to receive the document; and iii) if the document was prepared for the benefit of the party requesting it or if it was prepared in connection with a relationship between the parties.

The reforms retain Article 312, but they allow the possessor of the document to refuse to produce it on the basis of four limited grounds: i) if the document would incriminate the person, his or her spouse, or a relative; ii) if the document contains a government secret and the relevant agency has not authorized production; iii) if the documents are subject to various privileges, such as an attorney-client privilege or a doctor-patient privilege; and iv) if the documents are used solely by the party possessing them. The objective of the reforms is to make document production more accessible. If a party refuses to produce a document, the court may accept as true an assertion by the requesting party as to the contents of the document (Davis, 1996).

Discovery. The reforms provide a limited form of discovery, similar to interrogatories used in the United States. Parties can send written questions to opposing parties on matters related to preparation for the clarification of issues and identification of evidence during the preparatory procedure. No sanctions are available in the event of a refusal to comply. The opposite party is required to produce answers within a reasonable period of time. The request should not be overly burdensome and should not ask for views or opinions.

Protection of Secrets. In Japanese courts today, there is a great deal of evidence that constitutes trade secrets, proprietary business information, or sensitive personal information. There is a tradeoff between keeping such information secret and maintaining courts that are open to the public. Given the high technology industrial base in Japan, the country has struggled with this issue. Access to the court record may be restricted with respect to records whose disclosure would hinder a person from leading a normal social life, and records that have trade secrets as that phrase is defined in the Law on the Prevention of Unfair Competition. Documents containing such secrets are also exempt from the requirements for the production of documents set forth above.

Public Interest Litigation

The United States is widely regarded both as a litigious society and as having probably the most developed procedural provisions to initiate complex and class action litigation. Standing rules in the United States, though subject to some tightening by courts in recent years, still are liberal in comparison to standing requirements in Western Europe and elsewhere. (Lindblom and Watson, 1992). U.S. courts, moreover, are equipped to handle mass claims of parties similarly situated, such as asbestos claimants.

A country that far surpasses the United States in its acceptance of public interest litigation, however, is India. Cassells (1989) states that the judiciary in India has loosened standing requirements "to the point that they may be said to have ceased to present any real obstacle to the public interest litigant."[9] Cassells further states:

> The Indian judiciary has shown a willingness to alter the rules of the game where necessary. Actions may be commenced not only by way of formal petition, but also by way of letters addressed to the court or a judge who may choose to treat it as a petition. There are reports of actions begun by postcard, and even of one judge converting a letter to the editor in a newspaper into a [public interest litigation] writ. Judges have been known to invite and encourage public interest actions.

Public interest litigation in India is led by the judiciary, as explained again by Cassells:

> Painfully aware of the limitations of legalism, the judiciary of India has struggled over the last decade to bring law into the service of the poor and oppressed. Under the banner of Public Interest (or Social Action) Litigation…and the enforcement of fundamental rights under the Constitution, the courts have sought to rebalance the distribution of legal resources, increase access to justice for the disadvantaged, and imbue formal legal guarantees with substantive and positive content. Originally aimed at combating inhumane prison conditions and the horrors of bonded labor, public interest actions have now established the right to a speedy trial, the right to legal aid, the right to a livelihood, a right against pollution, a right to be protected from industrial hazards, and the right to human dignity.

The Indian approach to public interest litigation is not necessarily appropriate in all countries or legal systems. When considering the feasibility of such litigation, one should examine the costs of its benefits. Public interest litigation inevitably involves tradeoffs.

On the benefit side, public interest litigation may serve to strengthen civil society. In countries with fragile or weak structures for civil society in the executive and legislative branches, such litigation may serve as a substitute for the means to seek redress from government. Or, it may serve as a complement to burgeoning civil society structures. There is a body of literature that asserts that public interest

---

[9] See *Maharaj Singh v. Uttar Pradesh*, A.I.R. 1976 S.C. 2602; *Mumbai Kangar Sabhha v. Abdulbhai*, A.I.R. 1976 S.C. 1455; *S.P. Gupta v. Union of India*, (1982) 2 S.C.R. 365, 520, A.I.R. 1982 S.C. 149, 189.

litigation may provide the means for the vulnerable and oppressed to have a stake or voice in society and to redress injustice.

The social costs of public interest litigation, however, may be significant. While some cases involving certain groups may be served by public interest litigation—such as a consumer suit to challenge a cartel—the institutional incentives created by public access provisions can create some socially wasteful litigation as well. There may be no way to separate socially beneficial or economically efficient litigation from socially wasteful or inefficient litigation. One may take a normative stance and provide for public interest litigation for groups that, for example, a legislature believes should receive gains from increased access to justice. Laws cannot be perfectly specified or interpreted, however, and a well-intentioned law may be used to accomplish socially wasteful rent seeking. In rent seeking, interest groups manipulate the court system in order to redistribute wealth from consumers and impose a deadweight loss in the form of reduced consumption or reduced consumer surplus (Ramseyer, 1990). The court system may also provide incentives for extortion and nuisance suits (Coffee, 1986). Conflicts may arise between the interests of attorneys and clients in public interest litigation, since the costs of litigation are not internalized by the parties to class action litigation. The lack of internalization of all of the social costs of litigation, including the costs of using the judiciary (including opportunity costs), indicates that the price of litigation may be too low and nonoptimal. This, in effect, results in a subsidy or wealth transfer to individuals with an incentive to bring litigation (Coffee, 1986).

Appellate Process Reform in Spain

Spain's reforms of the appellate process appear to be based predominantly on the view that adequate regulation of appellate procedure calls for its limitation to exceptional circumstances—that is, circumstances where there is a need to correct errors in the application of the law and the creation of case law in order to unify judicial interpretation. Cassation has been limited to cases where there has been an error in the application of the law, as for example when there has been an incorrect application of burdens of proof or an erroneous admission of evidence. De novo factual findings are no longer considered except in rare cases when a party must demonstrate "elements suitable to prove" a contradictory finding of fact.

Oral hearings in appellate cases are avoided where possible and only granted in serious cases or those involving large sums of money. Measures were instituted to limit appeals or cassations in civil cases to those that involve an amount in excess of a certain value threshold. One criticism of this amendment is that it encourages fraud regarding damages incurred. Another concern is that the change ignores the fact that some important issues do not always involve damages or a significant magnitude of damages.

Some of these initiatives have faced opposition from the bench. For example, Judge Andres de Oliva Santos has argued that it is impossible to urgently execute such dramatic reforms without making grave errors. He agrees that the courts are overburdened, but compares the proposed solutions to eliminating treatments and suppressing illnesses in response to an overburdened medical system. The proposed law would allow courts to deny admittance for cassation to cases that are "fundamentally lacking or which deal with issues similar to others which have been dismissed." Judge Santos finds this procedure unacceptable, contending that it denies the reality that the individual facts of each case are never the same, and that the time it takes to make the preliminary decision as to whether to take the case could more efficiently have been used to actually decide that case on its merits. He is of the view that it is better to hear repetitive cases than to risk a summary dismissal of a valid claim.

Alternative Dispute Resolution

The promotion of alternative dispute resolution (ADR) is one of the most prominent trends in judicial administration both in Latin America and elsewhere. This section describes recent ADR efforts outside of Latin America.

The jurisdictions with the seemingly most developed systems of ADR are the United Kingdom, Australia, Canada and the United States. Judiciaries in continental Europe have also experimented with ADR (Iwai, 1991). New Zealand launched a study of ADR in 1997 in order to determine whether it should be expanded beyond its current role as a parallel form of dispute resolution not connected with the courts. In some countries, such as China, litigation could be considered as an alternative dispute resolution. However, the informal models of dispute resolution in Asian countries may be too culturally specific to be candidates for transplantation to other countries.

The numerous types of ADR include negotiation, mediation, conciliation, consensus building and negotiated rulemaking, arbitration, early neutral evaluation, the mini-trial, the summary jury trial, referees and the use of ombudsmen (Goss, 1995). This section looks at the use of mini-trials, particularly in Alberta, Canada, and Japanese settlement-in-court procedures.

The Mini-Trial in Canada

Out of a concern for lengthy and protracted litigation of cases with the potential for settlement, the courts in Alberta, Canada have experimented with the use of mini-trials. The mini-trial does not fit within the classic definition of a trial as one would think of it under common law. Rather, it is a formalized structure for settlement negotiation. The mini-trial "is premised on the belief, which has largely proven to be correct, that the structured presentation of evidence and arguments, on behalf of the parties before a judge, enables the parties to settle the dispute themselves on the basis of non-binding opinion expressed by the judge at the conclusion of the process" (Moore, 1995). It can be, in essence, part of the pre-trial procedures in a case.

In Alberta, the mini-trial is offered without cost to the parties as an option by the courts—it is not mandatory. There are no formal rules governing its use, but the following guidelines are generally followed: 1) all parties must consent to the use of the mini-trial; 2) clients must be present while counsel present arguments and when the judge provides an opinion at the conclusion of the arguments; 3) no gowns are worn so as to provide an atmosphere of informality; 4) the parties are encouraged to provide a written stipulation of agreed-upon facts, along with expert reports; 5) no evidence is adduced at the mini-trial, but counsel must be prepared to present arguments; and 6) the non-binding opinion of the judge at the conclusion of the mini-trial is confidential and the judge will not discuss the opinion with any other judge (Moore, 1995). The judge's opinion is essentially pointed towards the parties, to inform them of the likely outcome of their case.

The mini-trial may not be appropriate for all types of civil litigation, although it has been used in Alberta even in complex commercial litigation. Essentially, it is appropriate when mediation would be.

Settlement-in-Court in Japan

Japan has developed a unique procedure in which judges who preside over cases actually become involved in facilitating settlement between the parties. Article 136 of the Japanese Code of Civil Procedure provides in part that "the court may, at whatever stage the suit may be in, attempt to carry out a compromise or have a commissioned judge or an entrusted judge try the same." This is a longstanding procedure that has existed in Japan since 1948. Judges, in essence, may become involved in the settlement process, even if they preside over the case. The procedure is used in both first instance and appellate courts.

When a judge presiding over a case believes that it is a good candidate for settlement, he or she will admonish counsel, in the courtroom, to attempt settlement. Parties may refuse, but the judge will seek other opportunities to raise the issue during the proceeding, although the judge has the power to transfer to the settlement process without the consent of the parties. Once the parties agree to follow the settlement procedure, the judge takes the initiative, even though he or she is the same judge who presides over the litigation. In some instances, the proceeding will switch back and forth between settlement and hearing modes, allowing parties the opportunity to present testimony that may influence settlement outcome. Some settlement meetings will be held ex parte.

The court will usually suggest the settlement process 1) at a very early stage of the case, possibly after exchange of initial submissions; 2) after the filing of major submissions and the submission of the principal documentary evidence to the court; or 3) after the court has examined all the major witnesses in the case.

The in-court settlement process occurs in three stages. First, the court sets a date for a "meeting for the arrangement of settlement" (Iwai, 1995). At this stage, the judge allows the parties to explain themselves and even to cover issues that are not the subject of the claims at issue in the case. In the second stage, the judge makes a wide range of recommendations for potential compromises. In the third stage, the court reviews the conditions for settlement proposed by the parties and submits a final proposal for their consideration if they are close to settlement. In this final stage, the judge will be candid about his views on the facts and law of the case, and on the appropriateness of the solution.

If a settlement is reached, it may be entered in the court registry and may have the same effect as a judgment. However, it is nonappealable.

Iwai (1995) summarizes the nuances of the settlement-in-court process as follows:

> Judges persuade parties by explaining the merits of a settlement compared with the result of formal court decision, by removing fundamental misunderstandings or obstacles in communication caused by lack or shortage of negotiation, and by making parties reflect more on the positive future course of their relationship rather than [on] the negative conflicts of the past. They must, of course, be very careful in persuading parties or putting forward proposals not to give the impression that the penalty for non-acceptance might be the loss of their case; such misunderstanding would provoke serious mistrust by the parties as to the fairness and impartiality of the court. If the process fails and a formal judgment is later delivered, the judge must also be extremely careful not to deliver a final decision whose content is inconsistent with the opinions disclosed in the course of attempting to persuade the parties to settle or in putting forth the proposals for settlement. This would likewise lead to serious mistrust and an impression that the court had, in the ADR mode, been irresponsibly trying to impose an unfavorable and ill-grounded solution. In order to avoid any such mistrust by the parties, therefore, the judges must examine all the arguments and evidence with as much care as if they were preparing to draft a final judgment, and must respect the feelings and the free will of the parties before them. In doing so, they must consider the extent and manner of disclosing opinions prudently and flex-

ibly in accordance with the characters or attitudes of the parties at each stage of the proceedings.[10]

The Japanese "mediation" procedure outlined above is not formalized in any detailed procedures but is individualized by each judge. Moreover, there is some question as to the advisability of a procedure in which a judge who presides over a case would also preside over settlement discussions or mediation. Finally, there is concern whether the procedure would comply with open court requirements typically found in constitutions and other fundamental laws governing judiciaries.

BEST PRACTICES IN CRIMINAL JUSTICE

Reform of Criminal Procedure in Italy

In 1989, Italy adopted a new Code of Criminal Procedure that resulted in fundamental changes. With its emphasis on procedural justice, the new code is a radical departure in a country where the legal system is firmly grounded in the civilian tradition.

The Italian reforms were deemed necessary because the former system was perceived as inefficient, too closed, and inconsistent with Italy's status as a democratic state. Under the prior procedures, the two principal stages of a criminal proceeding were a closed pretrial inquisitorial or instruction phase and a public trial phase. In the first phase, a judge would perform the roles of both investigator and judge. This first phase became so disproportionately powerful, however, that the trial phase diminished to a formality. As explained by Pizzi and Marafioti (1992):

> In theory, a public trial followed the examination phase, which developed all the evidence on which the defendant might be convicted. In practice, however, the examination phase grew in importance at the expense of the trial, and the trial became a purely formal exercise. The traditional principles of orality and immediacy were abandoned, and records and materials collected during the investigative phase became the basis of the verdict and sentence. In short, the trial merely confirmed

---

[10] In conjunction with the preparatory procedure, Japanese courts also use a "pleading-and-settlement" approach to facilitate settlement. In this process, the court essentially bypasses the lengthy and protracted formalized written submissions that characterize Japanese civil procedure. After the initial filing of the complaint and the defendant's response, the judge calls the parties to a meeting at the courthouse and goes through the entire case and the defenses in an informal discussion with the parties.

what had taken place during the pretrial examination phase. As a final twist, the examination phase was conducted secretly. The defense had no right to participate or even to be notified of the investigation.

The new code substantially changed this process by, among other things, separating prosecutorial and judicial functions and making clearer distinctions between the trial and investigatory phases (Freccero, 1994).

The reforms were also necessary because the prior procedural regime was inefficient. Some cases were delayed for over 10 years. Although efficiency does not necessarily follow from an increase in adversarial procedures, Italy adopted special procedures that have an effect similar to plea bargaining and in turn lead to speedier case disposition (Pizzi and Marafioti, 1992).

Italian criminal procedure works as follows:

1) A victim reports a crime to the police. Within 48 hours, the police are required to inform the prosecutor and provide all the information that they have gathered.

2) Upon being notified by the police, the prosecutor is required to record the crime in a crime register. This record triggers time limits within which the criminal investigation must be completed—it is, in effect, a speedy trial provision. In general, the prosecutor is required to complete the investigation within six months of the initial record of the crime. A judge may grant six month extensions up to a total of 18 months. The prosecutor has the primary responsibility for investigation, although a judge serves in an oversight function, and police work is carried out under the prosecutor's direction (Pizzi and Marafioti, 1992).

The new code curtails the prosecutor's ability to implement coercive measures during the investigative phase, such as lengthy pre-trial detention, restriction of a suspect's movements, house arrest, or injunction. Under the new code, the prosecutor must obtain the approval of a magistrate after a judicial proceeding prior to implementing pretrial detention. The reforms also create the position of a preliminary investigation judge separate and distinct from the prosecutor.

3) If a case is weak, the prosecutor does not have the right to refuse to prosecute. Like many civil law countries, Italy does not provide prosecutors with the discretion to decide whether or not to prosecute. A prosecutor may, however, request from a judge a judgment of dismissal, called a *decreto di archiviazione*.

4) A prosecutor or defense counsel may seek what in the U.S. system would be called a testimonial deposition of witnesses before trial. In Italy, it is called the *incidente probatorio*. The purpose of the procedure is to obtain the testimony of a witness who may not be available for the trial.

5) The new code provides for a preliminary hearing (*udienza preliminare*) held in camera. The judge reviews documents developed by the prosecutor during the investigation. Defense counsel participates in the hearing. No testimonial evidence

is presented; the parties argue from the investigatory file. The defendant, however, may request examination by the judge alone. Based on this hearing, the judge decides whether to set a date for a trial.

The preliminary hearing is largely a formality, because the judge applies an extremely lenient standard to the prosecutor's case. A weak case against the accused is not a basis for dismissal. Rather, a judge may dismiss the case only if he concludes that no crime actually took place, that the events described in the charges do not constitute a crime, or that the defendant clearly did not commit the crime. In short, the decision to dismiss the charge against a suspect after the preliminary investigation hearing amounts to a declaration that the defendant must be acquitted immediately without a trial (Pizzi and Marafioti, 1992).

6) The public criminal trial under the new code retains many civil law characteristics, with some notable departures. The new code limits written materials that a court may consider on its own in the trial to the charging documents, physical evidence and evidence resulting from the *incidente probatorio*. The parties must introduce all other evidence at the trial. Other features of the trial are participation by injured persons, opening statements, direct and cross examination of witnesses, closing statements and rebuttals. Continuing in the civil law tradition, defendants have the right to speak at any point to challenge testimonial evidence presented.

Freccero (1994) describes the trial as follows:

> The trial phase under the new code differs significantly from its predecessor. Under the old [code], a trial had been intended, in theory, as the oral confirmation of evidence gathered in the instruction phase of the process. In practice, however, the trial had "degenerated" into a formal reception of written summaries of the evidence that had been gathered in the earlier phases. Some critics had maintained that the former system was flawed because the trial court based its judgment on summaries of the testimony without ever having the benefit of hearing witnesses and viewing the demeanor while testifying.

The new code substantially increases the orality of trials. It contains evidentiary rules that prevent the use of written testimony except for impeachment, prohibiting the use of certain types of hearsay and prohibiting judges from using information not admitted at trial. The parties, not the judge, have principal responsibilities for presenting evidence. The parties ask questions directly of witnesses rather than first posing the question to the judge for review.

7) At the conclusion of the trial, the court is required to issue a decision and prepare a written opinion that explains in detail the reasons for it. If the court cannot prepare an opinion immediately after the trial, it is required to issue its opinion generally within 60 to 90 days. As is common in civil law systems, trials are

presided over by a panel of judges that in some courts includes a combination of lay and career judges.

8) The new code did not substantially alter the appellate review process for criminal appeals. The Italian system of appellate review retains the standard civil law characteristics for broad review.

The new code is designed to alleviate case backlogs through special, expedited procedures that depart from the general model described above. These special procedures are of two types: procedures that eliminate the preliminary hearing (number five above), and procedures that provide an alternative to trial (number six above).

No Preliminary Hearing

A preliminary hearing may be skipped in the case of either *giudizio direttissimo* or *giudizio immediato*. The *giudizio direttissimo* is available when 1) the defendant is arrested in the act of committing the crime; 2) the defendant consents; 3) the defendant is arrested in the act but the crime requires additional investigation, in which case the prosecutor may take up to 15 days to conduct the investigation before requesting the special procedure; and 4) the defendant makes a full confession to the prosecutor. These cases go directly to the trial phase.

The *giudizio immediato* is intended for use when the evidence against a defendant is overwhelming but does not strictly meet the requirements for a *giudizio direttissimo*. Either party may ask for a waiver of the preliminary hearing. The prosecutor may ask the judge to skip the preliminary hearing and set a date for trial within 90 days of commencing the investigation. The judge rules on the documents and does not convene a hearing.

Alternatives to Trial

Three alternatives to trial in the code are 1) the proceeding by penal decree; 2) a request for the application of punishment by the parties; and 3) summary trial. Each of these procedures is a limited form of plea bargaining. Pizzi and Marafioti (1992) describe the proceeding by penal decree, or *procedimento per decreto penale,* as follows:

> A penal decree is, in essence, a unilateral offer by the public prosecutor to resolve the case by a discounted fine. The defendant is free to accept or reject the offer. It is available only for minor crimes where the public prosecutor can ask the judge to sentence the defendant directly, resulting in a fifty percent fine reduction. There is no preliminary hearing and no trial—simply the direct imposition of the fine. The large discount in the

fine is obviously intended to encourage defendants charged with minor crimes to accept the penal decree. But, if the defendant is dissatisfied with the fine or desires a trial for other reasons, he is entitled to demand a trial any time within fifteen days after the judge imposes the fine.

This procedure was not introduced in the new code, but the new code made several changes to it.

The application of punishment upon request of the parties, or *applicazione della pena su richiesta delle parti,* is the closest procedure to U.S.-style plea bargaining in the Italian system of criminal justice. In this special procedure, the prosecutor and the defendant may agree on a reduced sentence and ask the judge to impose the agreed-upon sentence, or the defendant may request that the judge impose a reduced sentence if the prosecutor refuses to come to agreement. The parties cannot bargain over the criminal charge itself, since prosecutors have no discretion in this regard. The specified sentence can be reduced by, at most, one-third, and the reduced sentence cannot exceed two years. These sentencing limitations restrict the types of crimes that may be the subject of this procedure.

In the third procedure, the summary trial or *giudizio abbreviato,* the case is resolved expeditiously by the judge based solely on the documentary information in the investigative file and having the defendant as the only potential witness. The defendant who opts for this procedure obtains a substantially reduced sentence in the event that he or she is found guilty. The sentence, in general, is to be reduced by one-third. Although the defendant may request this expedited procedure, the prosecutor must consent. The summary trial can be used for many types of crimes, even quite serious crimes. The summary trial is, in some respects, even more expedited than the preliminary hearing. In the preliminary hearing, the judge may seek additional evidence from the parties, which he cannot do in the summary trial.

Pizzi and Marafioti (1992) have said that the summary trial "is the most important of the special procedures in the new Italian Code, because it is designed to resolve a substantial percentage of the system's criminal cases without a full adversarial trial." The summary trial, "by sparing the state a full adversarial trial, offers tremendous savings of judicial resources." Appeals from summary trial judgments are also limited; defendants cannot appeal acquittals, fines or suspended sentences, and prosecutors cannot appeal a sentence that does not impose a prison term.

Commentators have identified a number of concerns with the new Italian code, and particularly with the summary trial (Pizzi and Marafioti, 1992; Del Duca, 1991). The International Law Institute reports that the lack of institutional reform separating the prosecutor and the judge in different career tracks may be limiting the success of the procedural reform. The use of common law adversarial procedures may be problematic without reform of the bureaucratic framework governing civilian prosecutors and judges. In addition, there may be some concern about the permanence of this legislation in Italy, given the dramatic political changes that occurred in that country after 1988. Follow-up studies should focus on the continued implementation and operation of the code.

Boards of Conflict Resolution in Norway

The town of Lier in Norway has experimented with the use of a conflict resolution board or *Konflikrad* for resolving minor criminal offenses by youth offenders.

The basis for the project is the view that "informal mechanisms of social control are important in the prevention and interdiction of early criminal behavior" (Shaughnessy, 1992). The problem perceived by the creators of the Lier board was that juveniles were becoming increasingly isolated from adults in Norwegian society. People were no longer as socially connected as they were in the past, and depended on formal methods of social control, such as the police and the courts, for the handling of criminal activity by youth. The result was fewer incentives for youth to be accountable for their actions, given that these formal control mechanisms were likely to react slowly and less effectively to minor crime committed by youth. The board was established to deal with these shortfalls.

One of the rationales underlying the Lier program is that "the victim and the offender should face each other and talk it out...The networks of family and friends have begun to collapse in towns and cities. The issue is whether these can be built up again without unneeded bureaucratization and making people too distant from each other" (Shaughnessy, 1992).

The board's purpose is not to punish. Serious offenses are handled by the usual law enforcement methods, which includes police prosecutors and sentencing courts for some minor crimes. Use of the board system is voluntary on the part of both parties. If a complainant is unsatisfied with the outcome of a board proceeding, he or she may file a police complaint.

Any agreement to use the board system, as well as settlements reached in this system, must comply with laws relating to contracts by minors if a minor is a party to the proceeding. The board maintains records of cases, but the records cannot be accessed by official government organs. The plaintiff may obtain access to limited information for insurance purposes only. If a court requires information on a disposition by the board, board members can be called as witnesses.

The board's role is to bring parties together, not to have independent meetings or consultations concerning a matter. The idea is to have the parties themselves resolve the matter. Board members are mediators. The board maintains a secretariat and offices, and members are compensated for travel expenses and their time.

Shaughnessy (1992) describes the board process as follows:

The sergeant gets a telephone call from Peder Aos, owner of a house in Tranby. Someone has broken into his cellar the night before, while the family was out. But he came home in time to see the perpetrators disappear—two teenagers on a motorbike. From the description of the two teenagers and the bike the sergeant thinks he knows who this must be. He suggests that Peder Aos contact the Conflict-Board instead of making a police complaint. After a briefing about this system, Peder Aos accepts the offer.

The sergeant's office gives the secretary of the Conflict-Board the name of the plaintiff and the suspected persons. The secretary phones one of the two members of the Board living in Tranby. She is a teacher at the junior high school and knows the two boys. She talks to them after school, and they both agree to join her at the home of Peder Aos the same evening. At the arranged time, two members of the Board pick up the two boys and drive to Peder Aos' house. They all have a look at the damage in the cellar, and the two boys pick up the pieces of broken glass. They agree to compensate for a lock on the cupboard in the cellar and the broken window with 100 kr. per week for two weeks. This satisfies Peder Aos, and the two boys are brought home again. The secretary of the Board calls Peder Aos two weeks later to hear if the boys have paid as promised. If so, then the case is closed. The housebreak is not reported to the police, and the boys will not be registered by the police.

The Lier Board is only one example of the practice of "diversion" that is occurring in many countries. Diversion involves community treatment and the avoidance of official action in criminal cases (Brants and Field, 1995; Gelsthorpe et al., 1995; Hogarth, 1979).

Victim Participation

Germany

A common practice in civilian criminal justice systems is the participation of the victim in the criminal proceeding as a secondary accuser. In Germany, this is known as the *Nebenklage* procedure (Pizzi, 1996). In 1986, Germany instituted the following reforms in its victim participation procedure:

1) Victims must allege serious injury to themselves or to their reputation. The purpose of this reform was to stop insurance companies from using the procedure to obtain discovery for civil proceedings.

2) Sexual assault was explicitly added to the list of crimes eligible for the procedure. Previously, sexual assault cases had to qualify generally under the theory that they involved assaults, which were on the list.

3) Lawyers representing the victim can now participate in the pretrial proceedings. This is significant from the lawyer's point of view, because he or she can attempt to influence the prosecutor for factual investigations into certain areas.

4) Indigent victims can obtain legal aid, including for pretrial consultations.

These changes may provide guidance for reforming procedures governing victim participation in criminal proceedings at a time when there is significant public interest in victims' rights. Changes to victim participation procedures may serve to alter the negative perceptions of justice systems in some countries.

Belgium

Following the work of the Commission for Criminal Procedure Law, the government of Belgium approved a draft law on December 6, 1996 to more precisely regulate measures relating to judicial inquiry and examination. The legislation includes improved access by victims in the instructional stages of criminal prosecutions, overcoming exceptions based on principles of privacy.[11] The draft law provides victims with access to court files after receiving authorization from the instructional judge, and the possibility of an appeal before the grand jury (la chambre des mises en accusation). It also provides parties with the ability, as has always been the case for prosecutors, to solicit complementary investigations from the examining magistrate during and at the end of the proceeding. The project aims to reinforce the independence of the examining judge by taking away his role as a judicial police officer, placing him under the supervision of the district attorney (procureur général), and giving him the legal power to accomplish all of the necessary examination tasks.

The Belgian government has passed or considered several measures to promote the rights of victims, including the following:

1) The House of Representatives (Chambre des Représentants) approved a draft law on financial assistance for victims of intentional acts of violence. The decree providing for the enforcement of this law is being prepared and a public campaign for funding assistance was renewed in 1997.

2) A new final directive concerning the accommodation of victims in court and the prosecutors' offices was submitted to the Collège des Procureurs Généraux in 1997 to replace the provisional rules of July 13, 1993. It contains, among other

---

[11] In Spain, too, reforms call for a mechanism in which a case can go forward without the direct involvement of the prosecutor. The victim, with the help of an attorney, pursues the case.

things, dispositions on how victims and their families will receive assistance. Provision for social workers and counselors was also included.

3) The Minister of the Interior issued a circular on March 29, 1994 concerning the treatment of victims by the police. The document affirmed that police officers must be helpful within the limits of their duties; but the role of these officers is neither that of a therapist nor a social worker. The Minister of the Interior took several initiatives following this circular, including i) distribution of a brochure "You the Victim"; ii) integration of courses on treatment of victims into the training of police officers; iii) general education on police officer assistance for crime victims; and iv) establishment of a protocol between the Minister of the Interior and the Minister of Employment and Labor to organize training specifically geared towards the reception and treatment of victims of physical and sexual violence, in conjunction with the creation of local public hearings in certain police forces for these victims. In addition, districts developed offices managed by social workers to assist crime victims.

4) An entirely separate personnel structure has been established for treatment of victims. Since February 1994, each judicial department has had a reception service available for victims at the prosecutors' office and at the court of first instance. Courts have liaison judges for the reception of victims, a social worker, and a local counsel representing the policy in favor of victims. Other specialized offices have been established, including two national counselors, supplementary assistants for the reception of victims, and a special service in the central administration of the Ministry of Justice that is responsible for the preparation of policy decisions, logistical support, and the handling of victim complaints.

5) The Minister of Justice, along with the prosecutors' office, will take the interests of victims into account by systematically communicating with them about the steps being taken concerning their complaints, informing them of developments of the investigation, and ensuring that the identity of the victim or the victim's family cannot be discovered by the suspect or his attorney, except so far as it is necessary for the investigation. Crime reports must clearly state the damages incurred by the victim and a copy of this report must be given to the victim. The victim is asked if he or she would like to be informed of the status of the file. The victim's decision on this matter will be included in the report. Regulations will be elaborated to allow audiovisual testimony for vulnerable victims. Moreover, the Belgian government plans to study how the normal lives of victims and their families can be better preserved in terms of media coverage.[12]

---

[12] In addition, the Counsel of Ministers approved two draft laws on probation designed to replace the Law of May 31, 1998.

BEST PRACTICES APPLICABLE TO BOTH CIVIL AND CRIMINAL PROCEEDINGS

Specialization in Courts or Procedures

There is a significant trend towards the development of specialized courts for certain types of proceedings. The advantages of these courts is that they facilitate expertise in areas that tend to be more complex or where knowledge of substantive law will minimize arbitrary decisions. Moreover, they permit the development and use of specialized procedures tailored to the particulars of the problems in question.

Delaware in the United States has a long history of serving as the state of incorporation for over half of all publicly traded Fortune 500 companies and for more than 40 percent of all companies listed on the New York Stock Exchange (Dreyfuss, 1995). The Delaware Chancery Court, although not formally designated as a specialized court, decides predominantly corporate governance disputes.

North Carolina established specialized business courts in 1996, while New York City has had four specialized "Commercial Parts" since 1993 to hear complex commercial and business disputes (Garrou, 1996). There is also a long history of specialized courts in the United States in the areas of family law and juvenile justice.

Russia has had a long history of using economic courts, even during communist rule. The economic courts of the Soviet era decided disputes between state enterprises concerning the proper interpretation of the economic plan. Contracts in a planned economy are essentially state orders for the transfer of resources from one state entity to another. The successors to these economic courts are the Russian commercial courts. There are two independent court systems in Russia: the courts of general jurisdiction and the commercial courts (Maggs, 1995). The subject matter jurisdiction of the commercial courts includes business-related disputes among legal persons and sole proprietors, disputes between the government and its subjects or between its subjects, and bankruptcy cases. Many former Soviet bloc countries have similarly transformed their economic courts.

Of course, France and other civil law jurisdictions have a long history of specialized courts. France has commercial courts (*tribunaux de commerce),* labor courts (*conseils des prud'hommes),* rural courts (*tribunaux paritaires des baux ruraux)* and social security courts (*commissions de premiere instance de securité sociale* and the *commission technique de securité sociale)* (Kublicki, 1994).

Australia has used children's courts that divide into criminal and civil divisions (Swain, 1994). Some jurisdictions, such as New Zealand, have labor courts and land courts (Dannin, 1991; Goddard, 1996).

Court specialization may raise difficult questions concerning the allocation of resources. Does a state want to develop excellence in adjudication of business disputes in order to attract foreign investment, or does it want to allocate resources to prosecuting drug related or violent crimes (Dreyfuss, 1995)? The California Trial Lawyers Association, for example, opposed the creation in their state of a business court, asserting that the court would create a special class of litigants and deny equal access to justice to others, as well as misallocate scarce resources from other civil cases (Garrou, 1996).

Improvements in Legal Aid and Access to Justice

There has been discussion in the literature about options for reform of legal aid and access to justice, particularly regarding the method of legal aid funding. The discussion centers on the cost or funding of aid but not on the quality of representation.

Baauw (1996) has summarized the main options for the funding of legal aid as follows:

Model A:
The *profession* sets the fee level (in competition, or subject to statutory or professional regulation). The client either pays in full or is "'aided" from public funds.

Model B:
As A, but the authority providing the funds fixes maximum or banded fees for specified kind of work; i.e., the *state,* not the lawyer or the client, fixes a non-negotiable fee or fee-band.

Model C:
As A or B, but a global state budget is set, with some flexibility as to its distribution (i.e., by lawyers' professional bodies).

Model D:
Insurance against the risk of litigation, etc., publicly underwritten if the private insurance market cannot or will not offer it.

Model E:
Conditional and contingency fee arrangements. This applies to only those civil claims which, if successful, produce an award large enough to meet legal expenses.

Model F:
Reduction in [legal aid] funding requirements brought about by large-scale procedural reforms, e.g., allocating classes of cases to courts where fees are lower, limiting [legal aid] to certain stages (pre-trial advice, court

of first instance, etc.) and replacing judicial with administrative determination (with or without the possibility of judicial review) at the "public" expense.

Model G:
Distinguishing private practice lawyers from those specifically employed or retained to work in, for example, *publicly funded law centers*, voluntary legal "clinics," or as public defenders.

Model H:
Defining certain kinds of cases as deserving publicly-funded support, e.g., multi-party (group/class/representative) actions where a "public interest" can be shown; the possibility of such claims being pursued by public legal officials; cases involving new kinds of claims or arguing new points of law; and cases involving certain categories of party, e.g., minor children, and officials whose personal liability is to be tested.

Some of the relevant issues for further study concern the various structures for providing and funding legal aid and the incentives provided by these structures.[13] Some of the prevalent models are (i) the use of governmental or quasi-governmental organizations, such as an office of public defenders, funded directly by a government; (ii) the use of subsidies to the private bar or persons of limited means in order to provide access to justice; (iii) law school clinical programs; and (iv) public service requirements imposed on recent law graduates. These models are not mutually exclusive and each may exist independently to some extent in the same legal system. Moreover, an important consideration is whether models for legal aid vary depending on whether legal services are for access to civil or criminal justice.

Changes Relating to the Service and Tenure of Judges in Spain

Revisions in 1993 of Spain's Organic Law of Judicial Power brought significant changes in the selection and appointment of judges and magistrates. The revisions were made because of the growing need for judges and magistrates, and the inability of the current system to provide sufficient numbers. The changes are based on opening the judicial career track to a competitive process.[14]

---

[13] Chapter Two provides a detailed look at structures for funding legal aid, and at various legal aid service delivery models.

[14] Australia, Belgium and Denmark are also in the process of reforming their judge selection processes.

The new law creates a system for appointing established and respected members of the legal profession to the judiciary instead of just relying on career jurists to fill vacancies. This not only fills vacant positions but also rewards competent and deserving members of the legal profession and introduces new and varied perspectives by creating diversity within the judiciary.

One of four judges will be chosen from a competitive process among attorneys with a minimum of six years of professional experience. For magistrates, two of four will be selected from the highest level of judges, one through testing and from specialists in administrative and social issues among judges, and one from a competition among qualified attorneys with a minimum of 10 years of experience.

The procedure allows for a selection committee to review information about the candidates' professional lives and events that may affect their aptitude for the judicial role. Interviews will be conducted of selected candidates but will not function as "exams" in which they are asked substantive questions of law.

The revised law also enhanced disciplinary procedures and sanctions for judges, clarifying the sorts of behavior that are unacceptable and what sanctions may be imposed. Violations are classified either as very serious, serious or minor. Only very serious violations will result in removing a judge from the bench.

A shortage of jurists has created the need to create a flexible system that allows for temporary appointment of judges and for the temporary transfer of existing judges to jurisdictions other than their own. As in other countries such as Singapore, Spain has experimented with temporary appointments and with other means to allocate judicial resources on a temporary basis.

In 1996, additional amendments were recommended to the Organic Law of Judicial Power. The primary proposal was to allow judges and magistrates to leave office temporarily to occupy certain administrative or political offices. These judges must resign within eight days of accepting the position and are barred from sitting on the bench for three years after completing their tour of duty. Certain parliamentary and municipal positions are exempted because of their more significant electoral and political implications.

Recusal is particularly important, as judges come from other governmental offices, and when judges may have had prior affiliations with the parties (for example, as attorneys). Judges are required to recuse themselves whenever they may doubt their ability to be impartial.

APPENDIX 1.1

Excerpt: Order 10, Federal Court Rules of Australia

"Without prejudice of the generality of sub-rule (1) or (1A) the Court may:

(a)   make orders with respect to:
    i)   discovery and inspection of documents;
    ii)   interrogatories;
    iii)   inspections of real or personal property;
    iv)   admissions of fact or of documents;
    v)   the defining of the issues by pleadings or otherwise;
    vi)   the standing of affidavits as pleadings;
    vii)   the mode and sufficiency of service;
    viii) amendments;
    ix)   cross-claims;
    x)   the giving of particulars;
    xi)   the place, time and mode of hearing;
    xii)   the giving of evidence at the hearing, including whether evidence of witnesses in chief shall be given orally or by affidavit, or both;
    xiii) the disclosure of reports of experts;
    xiv)   costs; and
    xv)   the filing and exchange of signed statements of evidence of intended witnesses and their use in evidence at the hearing;

(aa) where, in any proceeding commenced in respect of any alleged or threatened breach of a provision of Part IV of the Trade Practices Act 1974, an order pursuant to section 80 of that Act is sought, direct that notice be given of the order sought by public advertisement or in such other form as the court directs;

(b)   notwithstanding that the application is supported by a statement of claim, order that the proceeding continue on affidavits;

(c)   order that the evidence of a particular fact or facts be given at the hearing:
    i)   by statement on oath upon information and belief;
    ii)   by production of documents or entries in books;
    iii)   by copies of documents or entries, or
    iv)   otherwise as the Court directs;

(ca)   order that an agreed bundle of documents be prepared by the parties;

(d)   order that no more than a specified number of expert witnesses may be called;

(da)   order that the reports of experts be exchanged;

(e)   appoint a court expert in accordance with Order 34, rule 2;

(f)   direct that the proceeding be transferred to a place at which there is a Registry other than the proper place. Where the proceeding is so transferred, the Registrar at the proper place from which the proceeding is transferred shall transmit all documents in his charge relating to the proceeding to the Registrar at the proper place to which the proceeding is transferred;

(g)   order, under Order 72, that proceedings, part of proceedings or a matter arising out of proceedings be referred to a mediator or arbitrator;

(h)   order that the parties attend before a Registrar for a conference with a view to satisfying the Registrar that reasonable steps to achieve a negotiated outcome of the proceedings have been taken, or otherwise clarifying the real issues in dispute so that appropriate directions may be made for the disposition of the matter, or otherwise to shorten the time in preparation for all at the trial;

(i)   in a case in which the Court considers it appropriate, direct the parties to attend a case management conference with a Judge or Registrar to consider the most economic and efficient means of bringing the proceedings to trial and of conducting the trial, at which conference the Judge or Registrar may give further directions;

(j)   in proceedings in which a party seeks to rely on the opinion of a person involving a subject in which the person has specialist qualifications direct that all or part of such opinion be received by way of submission in such manner and form as the Court may think fit, whether or not the opinion would be admissible as evidence."

APPENDIX 1.2

U.S. Federal Rules of Civil Procedure
Rule 16. Pretrial Conferences; Scheduling; Management

(a)   Pretrial Conferences; Objectives. In any action, the court may in its discretion direct the attorneys for the parties and any unrepresented parties to appear
before it for a conference or conferences before trial for such purposes as:
  (1)   expediting the disposition of the action;
  (2)   establishing early and continuing control so that the case will not be
        protracted because of lack of management;
  (3)   discouraging wasteful pretrial activities;
  (4)   improving the quality of the trial through more thorough preparation;
        and
  (5)   facilitating the settlement of the case.

(b)   Scheduling and Planning. Except in categories of actions exempted by
district court rule as inappropriate, the district judge, or a magistrate judge when
authorized by district court rule, shall, after receiving the report from the parties
under Rule 26(f) or after consulting with the attorneys for the parties and any
unrepresented parties by a scheduling conference, telephone, mail, or other suitable means, enter a scheduling order that limits the time:
  (1)   to join other parties and to amend the pleadings;
  (2)   to file motions; and
  (3)   to complete discovery.
The scheduling order may also include:
  (4)   modifications of the times for disclosures under Rules 26(a) and 26(e)(1)
        and of the extent of discovery to be permitted;
  (5)   the date or dates for conferences before trial, a final pretrial conference,
        and trial; and
  (6)   any other matters appropriate in the circumstances of the case.
The order shall issue as soon as practicable but in any event within 90 days
after the appearance of a defendant and within 120 days after the complaint has
been served on a defendant. A schedule shall not be modified except upon a
showing of good cause and by leave of the district judge or, when authorized by
local rule, by a magistrate judge.

(c)   Subjects for Consideration at Pretrial Conferences. At any conference under this rule consideration may be given, and the court may take appropriate action, with respect to:

1) the formulation and simplification of the issues, including the elimination of frivolous claims or defenses;

2) the necessity or desirability of amendments to the pleadings;

3) the possibility of obtaining admissions of fact and of documents which will avoid unnecessary proof, stipulations regarding the authenticity of documents, and advance rulings from the court on the admissibility of evidence;

4) the avoidance of unnecessary proof and of cumulative evidence, and limitations or restrictions on the use of testimony under Rule 702 of the Federal Rules of Evidence;

5) the appropriateness and timing of summary adjudication under Rule 56;

6) The control and scheduling of discovery, including orders affecting disclosures and discovery pursuant to Rule 26 and Rules 29 through 37;

7) The identification of witnesses and documents, the need and schedule for filing and exchanging pretrial briefs, and the date or dates for further conferences and for trial;

8) The advisability of referring matters to a magistrate judge or master;

9) Settlement and the use of special procedures to assist in resolving the dispute when authorized by statute or local rule;

10) The form and substance of the pretrial order;

11) The disposition of pending motions;

12) The need for adopting special procedures for managing potentially difficult or protracted actions that may involve complex issues, multiple parties, difficult legal questions, or unusual proof problems;

13) An order for a separate trial pursuant to Rule 42(b) with respect to a claim, counterclaim, cross-claim, or third-party claim, or with respect to any particular issue in the case;

14) An order directing a party or parties to present evidence early in the trial with respect to a manageable issue that could, on the evidence, be the basis for a judgment as a matter of law under Rule 50(a) or a judgment on partial findings under Rule 52(c).

15) An order establishing a reasonable limit on the time allowed for presenting evidence; and

16) Such other matters as may facilitate the just, speedy, and inexpensive disposition of the action.

At least one of the attorneys for each party participating in any conference before trial shall have authority to enter into stipulations and to make admissions regarding all matters that the participants may reasonably anticipate may be discussed. If appropriate, the court may require that a party or its representative be present or reasonably available by telephone in order to consider possible settlement of the dispute.

(d)   Final Pretrial Conference. Any final pretrial conference shall be held as close to the time of trial as reasonable under the circumstances. The participants at any such conference shall formulate a plan for trial, including a program for facilitating the admission of evidence. The conference shall be attended by at least one of the attorneys who will conduct the trial for each of the parties and by any unrepresented parties.

(e)   Pretrial Orders. After any conference held pursuant to this rule, an order shall be entered reciting the action taken. This order shall control the subsequent course of the action unless modified by a subsequent order. The order following a final pretrial conference shall be modified only to prevent manifest injustice.

(f)   Sanctions. If a party or party's attorney fails to obey a scheduling or pretrial order, or if no appearance is made on behalf of a party at a scheduling or pretrial conference, or if a party or party's attorney is substantially unprepared to participate in the conference, or if a party or party's attorney fails to participate in good faith, the judge, upon motion or the judge's own initiative, may make such orders with regard thereto as are just, and among others any of the orders provided in Rule 37(b)(2)(B), (C), (D). In lieu of or in addition to any other sanction, the judge shall require the party or the attorney representing the party or both to pay the reasonable expenses incurred because of any noncompliance with this rule, including attorney's fees, unless the judge finds that the noncompliance was substantially justified or that other circumstances make an award of expenses unjust.

APPENDIX 1.3

UNITED STATES DISTRICT COURT
EASTERN DISTRICT OF VIRGINIA
ALEXANDRIA DIVISION

Case No. CA 97-171

SCHEDULING ORDER

A pretrial conference will be held on this action on Thursday, July 17, 1997 at 10:15 a.m.

All discovery must be concluded by Friday, June 27, 1997.

Unless a later time has previously been allowed, any defendant who has not filed an answer must do so within 11 days from the date of this order.

All motions, except for summary judgment, shall be noticed for hearing on the earliest possible Friday before the pretrial conference. Ten working days notice is required for motions to dismiss, for summary judgment, for patent claim construction, and for judgment on the pleadings. Non-dispositive motions must be filed and delivered by the Monday before the Friday for which noticed, with responses due not later than the Wednesday before the hearing.

Expert discovery shall be conducted as provided in Local Rule 26(D). Experts not properly identified, and for whom a report has not been timely provided, shall not testify at trial for any purpose.

Fed.R.Civ.P.26(a)(3) disclosures must be made before the pretrial conference, and the parties must bring to the conference the disclosures and a list[1] of the exhibits to be used at trial, a list of the witnesses to be called at trial and a written stipulation of uncontested facts. The exhibits themselves or a copy should be exchanged with opposing counsel before the conference. Objections to exhibits must be filed within 10 days after the conference; otherwise the exhibits shall stand admitted in evidence. The original exhibits shall be delivered to the clerk as provided by Local Rule 79(A). Non-expert witnesses and exhibits not so disclosed and listed will not be permitted at trial except for impeachment or rebuttal, and no person may testify whose identity, being timely requested in discovery, was not disclosed in time to be deposed or to permit the substance of his knowledge and opinions to be ascertained.

---

[1] This differs from prior scheduling order requirements. The original exhibits now should not be brought to the conference, but filed with the clerk one business day before trial.

Depositions, interrogatories, requests for documents and admissions, and answers and responses thereto, shall not be filed except on order of the court, or for use in this action in connection with a motion.

In non-jury cases, counsel should file with the clerk at the beginning of the trial written proposed findings of fact and conclusions of law.

The trial of this case will be set for a certain day within 4-8 weeks of the pretrial conference.

(Signed)
United States District Judge

March 3, 1997
Alexandria Virginia

This order is being mailed to local counsel only

BIBLIOGRAPHY

Armstrong, Nick. 1995. Making Tracks. In *Reform of Civil Procedure, Essays on "Access to Justice,"* A.A.S Zuckerman and Ross Cranston, eds. Oxford: Oxford University Press.

Australian Law Reform Commission. 1996. Judicial and Case Management. Background Paper 3. December.

Baauw, Peter. 1996. Access to Justice and Legal Aid. Paper presented at the 26th Biennial Conference of the International Bar Association, Berlin, 20-25 October.

Black, C., J. Jenkinson, and J.J. Branson. 1994. Case: Trade Practices Commission v. Rank Commercial Ltd., 53 CFR 303, July-August.

Brants, Chrisje, and Stewart Field. 1995. Discretion and Accountability in Prosecution: A Comparative Perspective on Keeping Crime out of Court. In *Criminal Justice in Europe – A Comparative Study,* Phil Fennell, et al. Oxford: Clarendon Press.

Braunschweig, Dr. A. 1996. La Procedure Penale en Droit Français. *International Review of Penal Law* 64.

Cassels, Jamie. 1989. Judicial Activism and Public Interest Litigation in India: Attempting the Impossible? *The American Journal of Comparative Law* 37.

Chen, Kong-Pin, Hung-ken Chien, and C.Y. Cyrus Chu. 1997. Sequential Versus Unitary Trials with Asymmetric Information. *The Journal of Legal Studies* 26(1), January.

Chodosh, Hiram E., Stephan A. Mayo, Fathi Naguib, and Ali El Sadek. 1996. Egyptian Civil Justice Process Modernization: A Functional and Systemic Approach. *Michigan Journal of International Law* 17, Summer.

Clark, David S. 1990. Civil Litigation Trend in Europe and Latin America Since 1945: The Advantage of Intra Country Comparisons. *Law & Society Review* 24(2).

Coffee, John C., Jr. 1986. Understanding the Plaintiff's Attorney: The Implications of Economic Theory for Private Enforcement of Law Through Class and Derivative Actions. *Columbia Law Review* 86(4), May.

Cooter, Robert D., and Tom Ginsburg. 1996. Comparative Judicial Discretion: An Empirical Test of Economic Models. *International Review of Law and Economics* 16(3).

Dannin, Ellen J. 1991. Three Years Out: The Labour Court's Treatment of Dispute Resolution Procedures. *Victoria University Law Review* 21, Oxford University Press, New Zealand.

Davis, Joseph W. S. 1996. Changes to the Code of Civil Procedure. *Dispute Resolution in Japan.* Cambridge, MA: Kluwer Law International.

Dayton, Kim. 1992. Case Management in the Eastern District of Virginia. *University of San Francisco Law Review* 26, Spring.

De Clerk, Steffaan. 1998.Note de Politique Générale – Justice. Ministre de la Justice, Belgium, December.

Del Duca, Louis F. 1991. An Historic Convergence of Civil and Common Law Systems – Italy's New "Adversarial" Criminal Procedure System. *Dickinson Journal of International Law* 10(1), Fall.

Dreyfuss, Rochelle C. 1995. Forums of the Future: The Role of Specialized Courts in Resolving Business Disputes. *Brooklyn Law Review* 61, Spring.

Ervo, Laura. 1994. The Reform of Civil Procedure in Finland. *Civil Justice Quarterly* 13.

Freccero, Stephen P. 1994. An Introduction to the New Italian Criminal Procedure. *American Journal of Criminal Law* 21(3), Spring.

Garrou, John L.W., Esq. 1996. North Carolina – Establishment of a Business Court. *World Reports* 8(3), November.

Geslthorpe, Loraine, Mike Nellis, Jeannette Bruins, and Annelies Van Vliet. 1995. Diversion in English and Dutch Juvenile Justice. In *Criminal Justice in Europe – A Comparative Study*, Phil Fennel, et al. Oxford: Clarendon Press.

Goddard, Chief Judge T.G. 1996. Decision Making in the Employment Court. *New Zealand Law Journal.* November.

Goss, Joanne. 1995. An Introduction to Alternative Dispute Resolution. *Alberta Law Review* 34(1).

Ho, H.L. 1996. The Operation of Order 14A In Practice. *Civil Justice Quarterly* 15.

Hogarth, Dr. John. 1979. Tentative Policy Proposals on Diversion. In *Expeditious Justice – Papers of The Canadian Institute for the Administration of Justice.* Toronto: The Carswell Co. Ltd.

Iwai, Nobuaki. 1991. The Judge as Mediator: The Japanese Experience. *Civil Justice Quarterly.* April.

Jolowicz, J.A. 1996. The Woolf Report and the Adversary System. *Civil Justice Quarterly* 15.

Kessler, Daniel. 1996. Institutional Causes of Delay in the Settlement of Legal Disputes. Stanford University and National Bureau of Economic Research.

Kublicki, Nicolas Marie. 1994. An Overview of the French Legal System from an American Perspective. *Boston University International Law Journal* 12, Spring.

Landes, William M. 1993. Sequential versus Unitary Trials: an Economic Analysis. *The Journal of Legal Studies* 22(1), January.

Leopold, Dieter. 1995. Limiting Costs for Better Access to Justice: The German Approach. In *Reform of Civil Procedure, Essays on "Access to Justice,"* A.A.S. Zuckerman and Ross Cranston, eds. Oxford: Oxford University Press.

Lindblom, Per Henrik, and Garry D. Watson. 1992. Complex Litigation – A Comparative Perspective. *Civil Justice Quarterly* 11.

Maggs, Peter B. 1995. Russian Commercial Courts Expand Jurisdiction Over International Business Disputes. *International Practitioner's Notebook,* nos. 58 and 59, August.

Modona, Guido Neppi. 1994. Italian Criminal Justice Against Political Corruption and the Mafia: The New Model for Relations Between Judicial and Political Power. *Osgoode Hall Law Journal* 32(2).

Moore, The Honourable W.K. 1995. Mini-Trials in Alberta. *Alberta Law Review* 34(1).

Nakamura, Mutsuo. 1990. Freedom of Economic Activities and the Right to Property. *Law and Contemporary Problems* 53(2), Spring.

Osuka, Akira. 1990. Welfare Rights. *Law and Contemporary Problems* 53(2), Spring.

Pizzi, William T. 1996. Crime Victims in German Courtrooms: A Comparative Perspective on American Problems. *Stanford Journal of International Law* 32, Winter.

Pizzi, William T. and Luca Marafioti. 1992. The New Italian Code of Criminal Procedure: The Difficulties of Building an Adversarial Trial System on a Civil Law Foundation. *The Yale Journal of International Law* 17(1), Winter.

Ramseyer, J. Mark. 1990. Doctrines and Rents in Japan: A Comment on Professors Osuka and Nakamura. *Law and Contemporary Problems* 53(2), Spring.

Ramseyer, J. Mark, and Eric B. Rasmusen. 1996. *Judicial Independence in Civil Law Regimes: Econometrics from Japan.* Chicago Law & Economics Working Paper No. 37, 2nd Series, University of Chicago Law School.

Shaughnessy, Edward J. 1992. *Conflict Management in Norway – Practical Dispute Resolution.* Lanham: University Press of America.

Shavell, Steven. 1995. Alternative Dispute Resolution: An Economic Analysis. *The Journal of Legal Studies* 24(1), University of Chicago Law School.

Singapore Supreme Court. 1996, 1995. *Annual Report.* Singapore.

_____ . 1996. Speeches and Judgements of Chief Justice Yong Pung How. *FT Law and Tax Asia Pacific.* Singapore.

_____ . 1994. *The Re-Organization of the 1990s.* Singapore.

Swain, Phillip. 1994. In the Best Interests of Children – Alternative Decision-Making and the Victorian Children's Court. *Australian Journal of Family Law* 8.

von Mehren, Arthur Taylor. 1988. Some Comparative Reflections on First Instance Civil Procedure: Recent Reforms in German Civil Procedure and in the Federal Rules. Symposium on the Fifteenth Anniversary of the Federal Rules of Civil Procedure. *Notre Dame Law Review* 63.

Williams, Philip L. and Williams, Ross A. 1994. The Cost of Civil Litigation: An Empirical Study. *International Review of Law and Economics* 14.

Woolf, Lord, The Right and Honourable, Master of the Rolls. 1996. Access to Justice. Final Report to the Lord Chancellor on the Civil Justice System in England and Wales.

Zander, Michael. 1995. Why Lord Woolf's Proposed Reforms of Civil Litigation should be Rejected. In *Reform of Civil Procedure, Essays on "Access to Justice,"* A.A.S. Zuckerman and Ross Cranston, eds. Oxford: Oxford University Press.

Zuckerman, A.A.S. 1995. Reform in the Shadow of Lawyers' Interests. *Reform of Civil Procedure, Essays on "Access to Justice,"* A.A.S. Zuckerman and Ross Cranston, eds. Oxford: Oxford University Press.

CHAPTER TWO

EXPANDING ACCESS TO JUSTICE: LEGAL AID MODELS FOR LATIN AMERICA

Robert J. Rhudy

INTRODUCTION

This chapter provides a detailed analysis of models of legal aid and access to justice and describes the conditions under which they might be applied in Latin America and the Caribbean. It identifies and reviews several case studies of successful legal aid programs outside the region that might serve as best practices for further consideration.

The analysis focuses on legal aid models designed to serve indigent and lower-income groups—defined as those who cannot afford to pay for legal assistance at its customary cost without suffering substantial deprivation of other needs—as well as other under-served sectors that cannot be addressed through market mechanisms. The chapter looks at how delivery and financing mechanisms interact to determine the effectiveness and efficiency of a legal aid model. It also describes the services that such a system provides—legal information, legal assistance, public action review, law reform, and general access to justice—and analyzes the abilities of different legal aid models to perform these functions.

The chapter proposes several criteria to evaluate legal aid models and systems, including comprehensiveness, effectiveness, efficiency, competency, equity of cost-sharing, affordability, independence, credibility, accessibility, and flexibility. The focus is primarily on funding and service delivery models for civil legal aid systems, while considering distinctions encountered in the financing and design of systems to provide legal assistance in criminal defense. The chapter also discusses the incentives that development of a particular legal aid model would provide to various actors (i.e., governments, court systems, members and institutions of the organized bar, and consumers). Particular attention is given to incentives for court systems and lawyers to regard the general public as clients.

There are numerous local factors that can affect how and to what extent a particular legal service model might be developed in a given Latin American country. These include the level and nature of respect for the rule of law; the status of the judiciary and existing legal aid systems; the status and operation of the legal profession; and the nature of the intended client population. This chapter recommends establishment of a legal services development commission comprised of all concerned parties under appropriate national leadership. The commission can review local factors in relation to consensual legal service goals to determine how to proceed, taking into account the lessons and experiences of legal services from around the world. The final section of this chapter points to the importance of sequencing activities when creating or expanding legal aid systems.

The legal aid models discussed and evaluated on the basis of potential performance, incentives, standards and criteria include (a) private attorney delivery models without public subsidy; (b) private attorney delivery models with public subsidy; (c) legal insurance and prepaid legal assistance; (d) staff attorney models; (e) law school clinics; (f) nongovernmental public interest law reform centers; (g) governmental public interest law reform centers; (h) ombudsmen; (i) simplified dispute resolution centers; and (j) legal advice, brief service, screening and referral models.

The actual performance of any legal services program depends on many factors unrelated to the structure itself of the model. These include its leadership, governance structure, nature and amount of funding, and the environment in which it operates. Some models can be expected to perform certain functions better than others, and some models can be expected to receive more support from various sectors of society.

As publicly supported national legal services systems developed during the 1960s, many countries initially gave strong priority to particular models. Greatest attention was given to the subsidized private attorney delivery model, the staff attorney model, and the simplified judicial or administrative dispute resolution model. A review of more recent literature, national reports and current activities shows a growing consensus for a mixed model of service delivery that provides the desirable range and level of legal services and access to justice. This trend is consistent with this chapter's findings. The nature, ratios, components and timing of the mix should vary depending on local needs, culture and circumstances.

The chapter describes legal aid models in the abstract, discussing prevailing qualities and characteristics that are common to various national legal aid programs. The case studies, however, focus on the functioning of particular legal aid or community legal education systems incorporating a mix of models. Each legal aid model involves different financing and delivery systems that need to be considered to properly understand and review its operations. For instance, private attorney models can deliver legal aid for private client compensation at unregulated or regulated fee schedules, with or without contingency or fee-shifting mechanisms or legal risk or transaction insurance; and private attorneys can receive public subsidies to serve lower-income persons through various approaches. The effectiveness of the model in rendering effective legal aid will vary depending upon the interaction of the delivery and financing systems or mechanisms.

Four relatively successful legal services systems are reviewed and presented as case studies: the legal aid system in the Netherlands; legal aid in Quebec and Ontario (two distinct systems) in Canada; and the Self-Service Center of the Maricopa County Superior Court in Arizona in the United States. The Netherlands and Canadian provincial programs are relatively well-functioning examples of mixed model delivery systems. Activities are now underway, particularly in Ontario, to substantially increase the mix and diversity of the service models being implemented and evaluated. The Arizona system is a particularly strong example of a court-created legal information, advice and pro se assistance center. It uses telecommunications and computer technologies to provide a high volume of service.

Finally, the chapter provides information on various law school clinic programs and other models that merit further consideration.

Legal Aid Functions

Legal aid delivery systems can provide the following services:

1) Legal information that enables people to understand their legal rights and responsibilities, practices to prevent legal conflicts or violations, and institutions and procedures for the identification and resolution of conflicts;

2) Legal assistance to help people, organizations, and institutions implement their legal rights and responsibilities in the full range of civil and criminal defense involving private and governmental parties. This includes providing advice, counsel, legal research, interpretation of laws, preparation of documents, registration of legal rights, mediation or negotiation, fact-finding, and representation before administrative, judicial, executive or legislative institutions;

3) Public action review that involves representing parties in obtaining review and correction of actions by public administrative and executive agencies;

4) Law reform that advocates changes in public policies on behalf of concerned persons, organizations or matters through a range of research, litigation, lobbying and other approaches;

5) Improving access to justice and preserving the legitimate rule of law by ensuring access to justice for all and equitable application of the law.

Existing legal aid delivery models vary substantially in terms of how efficiently and effectively they provide these functions, as will be described in this chapter.

Legal Aid Financing

This chapter will describe and analyze various models for legal aid financing and delivery. While these two activities are closely entwined, it is useful to initially to discuss them separately.

In its basic form, legal assistance financing may consist of (a) individual consumer pay; (b) group consumer pay; (c) cost-shifting arrangements (i.e., loser pays); (d) contingency fees to an attorney from a portion of the plaintiff's monetary award from the defendant; (e) private third-party payment (i.e., legal or liability insurance); (f) partial or totally donated services (either voluntarily or by state or professional requirement); (g) services subsidized partially or entirely by local, national, regional or international private foundations, development agencies, or charitable sources; and (h) partial or complete state payment (with or without client copayments) for certain classes of individuals or matters. Most legal aid financing models consist of some mix of these financing mechanisms (with a number of hybrids) for certain types of legal aid services.

Legal Aid Delivery

The primary legal aid delivery systems that have been developed to perform these services include the following: (a) various private attorney (and related professional and para-professional) delivery systems; (b) legal insurance and prepaid legal assistance systems; (c) staff attorney delivery systems; (d) law school clinical delivery systems; (e) "public interest" law reform systems; (f) state ombudsmen systems; (g) simplified judicial/administrative dispute resolution systems; and (h) legal advice, assistance, screening and referral systems. In practice, existing legal aid systems may be relatively simple or may incorporate a combination of models involving several financing approaches (in greatly varying levels) and a mix of delivery systems providing some or all of the possible legal aid functions as briefly described above.

CRITERIA FOR MODEL ANALYSIS

It is necessary to identify and describe the criteria and standards used in this chapter to analyze and evaluate the various legal aid models and systems and to identify the best practices for legal aid or community legal education programs. The chapter examines the advantages and disadvantages of each model and describes the conditions under which such models could be applied in Latin America. It also discusses the incentives to implement these models for governments, court systems, the bar, intended consumers, and other interested persons, with particular attention to incentives for the court system and involved lawyers to regard the general public as their clients.

This analysis involves several related but also somewhat distinct tasks, including evaluations of each model based on (a) an appropriate set of goals and objectives for a legal aid system; (b) the incentives (from the sometimes conflicting perspectives of involved major groups) for and against implementation of a legal aid model; (c) the incentives provided in a particular model for the court system and involved lawyers to regard the general public as their clients; and (d) the conditions under which such models could be applied in Latin America.

A legal aid system, as well as the various financing and delivery models within that system, should be evaluated on the basis of the following:

• *Comprehensiveness.* Can the system/model provide the full range of legal aid functions as identified above to all appropriate clients, causes and matters? (Indicators: evaluation of functions performed by the system, range of population served, and subject matters addressed).

• *Effectiveness.* Can the system/model provide legal aid effectively and successfully fulfill its functions? (Indicators: does it accomplish its intended tasks?)

• *Efficiency.* Can the system/model render legal aid in a cost-effective manner? (Indicators: cost of service—per consultation or court representation unit, for example—relative to other delivery modes rendering equivalent service.)

• *Competency.* Can the system/model competently provide the desired legal aid functions? (Indicators are normally determined by attainment of objective professional performance standards.)

• *Equitable cost sharing.* Is the cost of operating the system/model equitably shared, in terms of benefits received, among interested parties such as clients, the state, the legal profession, defendants and other involved parties? (Indicators: an appraisal of service cost allocations between actors relative to benefits received and abilities to pay, using cost to ration demand of a scarce service resource, establishing cost reallocations to deter undesired behavior, etc.)

• *Affordability.* Can the legal aid system/model be affordably established, operated and maintained? (Indicators: system expense as a percentage of the GDP—relative to other similar states/countries, for example, or as a percentage of annual budget—analyzed for inflation over time in relation to similar expense items.)

• *Independence.* Can the legal aid system/model be assured independence from undue and inappropriate interference in carrying out its functions and its responsibilities to clients? (Indicators: system structure and decision analysis and perceptions of knowledgeable observers about the operations of the system.)

• *Credibility.* Can the legal aid system/model be operated in a manner that consistently has the credibility and trust of intended clients, state institutions, the legal profession, and other relevant parties? (Indicators: perceptions of persons using or otherwise knowledgeable about the system.)

- *Accessibility*. Can the services of the legal aid system/model be uniformly used by all intended parties regardless of geographic location, race, language, culture, disability or other potential barriers or circumstances? (Indicators: analysis of the barriers to service accessibility, and assessment of the system design with respect to avoiding or minimizing such barriers, i.e., distribution and placement of offices or outreach approaches, services provided in languages used by service population, etc.)
- *Adjustability*. Can the legal aid system/model be adjusted and modified to respond to relevant changes in circumstances? (Indicators: analysis of the system's ability to identify and implement necessary policy changes in response to changed conditions, with an assessment of past responses to changes.)
- *Supportability*. Can the legal aid system/model attract and maintain the necessary support from clients, the state, the courts, funding sources, the legal profession, and other parties? (Indicators: magnitude and longevity of financial and other forms of support for the system/model from significant parties.)

An excellent legal aid system (which would likely include a mix of models) should rate positively on these criteria, which will be applied in evaluating the models and case studies presented in this chapter.

Incentives and Disincentives for Implementing Legal Aid

There are various forms of incentives and disincentives that can be expected to impact major actors involved in the development of expanded legal aid and access to justice systems. As will be noted more specifically below, these incentives and disincentives will vary depending upon national circumstances and the nature of the legal aid model under development. Major actors to be considered include governments, court systems, the bar, intended consumers and other interested groups.

For governments, a major incentive to expand legal aid and access is the understanding that governing under the rule of law requires providing systems to ensure that all persons and groups subject to the jurisdiction of the state can understand their rights and obligations and obtain the protection of the law. Conversely, governments that rule authoritatively have a disincentive to support legal aid and expand access to justice. Uniform access to justice also increases popular confidence in governments and support for them, as well as public participation in the affairs of the state. A strong, independent judiciary broadly accessible to the public increases public confidence in the reliability of economic transactions and stimulates economic development.

Governments aim to provide legal aid and access to justice in a cost-efficient manner so as to allocate public resources most effectively while supporting the orderly administration of justice. Providing legal aid helps promote implementation of laws and regulations promulgated by legislative and executive bodies. In some instances, governments have an incentive to support the functions of legal aid that help effectuate a particular law reform or economic redistribution policy. Through regulation or public subsidy, governments may choose to stimulate the availability of legal aid so as to support certain public policies (i.e., child welfare, workers' rights, land contracts), even while restricting legal aid and access to justice in other areas. Governments are increasingly under pressure from international law, commerce and public opinion to respect the rule of law and assure human rights and access to justice for their citizens. This pressure is brought to bear through such incentives as international trade and development funding and such disincentives as restricted trade and other sanctions that may be applied in extreme circumstances.

The incentives and disincentives for court systems to expand legal aid are somewhat complex. Expanding legal aid can substantially improve the availability of justice for persons otherwise denied access to the court, and can help promote judicial administration and operation. These effects can produce greater professional satisfaction for the judiciary and increased public respect for the courts and the law in general.

However, expansion of legal aid achieves these beneficial effects in part by bringing a greater number of complaints before the court system, increasing legal representation to a greater number of litigants, and helping to review judicial behavior. As a result, increasing legal aid can strain judicial resources and challenge existing judicial practices. Perhaps unfortunately, the compensation of judicial personnel (including judges, prosecutors, public attorneys, clerks and bailiffs) is generally not established in relation to judicial volume. So overall public expenditures for the judiciary may need to be increased in response to greater demand generated by increasing access to justice. In some instances, however, increased legal aid can foster a more efficient judiciary by helping potential litigants better understand and clarify their legal demands and defenses, by providing legal education to prevent legal problems, and by helping to settle through negotiation, mediation or alternative dispute resolution issues that would otherwise require judicial resolution.

Various financial, professional and personal incentives have an effect on members and institutions of the bar in expanding legal aid. Such incentives can include charitable and civic motives, general professional advantage, and individual financial reimbursement.

Permission to practice law is generally regulated by the state and professional associations, and in many countries legal professionals are required or expected to help provide legal aid to indigent persons in some criminal and civil matters as a condition of practice. The relative monopoly granted to members of the bar to render certain services is sometimes premised on the profession's assurances that its services are available to all members of society. Generally, however, this regulatory incentive does not appear to be strongly or uniformly applied to such an extent as to assure adequate access to justice.

In some countries, bar leadership strives to increase public support for the legal profession and the rule of law by supporting professional and public policies that assure more uniform access to justice. In others, failures by the bar to adequately render legal aid may result in state threats to erode the profession's monopoly position by allowing other providers (i.e., paralegals, notaries, and insurance companies) to render certain services at lower cost. This can prompt the legal profession to increase the amount of uncompensated services provided by its members or to support public funding for legal aid that either pays private attorneys for certain services (usually at fee levels below private rates), or creates legal aid offices staffed by salaried attorneys, which releases private attorneys from prior uncompensated pro bono obligations.

In many countries, a substantial percentage of the bar provides legal services to a middle-income clientele with legal needs similar (with some distinctions) to those of the poor. Pay for these attorneys is below the average for their profession. Some of these attorneys have a personal interest in serving the poor and improving access to justice, and provide such service without charge or at reduced rates as their practice can afford. Such attorneys would be interested in receiving public support for helping to provide legal aid in criminal and civil cases. In addition to this financial incentive, other attorneys (normally a small percentage of the national bar) have a personal and ideological commitment to establishing full-time careers as legal aid attorneys serving the poor and promoting social justice, and are willing to accept lower incomes for this career choice. To a great extent, attorneys who work in law school clinics and in nongovernmental legal advocacy organizations operate under similar incentives. Law schools also use clinics serving the poor as an educational tool to help train students in the practice of law.

The primary incentive for low-income and other intended consumers to support expanded legal aid and access to justice is the belief that they will be able to obtain assistance to help them understand their legal rights and responsibilities, prevent legal problems, and gain increased benefits and protections through the legal system. Because of past interactions with the justice system and legal profession in their countries, many consumers must first be educated to better understand the potential benefits of legal aid and greater access to justice for them, their families and communities, including reasons to believe that judicial and governmental institutions will serve them justly.

Some consumers will support expanded legal aid as part of law reforms covering a range of public policies, including police behavior, economic and human rights, land distribution, employment practices, child protection, women's rights, and indigenous issues. Organizations that work in these fields or support public policy reforms, including nongovernmental advocacy groups, churches and labor unions, understand the role of legal advocacy in support of such activities and have an incentive to support expanded legal aid that promotes such law reform.

DESCRIPTION AND ANALYSIS OF LEGAL AID MODELS

This section describes eight primary models of legal aid delivery used around the world, followed by an initial evaluation of each model according to the criteria set above.

It is difficult to provide a current and comprehensive international status report on legal aid from existing data sources, since practices have been in transition over the past decade. Appendix 2.1 presents an overview of legal aid practices around the world and summarizes portions of a 1984 survey on national legal aid practices conducted by the International Bar Association and published as the *International Directory of Legal Aid* (International Bar Association, 1985). While the survey is dated, most of the information regarding national authority for legal aid, types of services provided, primary legal aid models used, and permissible attorney fee arrangements is generally accurate and unchanged.

Private Attorney Models

Many countries primarily use various private attorney models to provide legal aid and access to justice for the poor. These include most European countries, Australia, most of the Canadian provinces, and New Zealand. The specific operation of such models, including services provided and funding mechanisms, varies substantially from country to country.

This chapter uses the term "attorney" to describe members of the legal profession who are authorized to provide the full range of legal services, including such professionals who do so in a private attorney-client relationship, in public service on behalf of a governmental organization, or as staff in a private for-profit business entity or nonprofit organization. In some countries, attorneys are differentiated between those authorized to appear before courts, and those who draft contracts, render advice, and otherwise counsel and represent clients outside of judicial fora. (These are referred to as barristers and solicitors, respectively, in Great Britain). In many civil law countries and in some Canadian provinces, other law-trained professionals called notaries perform various services concerning land transfer and recording, as well as prepare wills, contracts, and other conveyances. Services by all such professionals may be encompassed in a legal aid system, and they are thus included here under the discussion of attorneys, the bar and legal services generally.

Private Attorney Assistance Without Public Subsidy

The primary arrangement for obtaining legal services from private attorneys is through payment by the client either as a specific fee for the transaction or service, or on a hourly basis for work performed. In some instances, services are provided by the private bar on the basis of fees determined by the state or the bar association, taking into consideration such factors as the nature and complexity of the service and the dispute, experience of the attorney, and the ability of the party to pay. There is also some expectation that a minimum of services will be available to lower-income persons in certain areas (such as criminal defense and divorce, for example). In some countries, attorneys are expected by the government or bar association to provide some services without charge. Attorneys frequently constrict the provision of such reduced fee or free services to cases in which they determine that there is substantial merit to the matter in controversy.

In a few countries, including Argentina, Brazil, parts of Canada (British Columbia, Manitoba, and Quebec), Chile, India, Indonesia, Israel, Paraguay, the Philippines, Turkey, and the United States, attorneys provide legal assistance for disputes involving efforts to recover property or a monetary award for a fee that is contingent upon winning the case. This fee is set as a percentage of the amount collected, and no fee is assessed if the case is not successful. This contingent fee arrangement is a successful mechanism for providing legal services to plaintiffs in cases involving a sufficient monetary amount and which exhibit a reasonably high likelihood of success. The contingent fee arrangement does not address the legal needs of the defendants in such actions or of parties to small claims or plaintiffs with marginal chances of prevailing. Nor does it address legal needs not involving monetary claims, or family law actions.

In most countries, such contingent fee arrangements are prohibited for improperly biasing the professional objectivity of the attorney or for other reasons. A limited development of contingent fee arrangements is slowly evolving or under review in a few such countries, however, including Great Britain and Canada. The Hong Kong government has recently established a unique legal aid contingency fund, which low-income clients may draw upon in monetary cases deemed potentially meritorious to retain an attorney to represent their claim. They are required to repay the fund upon receipt of their claim if successful. A limited exception to the general prohibition on contingent fees has developed in the Netherlands' legal aid program. Eligible legal aid clients seeking damages may be provided with a provisional voucher to obtain private attorney representation in the suit, which will be revoked if damages are received from which the attorney can be paid.

In most countries (but generally not Chile, Spain or the United States), the court can assess the losing party to litigation with attorney fees and court costs of the prevailing party. While plaintiffs and defendants are normally expected to advance their own attorney fees to initiate the litigation and defense, this fee-shifting arrangement does provide some legal aid in litigated matters. However, the arrangement has most of the same deficiencies described above regarding contingent fee arrangements. The risk of paying all attorney fees can deter parties (particularly lower-income persons) from bringing litigation, but may also help to stimulate out-of-court settlements. Whereas in the United States each party is generally required to pay its attorney fees regardless of the outcome of the litigation, fee-shifting is established by federal or state statute in certain areas of litigation, including consumer fraud, employment discrimination, and certain claims against the state.

Countries also differ in terms of whether class-action litigation can be brought to try the substantially similar claims of numerous plaintiffs or defendants in one lawsuit. Primary examples include product liability actions against a corporation or damage claims against a governmental entity. Where permitted in countries allowing contingent fees, attorneys can bring a claim on behalf of perhaps hundreds or thousands of litigants with a very substantial monetary amount in controversy even though each individual plaintiff's damage is minor. These cases present the opportunity to receive a large contingency fee.

Forms of legal liability insurance and prepaid legal services plans provide a further variation on the client payment to private attorney model. This model is discussed separately in the section below.

All of the above-mentioned approaches involve either private reimbursement (by the individual client consumer, the litigation loser, or the third-party private insurer) for legal services rendered by private attorneys, or the provision of some level of uncompensated pro bono legal assistance to indigents by private attorneys.

Publicly Subsidized Private Attorney Assistance

Many countries also offer legal aid to income-eligible persons in certain civil and criminal defense matters by providing public funding to private attorneys for such services. This is the primary legal aid delivery model for civil and criminal defense assistance in Great Britain and Wales, Australia, most of Canada, the Scandinavian countries, and the Netherlands, and is a substantial component in many other national legal aid systems (including criminal defense representation in many U.S. states).

In virtually all these countries, the public payment for legal services rendered by private attorneys is substantially below prevailing private fees. Financial eligibility for legal aid is generally set by statute or administrative regulation, with many programs giving consideration to family income and resources (savings, property, etc.) and the likely expense of the legal service requested. Under some national programs, legal aid to qualified persons is rendered without fee to the client, or upon payment of a minor application fee. Other programs (including that of the Netherlands, where nearly half the adult population is eligible for publicly subsidized legal aid) assess a sliding fee copayment toward the attorney fee for persons at the upper ranges of the eligibility scale.

There are various systems for structuring and administering publicly subsidized private attorney legal aid. Two prevalent ones are a certification or voucher program (frequently called "judicare") and a "duty counsel" or "day counsel" program.

Under a judicare program, income-eligible persons who are determined to need attorney services in an eligible problem area (and which may have been determined to be a merit-worthy claim or defense) are referred to a private attorney participating in the program. Or they may select any attorney who agrees to accept judicare-level fees for the requested service. Upon rendering the approved service, the attorney is paid by the publicly funded judicare program. Judicare rates may be set as per the service performed (i.e., a flat fee for an uncontested divorce) or per hour, with caps regardless of time expended. Judicare is frequently operated as a national program with local administration, which may be governmental or under the bar association or foundation. In some instances, a somewhat less formal program exists whereby judges refer indigent parties needing legal assistance to attorneys, who submit bills for services provided to the court for review and payment.

Under duty counsel programs, private attorneys are paid by the court or the local legal aid authority on a daily basis to be in the courthouse and provide advice, counsel and representation to indigent persons appearing without counsel before the court on that day. As with judicare, such services are provided at daily charges below normal private attorney rates. Duty counsel is part of legal service systems in many countries (including Canada, England, the Netherlands and Sweden), frequently in combination with other legal aid models. This model can be a reasonably convenient and efficient approach to helping indigent persons in litigation, though it generally does not assist with other legal needs outside the court setting. Even in litigated matters, however, the duty counsel system fails to provide pre-litigation services to a party to resolve matters before trial, assist with discovery, or help with identifying, preparing and bringing witnesses before the court (unless the court routinely grants continuances to allow for such services in appropriate cases). Duty counsel systems appear to be appreciated by courts, however, because they can help with efficient trial administration.

Judicare and other models using public funding to pay private attorneys for providing legal aid have both strengths and weaknesses. Many countries have an available supply of private attorneys interested in providing such services as a part of their practice at a fee which is discounted from their private billing, and capable of competently providing assistance in many of the types of routine civil and criminal legal matters encountered by both low- and middle-income persons. The private bar appears to have had some success in some European countries and Canadian provinces in helping to secure relatively high levels of public funding for such legal aid. However, private attorney models are generally weak in providing law reform or public policy advocacy, and in rendering assistance in matters unique to the poor, indigenous groups, and other weaker minorities. Private attorneys are generally not located in low-income communities or rural areas.

Legal Insurance and Prepaid Legal Services

Legal liability insurance exists in most countries for a range of risk-generating activities such as operating motor vehicles, conducting a business, and providing medical and other professional services. Under this system, people and businesses obtain private insurance policies that include coverage for legal representation for initiating and defending against legal claims for damages. Over 80 percent of the population of Sweden is covered by legal liability insurance (because of national requirements) and approximately 50 percent of the population of Germany. Most licensed drivers in the United States are required by law to maintain automotive insurance as a condition of car registration. Legal assistance in such matters is thus prepaid, with the cost spread throughout the insured population and attorney compensation rates negotiated by the insurance companies. The insurance companies are able to receive substantial discounts in attorney fees in exchange for a high volume of guaranteed business. The insurance bar has developed management practices to efficiently provide legal assistance through specialization, automation, extensive use of para-professionals, industry-accepted settlement standards, and other approaches.

In a substantially smaller number of countries, including the United States, a further form of general prepaid legal insurance has been developed in recent years to provide legal services for a broader range of matters. These may include providing basic advice and counsel on personal and small business concerns, drafting wills and administering estates, drafting and implementing contracts, negotiating and litigating divorces, carrying out adoptions, and providing some criminal defense representation. While such prepaid legal insurance was initially developed and provided as a group benefit to members of labor unions and other organizations (including most notably the United Auto Workers Legal Services Plan in the United States and Canada), it is now sold on the private market, primarily to a middle-class clientele. Similar prepaid legal insurance plans are available or under development in some South American countries. Like the liability insurance bar described above, the prepaid legal insurance bar has implemented cost saving and efficiency standards. However, there are few if any publicly subsidized prepaid legal insurance programs for the poor that might be comparable to public Medicaid programs in such countries as the United States, Canada and Great Britain. Such a model deserves consideration as a way to provide a broad range of legal assistance under public regulation and review. It could include potential cost-containment and efficiency features if the public and legal profession were to accept some level of bureaucratic administration and control.

The simplest form of a legal service plan is the group discount plan. Under this arrangement, an individual member of the group is referred to a lawyer or law firm recommended by the group leadership. In return, the lawyer may provide free or low-cost advice and consultation plus additional services according to a plan fee schedule or at some fee discount.

Most prepaid legal service plans are more complex than the group discount plan. The "access plan" generally provides legal advice and consultation by telephone. This service may also include brief office consultations, the preparation or review of a simple legal document such as a will, and the writing of short letters or the making of phone calls by a lawyer to an adverse party. If additional services are needed, the plan member is referred to a local attorney who has agreed in advance to provide such services at discounted fees.

The more comprehensive prepaid legal service plans are designed to cover 80 to 90 percent of the average person's legal service needs in a given year. Once the fee has been paid under this plan, benefits are available at no additional charge, except for deductibles and copayments that may apply to certain kinds of services.

A comprehensive plan may provide access services—i.e., legal advice and information by phone—plus coverage for a wide variety of legal work. The plan depends heavily on risk-spreading principles, and assumes that only a certain proportion of the enrolled members will actually use the benefits each year.

Benefits can be stated in terms of either the type of legal problems covered or the type of legal service for which the plan will pay. For example, one plan may provide full coverage for problems involving wills and estates, purchase or sale of a residence, consumer disputes, uncontested divorces and landlord/tenant problems, with partial coverage for traffic matters and other criminal offenses. Another plan may cover unlimited legal advice and consultation by telephone, and pay up to a certain amount for services performed by the lawyer in the office, charging the participants additional amounts for matters involving administrative and judicial proceedings.

All plans limit coverage in some way in order to control cost. Coverage limits may be specified either in terms of money or by stating the number of hours of attorney time for which the plan will pay. Alternatively, the benefit schedule may specify each service for which the plan will pay or provide, regardless of the cost or the time spent. Deductibles and copayments can be applied to some benefits in order to limit the cost of the plan and to discourage frivolous use.

As in other insurance-style arrangements, an administrator handles plan finances, collects contributions, enrolls members, provides plan descriptions and forms to members, processes and pays claims, and files reports required by regulatory agencies. The administrator also establishes and maintains complaint mechanisms to serve the needs of both plan members and service providers who may have a dispute regarding plan coverage, rules or claims.

People enroll in a legal service plan either on a "voluntary" or "true group" basis. In the voluntary model, each potential plan member decides whether to enroll and pay the membership fee or insurance premium. Under a true group arrangement, each person in the group is automatically enrolled by virtue of his or her group membership. The best example of this latter arrangement would be the employer who decides to give all employees legal services as a benefit.

Under a voluntary enrollment model, the rate at which plan members will seek services will be two to four times higher than in a true group situation in the first few years. This is due to the fact that most people who choose to join a prepaid legal service plan either have immediate need for legal services or contemplate such a need in the near future. In a true group plan, some members will have immediate legal problems, while others may never need to use a lawyer.

A prepaid legal service plan can be operated without a legal service provider system. The simplest form of a prepaid legal expense insurance policy promises to reimburse the policyholder for legal service expenses according to a schedule of benefits. The policyholder seeks out an attorney on his or her own, has the services performed, pays the attorney, and submits a claim to the insurance company for reimbursement,

However, very few plans today operate in this manner. Normally, there is some sort of system that organizes lawyers into a contract service provider panel. This panel may consist of one lawyer or a group of lawyers who agree to the terms and conditions under which the plan is operated.

In some plans, legal advice by telephone is provided by one law firm or a small group of law firms in each state, retained specifically for this service. Plan members are referred to local firms for additional legal representation as needed. Other plans contract with lawyers in areas where they have members to handle all covered services, including telephone legal advice.

Legal service plans usually state criteria that lawyers must meet in order to become legal service providers. Professional liability insurance, relevant professional experience, convenient office hours and an adequate phone system are among the most common requirements. A few plans need specialists in certain areas of the law, but most concentrate on recruiting experienced general practitioners in the geographic area where they have members.

Staff Attorney Models

After private attorney models, which continue as the predominant legal aid delivery system for most of the world, the most common legal aid model is the staff attorney program. Staffed legal services offices are the primary legal aid system for providing civil legal assistance to indigents in the United States, where many states also use staffed public defender offices for indigent criminal representation. In Quebec, Canada, staffed legal offices provide over half of the services in civil matters and a smaller portion of criminal defense services. A few other countries, such as Ireland, rely primarily on staffed legal aid offices for civil or criminal representation, while such offices play a proportionally smaller role in the Netherlands, other Canadian provinces, parts of Australia, Indonesia, Israel, Paraguay, Sweden, the Philippines, Great Britain, and Korea. In these countries or regions the legal aid offices work in conjunction with various private attorney models, law school clinics, nongovernmental legal advocacy organizations, government-employed attorneys, and other programs.

The most comprehensive staff attorney program in the world has been established in the United States to provide civil legal assistance to the poor. Now under the national authority of the Legal Services Corporation created by the U.S. Congress, this program began in the mid-1960s with an emphasis on law reform. That laid the foundation for constant political conflict, and evolved in more recent decades into more of an access to justice delivery system.

This section summarizes the development and operation of the U.S. Legal Services Corporation as an example of the staff attorney model (and, particularly during its initial U.S. Office of Economic Opportunity phase, as an example of a "public interest law" model).[1] The section also describes operations of this model when it is part of mixed model delivery systems, as in the cases of the Netherlands and the Canadian provinces of Quebec and Ontario.

The origins of the U.S. legal services program date to the establishment of the German Legal Aid Society in New York City in 1876, initially to aid German immigrants with civil and criminal matters. For the next 89 years, legal aid offices in the United States were supported primarily by bar associations and private charity. By 1965, these organizations were supporting 236 local legal aid organizations that financed the equivalent of 400 full-time attorneys providing assistance in civil and criminal matters on behalf of more than 50 million indigent Americans.

During the early 1960s, the Ford Foundation and other private foundations funded a small number of model inter-city legal services offices to undertake legal advocacy on civil issues affecting large numbers of poor persons. These neighborhood law offices, focusing on community legal education and law reform activities, became the prototypes for the first federally-funded legal services program established in 1965 by the U.S. Office of Economic Opportunity (OEO) as a part of President Lyndon Johnson's "War on Poverty." By 1974, the program provided funding to state and local legal services employing 2,660 attorneys, with support staff working in over 850 offices in more than 200 cities and towns throughout the United States.

The OEO Legal Services Program established the primary structures of federal and local relationships that exist to the present day. The federal agency did not work with state or local governmental units, but made grants to local nonprofit organizations of attorneys to provide civil legal services to indigents within a given geographic and political service area (i.e., from one to more than 20 programs per state), normally providing only one grant per service area. OEO grants were given

---

[1] See Rhudy (1994).

on an annual basis and grantees were selected based on compliance with OEO standards to provide legal assistance that emphasized representing client organizations and attacking the causes and effects of poverty. The OEO also required the inclusion of the poor on grantee governing boards, encouraged services to organizations of poor persons, and required provision of community legal education and preventive law activities. While many grantees were pre-existing local bar association-controlled legal aid offices (which previously had more traditional individual case service practices, often provided by private attorneys for reduced fees), others were created in response to the OEO legal philosophy and new federal funding.

In addition to these neighborhood service programs, the OEO program made substantial grants to specialized national support centers focusing on particular subject areas (such as housing and welfare reform) or on particular client groups, including the elderly and Native Americans. These centers undertook national advocacy through litigation and through legislative or administrative agency representation, and they sought to develop the expertise of the neighborhood programs. Grants were also given to a few model state support centers that provided similar functions on a state level. Virtually all of these programs (neighborhood offices, national and state support centers) employed full-time, salaried staff attorneys.

During their brief history, OEO-funded legal services attorneys aggressively represented their poor clients before state and federal courts, agencies and legislatures against landlords, financial institutions, corporations and, particularly, state and federal governments. Their advocacy literally created a new body of poverty law in the United States. Legal decisions were won that created new or expanded rights of tenants, welfare recipients, debtors, migrant farm workers, and many other low income groups. Earl Johnson, Jr., who directed the OEO Legal Services Program during 1966-68 and now serves as a justice on the California Court of Appeals, wrote:

> In the entire 89-year history of the legal aid movement from 1876 to 1965, not one legal aid staff lawyer had taken a case to the United States Supreme Court. Yet in five years—from 1967 to 1972—219 cases involving the rights of the poor were brought to the high court, 136 were decided on the merits, and 73 of these were won. (Johnson, 1978, p. 189)

The successes of these OEO-funded legal aid attorneys quickly generated substantial opposition. There were continuous efforts by the states and the U.S. Congress through the late 1960s and early 1970s to drastically restrict or eliminate the program. The Legal Services Corporation Act of 1974 was a culmination of efforts to insulate the federal legal services program from political pressures while addressing some of the criticisms made of OEO law reform activities. As the successor to the OEO, the Legal Services Corporation (LSC) is an autonomous non-profit corporation, not within a federal agency. It is governed by a Board of Directors whose 11 members are nominated by the U.S. President and confirmed by the U.S. Senate for three-year terms. Not more than six members of the board can come from one political party. The LSC Act requires that persons eligible to receive legal services be on the board, and all LSC boards have maintained two client-eligible members. The remainder are attorneys. The board serves without compensation and selects the full-time president who serves as chief executive officer, hiring and directing all remaining staff for the corporation. The LSC reports annually to the U.S. President and Congress, receives annual Congressional appropriations for its activities, adopts regulations, and makes and reviews legal services grants.

Generally continuing the earlier OEO role, the LSC Act does not permit the corporation to directly provide legal assistance to indigents, but empowers it to make grants to and contract with nonprofit organizations, attorneys or other entities for the delivery of civil legal services to low-income persons throughout the United States and its territories. The LSC can make grants for basic field service, on behalf of particular client groups (i.e., Native Americans, migrant farm workers), and (until Congress amended its funding in 1996) for national or state support centers. The LSC can also conduct research and training and provide technical assistance, as well as perform other activities to support, improve and expand civil legal services for the poor. Like the OEO, the LSC has virtually no relationship with state or local governmental entities.

Each grantee program receiving LSC funds is required to be governed by a board of directors. The boards are primarily made up of attorneys, but at least one-third of their members must be client-eligible persons. Board members are selected by and from local bar associations, community action programs, client organizations, and other entities. A majority of the board must be attorneys appointed by the governing boards of state or local bar associations in the program's area. Because the LSC has never been adequately funded to serve more than a small percentage of the need for its services, the grantee board is required by the LSC Act and subsequent regulations to establish priorities to determine what kinds of issues, cases or persons will receive legal assistance.

The LSC Act also includes a comprehensive list of restrictions on the corporation and its grantees regarding activities that had generated substantial opposition when undertaken by OEO-funded legal services offices. Some restrictions are outright bans on particular types of activities, such as political involvement and demonstrations, or bans on substantive case areas such as school busing in pursuit of racial integration and abortion-related litigation. Other restrictions create specific requirements and procedures regarding the provision of certain client services, such as class action representations and legislative or administrative advocacy. Generally, however, the LSC Act in 1974 continued an expansive view of the classes of legal concerns and types of services that could be provided, and whatever Congressional intent existed to reduce policy advocacy and law reform activities had very limited effect until the 1990s.

The LSC Act clearly intended to shift the OEO Legal Services Program's law reform focus toward an emphasis on providing access to justice. By 1976, the newly confirmed LSC Board of Directors adopted a "minimum access" standard in furtherance of this goal and to justify increased federal funding for the program. Minimum access was a proposal to provide and equitably distribute one LSC-funded attorney per 5,000 low-income persons throughout the United States. The LSC's minimum access proposal was successful with Congress, and the corporation's appropriations grew from $91 million in fiscal year 1976 to $321.3 million in fiscal year 1981, at which point the minimum access goal had essentially been achieved.

Minimum access was not intended, however, to ensure any particular person legal assistance in any given legal matter anywhere in the United States. It was simply a formula to allocate funding to legal services programs for minimal attorney staffing at the 1/5,000 ratio. (By comparison, the current ratio of attorneys to the United States population is approximately 1/335.) Each program receiving an LSC grant was required to establish priorities indicating what type of client and legal matter would receive what form and level of service, while not establishing a right to service for any individual.

By 1981, the LSC was making annual grants to 323 nonprofit legal services programs, including 290 basic field programs and 33 specialized grants to offices in all 50 states, the District of Columbia, the U.S. Virgin Islands, Puerto Rico, the Micronesian Trust Territories, and Guam. During that year, these programs employed 6,218 attorneys and 15,293 total staff in 1,425 offices, and provided legal assistance in just over 1.2 million matters.

In 1980, federal funding for the LSC was reduced, resulting in a substantial cutback from minimum access staffing levels and reduced legal services. National legal services policy development essentially ceased during this period as the result of a stalemate between persons nominated to the LSC by President Reagan, perceived as hostile to the program, and the corporation's grantees, the ABA, legal services advocates, and the U.S. Congress. The LSC's appropriations increased from $308.5 million in fiscal year 1989 to $357 million in 1993 and to $405 million in 1995 under a Democratic Congress, but dropped again in a Republican-controlled U.S. Congress to $283 million in 1998, well below the $321 million in fiscal year 1981, when adjusted for inflation and increases in the number of people living in poverty.

The stalemate and retrenchment in federal legal services policy throughout the 1980s stimulated some positive developments in both voluntary attorney services and legal services policy at the state level. Following the lead of the ABA to expand voluntary private attorney pro bono services, an estimated 135,000 attorneys currently participate in state and local programs cooperating with LSC grantees to provide civil legal services to indigents. Also, since 1981, interest on lawyer trust accounts (IOLTA) funding programs has been established in every state and the District of Columbia to help fund civil legal services activities within those jurisdictions. These IOLTA programs are the second largest funding source in the United States, after the LSC, for civil legal services to the poor, making grants of up to $100 million annually to LSC grantees and other programs.

Other state and local governmental funding for legal services also increased substantially over the period. In 1981, all state and local government funding to LSC grantees totaled approximately $5 million, increasing to approximately $50 million annually by 1990 and over $100 million by 1998. Many new state organizations that administer IOLTA and other state-generated revenues are now playing a major role in legal services development, actively participating in legal services funding, delivery innovation, grant making, monitoring, and policy development. Such state activity did not exist in 1981.

Despite nearly 30 years of federal funding and more recent state efforts to provide civil legal services to indigents in the United States, most poor persons needing legal assistance go unserved. Recent studies at the state and national level have consistently concluded that less than 20 percent of the need for legal assistance by poor persons in civil matters is being met under current program resources and practices.

The staff attorney model is generally viewed as affording increased specialization with legal problems unique to low-income persons and distinct subgroups (i.e., rural farmers, native peoples, children), and being better suited for law reform activities. It may also be used to establish services in locations not served by the private bar. In the United States, however, the staff attorney system has failed to develop government support for the level of public funding received in other countries by various private attorney judicare systems. One major impediment to funding in the United States has likely been the U.S. system's initial emphasis on law reform, which engendered political opposition to the program that continues to the present day.

Law School Clinical Model

Legal services in civil matters (and criminal defense to a much smaller extent) are provided by law school clinic programs in many countries, including Canada, Colombia, Finland, Great Britain, Guatemala, India, Nepal, the Netherlands, Panama, the Philippines, South Africa, Sri Lanka, Sweden and the United States. The law school clinic has two purposes: (1) law student training in practical skills in the provision of direct client services, in a controlled setting under the direction of clinical professors or practicing attorneys; and (2) the provision of client services. In most law school systems, the primary purpose of clinics is educational. Since this model calls for a fairly low student-faculty ratio and client-student ratio, other models can generally provide most legal aid functions or services more cost-effectively. While law students are relatively "cheap," they are generally inefficient in relation to more experienced (and expensive) legal assistance advocates, and they require higher levels of supervision. When the ratio of students to supervisors is increased substantially to provide service to greater numbers of persons, there will be concerns about quality control of the student work. Clinics may provide a general range of services in routine civil or criminal defense matters. More frequently, they focus on certain legal issues (divorce, disability rights, rental housing disputes, etc.) or client populations (women, children, native peoples, immigrants, etc.).

The law school clinic model appears to have received the greatest attention in the United States. Despite having developed only since the late 1960s, civil law clinics now operate in over half of the 174 U.S. law schools. They employ approximately 400 full-time clinical professors or supervising attorneys, who manage a broad range of family law, juvenile justice, disability advocacy, public entitlement, housing, senior citizen and other clinic programs. Funding for these programs comes primarily from traditional law school revenues (i.e., tuition, public support, private contributions), as well as about $15 million annually from the U.S. Department of Education, $1 million in grants annually from state interest on lawyer trust account (IOLTA) foundations, private foundation grants, and approximately $1 million annually (from 1984 to 1994) from the U.S. Legal Services Corporation (Legal Services Corporation, 1992; Trubek, 1994.)

A few U.S. law schools require clinical experience, internships, externships, or other forms of structured and supervised public interest experience as a condition for graduation. A small number of U.S. law school clinic directors and professors have experience in helping to establish clinic programs in other countries, including some Spanish-speaking attorneys with particular interest in Latin America.

A program that deserves attention in terms of the potential expansion of law school clinical services in a developing country is the National Law School of India at the University at Bangalore, India. It was founded in 1986 by the Bar Council of India as a "model institute for pioneering legal education reforms [and]…imparting a socially relevant and professionally competent scheme of legal education" (Menon, 1996). The curriculum emphasizes problems of poverty, caste-based socioeconomic disabilities, gender-based discrimination, and the impact of long periods of colonial rule. To help students understand the legal work involved in different areas, the law school places them for two months each year with different NGOs, law offices, companies, political parties, government offices, and social activists. There is an annual community-based law reform competition to help develop these skills and encourage attention to social engineering through application of the law. The law school also promotes a range of legal aid outreach activities to various community and institutional settings on behalf of children, prisoners, consumers, human rights, welfare reform, and other issues.

While law school clinics generally focus on individual client services, some clinics in the United States and other countries have undertaken law reform (or "impact") work in various areas to develop new public policies. Where such law schools depend on public funding or other support, however, and where their advocacy runs contrary to prevailing state directions, such law reform activities are likely to be minimal (Kharel, 1996). Commenting on a gender discrimination public interest lawsuit successfully brought before the Supreme Court of Nepal in part by a law clinic at Tribhuvan University, Nepal, Kharel states:

> In Nepal, 97 percent of the Tribhuvan University's budget is granted by the government. Being an employee of such an institution it is really hard to get support from higher authority of the University or faculty in initiating any public interest law case against the government. The term academic freedom is being used only for lip service, indeed. For any teacher seriously involved in such activities, it is common to receive express or implied threat of termination from their job. Usually, in any case that may lead to serious effect to the government, students or teachers are not allowed to mention the name of the faculty. (Kharel, 1996, pp. 94-95)

Another occasionally used legal aid model uses recent law school graduates in law school or public clinics. In various countries, law school graduates are required to serve a period of supervised work experience under a licensed attorney (usually at little or no salary) before they are eligible to seek admission to the bar. Partially in response to the difficulties that black law student graduates in South Africa encountered in being accepted for such work experience, a law school clinic was established to provide them with supervised internships while providing legal assistance to indigent native persons and groups. Other countries (i.e., Barbados) provide state scholarships for law students in exchange for a service requirement in public clinics on a full or part-time basis upon graduation and admission to the bar. Guatemala has also operated such clinics with recent graduates.

While the law school clinical model may be relatively inefficient due to its dual teaching and service roles and limited by only being able to provide services close to law school settings, it can nevertheless contribute to improving access to the justice system. These contributions include the following: (1) law schools often enjoy some status within a country, so the activities of their clinical programs can increase the overall legitimacy of efforts to improve access to justice; (2) even in countries where there is relatively little governmental support for access to justice, law schools and their clinical programs may be somewhat more insulated from governmental opposition than similar nongovernmental "public interest" law reform programs or other related entities working toward the same objective; (3) law school clinical experiences can help orient law students who may not otherwise have contact with the poor and their legal rights and problems; and (4) law school clinicians may be in a position to promote, direct and undertake research and practice that specializes on the legal problems and public policy needs of poor and other underserved people, groups and issues.

To a fairly consistent extent, law school clinic attorneys (i.e., clinical professors or directing attorneys) have personal motivations to help provide the poor and underserved with better access to justice and view them as their clients. In their educational and supervisory roles overseeing the delivery of legal services, these attorneys strive to impart their personal values to students.

Because of the inherent cost inefficiencies in providing quality service, the law school clinic model generally is not suited to provide services on large scale to improve access to justice. Nonetheless, it can make a key contribution by promoting the importance of access to justice, both to the general public and within the legal profession, by fostering professional understanding of the legal issues and problems of the poor and underserved.

The Law Reform Public Interest Model

There are nongovernmental legal advocacy organizations in nearly every country of the world that play some role in helping to preserve, protect, promote or advance the legal rights, interests and protections of various people, groups or causes. A directory published by the International Human Rights Internship in 1997, *Legal Aid and Public Interest Law Organizations,* identified more than 350 such public interest programs in developing countries. These NGO-operated legal advocacy centers function in a variety of ways. They have an assortment of private and public funding sources and perform some or all of the legal assistance functions discussed earlier in this chapter. A major focus has been the protection and advancement of human rights, civil rights and liberties, environmental protection, consumer protection, and the protection and expansion of the rights of indigenous peoples, racial, religious or ethnic minorities, women and children.

The current and potential contribution of this "public interest" law reform model to increasing legal assistance and access to justice for the poor is significant in some settings but limited in the range of services provided. To give some scale, of nearly 900,000 licensed attorneys in the United States, of which approximately 20,000 are publicly-funded public defender and civil legal aid staff attorneys, there are only about 1,500 to 2,000 "public interest attorneys" working in nongovernmental organizations on behalf of such issues as civil rights, civil liberties, environmental preservation, human rights, consumer law, women's rights and juvenile protection. The public interest bars in other countries are even smaller, despite the fact that the model has developed around the world over the past 30 years. Yet in some areas and instances, the impact of public interest lawyers on the law has been substantial, even while their quantum of direct services in individual cases has been minor.

While public interest law centers may perform a variety of roles in some countries, their primary function is change or reform of the law on behalf of their client group. They use a variety of strategies to publicize abuses, change public opinion, and advocate for preferred public policies through public relations initiatives, community organizing, major test case litigation by class actions or high court appeals, petitions for legislative action (i.e., "lobbying"), and political action. A few governments (i.e., Indonesia, Nigeria) have severely punished (including prison, torture and death) some public interest advocates for their efforts to reform the law.

The line of demarcation between a private NGO staff attorney clinic and a public interest law reform office is not always clear. While some NGO centers limit their services to community legal education and basic client services, the public interest offices normally employ a "macro" approach (i.e., focused on redirecting legal, governmental, economic and social policies and systems) rather than on helping people individually with their legal problems. It is generally the responsibility of other models discussed in this chapter to apply the law in day-to-day cases.

Staff attorneys working in these areas are primarily supported by private contributions from individuals and foundations, with some minor support from attorney fees and other funding sources. In some countries, these law centers have contracts with agricultural communes, rural co-ops, trade unions or women's centers to represent the organizations or their members (which helps to assure client control, as discussed below). NGO legal advocacy centers, some of which focus on law reform, provide services throughout Latin America and the Caribbean for a range of human rights and various other causes. In such countries as India, Nigeria, Pakistan, Philippines and Sri Lanka, public interest law centers begun by or affiliated with prominent national attorneys have made substantial contributions to preserving or expanding the legal rights and protections of indigent persons and classes.

Regardless of country, clientele or purpose, public interest legal centers are normally funded by private sources such as foundations, membership fees, donations, court awards or partial client fees. A variation of this model is the small number of publicly funded public interest legal offices that provide certain public oversight and advocacy functions. One example was the New Jersey (U.S.) Department of Public Advocate, which had advocacy responsibilities on behalf of the state's mentally ill, mentally retarded, prison inmates, consumer representation concerning public utilities, and various other citizen complaints. The department was created in 1974 and abolished in 1994 when a more conservative governor was elected. A more limited example is the People's Counsel to the Maryland Public Service Commission, which serves as a public advocate in rate hearings and other public utility regulatory and legislative actions. This model appears to have the potential to be relatively effective and credible when functioning in a time of supportive governments, but to be subject to drastic declines in influence (even existence) when governments change.

The primary incentive for attorneys working in public interest law reform centers is the personal and professional satisfaction of changing public policies in ways that reflect their values. To some extent, such attorneys select their clients and issues from the national circumstances in cooperation with their philanthropic funding sources. The challenge in implementing public interest law reform lies in defining the clients to be served, while assuring that those clients establish which issues and priorities to address and which policies and remedies to pursue.

Ombudsmen

The ombudsman model originated in Sweden in 1713 and has been implemented in other parts of Scandinavia, Western Europe, Israel, parts of Australia, Canada, the United States, and a few other countries. Its purpose is to investigate, mediate and resolve citizen complaints against the actions of public officials. The ombudsmen movement expanded substantially during the 1960s and 1970s, backed by such organizations as the United Nations, the International Bar Association, the International Commission of Jurists, and the Council of Europe. Their interest was in encouraging development and use of this model principally to protect human, civil and political rights against autocratic or arbitrary state actions. The model and concept have also been applied in various other private settings such as consumer complaints against businesses and intra-organizational complaints.

A 1974 International Bar Association resolution provides a brief description of the ombudsman:

> An office provided for by the constitution or by action of the legislature or parliament and headed by an independent, high level public official who is responsible to the legislature or parliament, who receives complaints from aggrieved persons against government agencies, officials, and employees or who acts on his own motion, and who has the power to investigate, recommend corrective action, and issue reports.

Wherever conditions exist to establish an ombudsman office with the requisite independence, authority, power and credibility, it can be a highly efficient and effective model to provide legal assistance, oversee public action, and perhaps undertake law reform in matters concerning public agency activities.

Simplified Judicial or Administrative Dispute Resolution Model

Each of the models discussed prior to the ombudsman model focuses on ways to provide attorneys to help people understand and implement their legal rights, responsibilities or remedies. But countries have an alternative course of action available to provide their citizens access to justice, as recognized by major international human rights decisions: providing simplified legal procedures for implementing legal rights and settling disputes.

One of the earliest major examples of this approach was the development of small claims courts in various countries throughout this century as a forum to settle, in a simplified fashion, a fairly high volume of disputes involving small financial claims. In some instances, other routine disputes such as landlord-tenant claims and divorce have also been simplified. Courts similar to small claims courts (sometimes referred to as "Magistrate's Courts" or "Justices of the Peace") have been developed for minor criminal charges.

A parallel movement has been the development of administrative dispute resolution procedures, particularly for claims involving governmental action that originally required judicial determination. Examples include labor and employment claims, insurance disputes, welfare determinations, and disputes over licenses and permits. A further relatively recent movement is the development of other alternative dispute resolution mechanisms (primarily mediation or arbitration, but also ombudsman offices as a specialized model) that are available or required either privately or through public offices to resolve conflicts that would otherwise have required judicial intervention. Under most of these approaches, parties generally can appeal for judicial review of the small claims ruling, administrative determination, or other alternative resolution for judicial review or determination.

Various aspects of this model should be implemented whenever feasible, with the understanding that these services require adequate public resources, management and review. The primary challenge for these approaches lies in the recruitment, training and management of people who can efficiently provide these services in an objective, timely and professional manner. Adequate salary levels must be established to attract and retain qualified personnel, working under standards to maintain appropriate service.

Legal Advice, Assistance, Screening and Referral Model

Providing a large volume of information, education, advice and assistance to low and moderate income persons with legal questions and problems is one approach to improving access to justice that is receiving considerable attention in several countries. This model may be developed and operated by court personnel, legal aid staff, law school clinics, nonprofit public interest centers or other organizations.

It often uses paralegals, other non-attorney staff and volunteers under the general supervision of attorneys, and uses computers and telecommunications to increase the efficient delivery of its services.

Various service techniques associated with this model have been developed and applied by legal aid staff offices or prepaid legal insurance programs in the United States, Canada, Australia, and other areas. Recently there has been renewed interest (partly driven by cost-containment needs) in expanding the use of this model to assist persons seeking legal information and access to the courts. One good example is the Self-Service Center of the Superior Court of Maricopa County in Arizona (U.S.). The Australian province of New South Wales is also devoting considerable attention to the development of high volume legal information and self-help services. Through a project using a combination of private foundation and public funding, the state of Maryland (U.S.) is in the process of establishing a Maryland Legal Assistance Network. It relies on telephone information and advice services, an Internet-based "People's Law Library," and expanded applications of brief, discrete task "unbundled" attorney services, among other approaches. The network is serving as a national demonstration project of this information service model.

Current efforts in various countries to expand basic access to legal assistance through this approach, combined in some instances with simplified judicial and administrative or "alternative" dispute resolution mechanisms, are similar to models implemented with varying levels of success in several Central and Eastern European countries following World War II. As described by Vittori Denti in Zemans (1979, pp. 355-56):

> The situation in socialist countries must be examined separately, since the problem of the right to counsel is seen in a different perspective—even the concept of "underprivileged" cannot be clearly defined. The basic principle of socialist legal systems is the attainment of substantial equality through simple, free procedures which enable all citizens to assert their own rights quickly and at no cost. According to a principle common to the procedural codes of all socialist countries, the judge is to assist all parties by intervening in the drafting of the complaint (which can be presented orally) and by giving appropriate directions during the proceedings. This is a duty, not a discretionary power of the judge; and in some systems its violation may lead to the invalidation of the proceedings.

> According to the socialist system, the assistance of counsel in civil actions is not compulsory. As a consequence, the problem of providing counsel for persons unable to pay for a lawyer does not arise. Moreover, hiring a member of a bar association is fairly easy since fees are low, and can be reduced even further if necessary.

Legal expenses are also treated differently in socialist countries. Exemption is granted not in relation to the economic status of the parties but as a priority for given categories of conflicts (labor, alimony, damages for work accidents, etc.).

Individual exemptions can be granted on the discretion of the judge, on the basis of economic conditions. A similar discretionary evaluation is made by the chairmen of the collective of attorneys upon a request for free legal assistance.

The organization of lawyers into public offices provides legal advice on a general basis. The group of attorneys must offer free oral advice to all those who ask for it, while for written advice a small fee is charged. It should be emphasized that the judge himself fulfills an advisory function, since he is obliged to assist all parties throughout the proceedings.

Finally, socialist countries meet the need for more accessible systems of justice through public bodies peculiar to these countries. For example, the public prosecutor can bring civil actions on behalf of an individual if the individual is unable to act because of economic constraints. Social organizations such as trade unions can also intervene in the proceedings in support of a party; and there are social courts, which are special jurisdictional bodies entrusted with the resolution of minor disputes. There has been a recent tendency in the socialist countries to increase the parties' responsibility in the proceedings. This trend increases the need for counsel in civil proceedings, thus extending the tasks of lawyers' organizations as far as legal assistance to economically weak parties is concerned.

It is noteworthy that Denti believed that developing countries, primarily because they could not afford an attorney-based legal aid system, should provide access to justice primarily through simplified dispute resolution approaches. His recommendations remain relevant today, lending support to implementation of the more recent generation of legal information, advice and self-service systems as a foundation for access to justice. Denti further writes:

The problems of legal aid in the developing countries deserve special attention. In these countries, it is necessary to reconcile the restructuring of the legal system with the concept of access to justice for the majority of the population which is still bound to dispute settlement through tribal or customary law.

Developing countries have directed their reform attempts towards reducing the pluralism which exists in the administration of justice and in substantive law. This implies a restriction of customary law, which is itself an obstacle to access to justice for the poor. The centralization of courts and the rationalization of the law require more professional judges and the assistance of a lawyer.

Professional specialization stresses the need for legal aid. At this point, however, there is a danger of the monopolization of counseling by the few lawyers available, who are mainly concentrated in the capital cities.

On the other hand, the cost of a truly efficient legal aid system would be unbearable for these poor countries. As a consequence, legal aid on a universal basis is not yet feasible, at least as far as civil cases are concerned. It has correctly been observed that an efficient legal aid system requires a high national economic standard, a relatively small proportion of poor people, the availability of many lawyers willing to perform a socially oriented activity, the independence of courts, and the existence of constitutional principles regulating fundamental guarantees in the administration of justice. The absence of these conditions in developing countries indicates that access to justice can be attained not through the introduction of legal aid schemes such as those found in Western countries, but by eliminating the need for representation by counsel. This means simpler procedures, initiative powers for the judge with respect to the course of the proceedings and to the assembly of evidence, and the creation of special conciliation boards and greater utilization of small claims courts. The maintenance of legal pluralism and of traditional dispute settlement techniques typical of customary law is regarded as necessary to a certain extent. (Zemans, 1979, pp. 356-57)

Evaluation of Legal Aid Models

Table 2.1 evaluates the various legal aid models described in this chapter in terms of their ability to provide access to justice and deliver legal services to the poor. Some substantial reservations regarding such a simplified evaluation approach need to be discussed at the outset. In spite of such reservations, however, the table is useful to show the salient characteristics and general strengths and weaknesses of the 10 models evaluated.

First and foremost, the actual performance of any legal services delivery program or system will depend on a number of key factors, particularly leadership, governance structure, funding level, and the nature of the legal, governmental, economic, cultural and institutional environment in which it operates. None of these factors are reflected in Table 2.1. Secondly, any legal services model can reflect a wide range of variations in its activities and operations. For instance, a staff attorney clinic may or may not provide a large amount of legal information services or undertake law reform activities. Such choices will determine if this particular staff attorney program is evaluated as high or low on these functions, and on such standards of comprehensiveness, effectiveness and supportability. (Most staff attorney programs provide a moderate to high level of legal information and a low to moderate amount of law reform services.) The evaluations in Table 2.1 reflect only perceptions of the nonexistent "average" staff attorney model (or law school clinic model, or subsidized private attorney model, etc.). Finally, the table and its ratings reflect the perceptions, experiences, findings and biases of the author.

The 10 models considered are those described in this chapter, as follows: (i) three variations of the private attorney model (private attorneys operating with no public subsidy, providing services either for private fee or without compensation, voluntarily or upon court or other order; private attorneys receiving a public subsidy such as in a judicare or duty counsel program; and private attorneys operating within a legal insurance or prepaid legal assistance program); (ii) staff attorney model; (iii) law school clinic; (iv) nongovernmental public interest law reform center; (v) governmental public interest law reform center; (vi) ombudsmen; (vii) simplified dispute resolution center; and (viii) legal advice center. The table uses a system of three ratings or grades: low (L), moderate (M), and high (H). For example, the model being evaluated might be determined to normally have provided a low (L) amount of legal information, or it might have been rated high (H) regarding the benefited public as its client. In some instances, ratings of L-M or M-H and even occasionally L-H are provided. A question mark indicates that there is too little information to attempt an assessment.

Models are evaluated on their perceived average and potential performance of five legal service functions described in this chapter: the provision of legal information, legal assistance, public action review, law reform, and access to justice activities. They are also evaluated as per the incentives discussed in the chapter; that is, according to the incentives they offer to service providers to regard the benefited public as their clients, and incentives they provide to the court, private attorneys and bar associations, the public interest bar and government to support that particular model. It must be cautioned that the characteristics and attitudes of such actors may differ considerably from one country to another. Finally, the models are evaluated on seven standards proposed, described and defined in this chapter: comprehensiveness of services, effectiveness, efficiency, affordability, accessibility, adjustability, and supportability.

Four criteria for evaluation that are discussed in this chapter are not included in the table because they present factors that are characteristic more of an actual program or system than of a model. These four criteria are competency, cost sharing capabilities, independence, and credibility. It should be noted, however, that two of the 10 models (the nongovernmental public interest model and the ombudsman model) exhibit institutionally higher levels of independence than the other eight.

FACTORS AFFECTING DEVELOPMENT OF MODELS OF LEGAL AID AND ACCESS TO JUSTICE IN LATIN AMERICA

Expanding legal aid and access to justice in Latin America requires taking into account a range of factors similar to those that have come into play in judicial reform programs that have been or are being implemented in the region. The presence, nature and interplay of these factors in the various and diverse countries of the region will affect the likelihood of expanding the level and quality of legal aid and access to justice. Factors to be considered include:

• *Respect for the rule of law.* Does the state respect the rule of law for all members of society, or does it govern in an authoritarian manner without respecting the legal rights of all persons within its jurisdiction? Without governance under the rule of law, it is unlikely that efforts to expand legal aid and access to justice will be successful. While it may be possible, though difficult, to establish various legal aid institutions in such a situation, these institutions will have very limited success in expanding actual access to justice for their clients beyond certain proscribed areas. Does the state have the willingness and financial ability to provide public funding for legal aid? Will the government be supportive of law reform activities in addition to basic access to justice services?

• *Status of the judiciary: independence, integrity, competence, efficiency, and respect.* Is the judiciary assured independence from the other branches of government and other elites in its operations and decision-making? Are the members of the judiciary relatively immune from undue influence and corruption, and capable of rendering decisions that are not biased by the class, race, ethnicity, gender or other improper distinctions of the parties? Is the judiciary composed of competent persons? Does it have adequate resources, and are they administered in a reasonably efficient manner? Are the state's judicial institutions sufficiently respected to be used by citizens in a wide range of disputes? What other state institutions and mechanisms exist to resolve disputes, how well do they operate, and are they widely used? The status of the state judiciary and other dispute resolution institutions is a crucial factor to be considered in determining what functions a legal aid system can provide and what legal aid model is most likely to successfully provide them.

• *Status and operation of the legal profession.* Is the legal profession substantially regulated by the state or by professional associations, or relatively independent?

Table 2.1 Summary Evaluation of Legal Aid Models

Legal Aid Models	Rating	Comments
Private Attorney 1 - No Public Subsidy		
FUNCTIONS		Ratings for this model are in regards to its services to indigent and lower in-come persons rather than relatively middle or higher income clients. If private attorneys under this model do not provide discounted or reduced fees for these groups, their services are normally very difficult to afford in most parts of the world except in those instances where fee shifting is allowed (i.e., contingency fee or "loser pays" circumstances) in cases with a relatively high probability of winning. If provided without charge upon court order, requirement of licensure, bar association expectation, or even at a substantially reduced rate, such services tend to be limited in scope and availability, and do not provide an incentive for the attorney to regard the benefited person as a client to the degree accorded a full-paying client. Such a system receives very limited actual bar support, except to the extent that it maintains the monopoly of the profession to provide legal services to the paying public. The model is affordable by the state, in that virtually no public funds are required for its operation, but substantially unaffordable by the intended users. And it is supportable because of a low public cost and little opposition from the legal profession so long as the actual expectation of free or reduced cost services to indigent and low-income persons is minimal.
LEGAL INFORMATION	L	
LEGAL ASSISTANCE	L	
PUBLIC ACTION REVIEW	L	
LAW REFORM	L	
ACCESS TO JUSTICE	L	
INCENTIVES		
REGARD BENEFITED		
PUBLIC AS CLIENT	L	
COURT SUPPORT	L	
PRIVATE ATTORNEY BAR		
SUPPORT	L-M	
PUBLIC INTEREST BAR		
SUPPORT	L	
GOVERNMENT SUPPORT	M	
COMPREHENSIVENESS	L	
EFFECTIVENESS	L	
STANDARDS		
EFFICIENCY	L	
AFFORDABILITY	L	
ACCESSIBILITY	L-H	
ADJUSTABILITY	L	
SUPPORTABILITY	M	
Private Attorney 2 - Public Subsidy		
FUNCTIONS		This model generally receives substantial support from private attorneys and the bar because it provides public financing for private attorney services while otherwise preserving the traditional roles of the legal profession. While at a rate substantially below prevailing private fees, the compensation provided is relatively assured and generally at a sufficient level to be attractive to at least some private attorneys. In some countries, such attorney and bar "special interest" support helps to expand the available level of public expenditures for legal services to indigents and low-income persons. This model frequently receives less support from the public interest bar because it competes or is perceived as competing for public revenues for preferred models, i.e., the staff attorney, law school clinic, and public interest law reform programs. Limited support comes also because of the private attorney model's primary attention to criminal defense and family law matters rather than other civil legal problems that are seen as more critical to the poverty law community (i.e., housing, employment, human and civil rights). This model can be more affordable to the low-income client than the first model, with services either free or requiring a sliding fee copayment. Yet in some national legal services systems this model has temporarily driven up public expenditures beyond supportable levels, resulting in fee and service reductions and the development of other delivery models for a mixed model system. Such factors as efficiency and effectiveness depend upon the individual attorney and national, provincial, state or local legal services governance design and management systems employed to oversee operation of the delivery system. In common with other private attorney models, it rates low on law reform and public action review functions, which are the model's primary deficiencies in comprehensiveness. Accessibility under this model can vary by region and country. Generally the distribution of attorneys is low in rural and lower-income areas, among native peoples, and among other such groups. This model will normally need to be supplemented by other approaches (i.e., staff attorney clinics) in such areas to better equalize accessibility.
LEGAL INFORMATION	M	
LEGAL ASSISTANCE	M-H	
PUBLIC ACTION REVIEW	L	
LAW REFORM	L	
ACCESS TO JUSTICE	M-H	
INCENTIVES		
REGARD BENEFITED		
PUBLIC AS CLIENT	M-H	
COURT SUPPORT	M-H	
PRIVATE ATTORNEY BAR		
SUPPORT	H	
PUBLIC INTEREST BAR		
SUPPORT	L	
GOVERNMENT SUPPORT	M	
COMPREHENSIVENESS	M	
EFFECTIVENESS	M	
STANDARDS		
EFFICIENCY	L-M	
AFFORDABILITY	L-M	
ACCESSIBILITY	L-M	
ADJUSTABILITY	L	
SUPPORTABILITY	M-H	

Legal Aid Models	Rating	Comments
Private Attorney 3 - Legal Insurance		
FUNCTIONS		This model often provides basic information and advice by telephone and by contract with local private attorneys in areas with high concentrations of plan members or clients. It rates high in the provision of legal information, basic legal assistance, and access to justice for its paying members, and could probably do so for indigent and low-income persons with public subsidies for such services. It rates low in law reform and public action review. Support by private attorneys and the bar varies depending upon understanding, level of development of the model in that jurisdiction, perceived competition, and other factors. Neither the courts nor the public interest bar appear to have strong feelings one way or the other about this model, even in those countries where it is beginning to deliver a significant amount of general consumer legal services. Its supportability is therefore difficult to assess.
LEGAL INFORMATION	H	
LEGAL ASSISTANCE	H	
PUBLIC ACTION REVIEW	L	
LAW REFORM	L	
ACCESS TO JUSTICE	M-H	
INCENTIVES		
REGARD BENEFITED PUBLIC AS CLIENT	M-H	
COURT SUPPORT	?	
PRIVATE ATTORNEY BAR SUPPORT	L-M	
PUBLIC INTEREST BAR SUPPORT	?	
GOVERNMENT SUPPORT	?	
COMPREHENSIVENESS	M	
EFFECTIVENESS	M-H	
STANDARDS		
EFFICIENCY	H	
AFFORDABILITY	M-H	
ACCESSIBILITY	M-H	
ADJUSTABILITY	M-H	
SUPPORTABILITY	?	
Staff Attorney		
FUNCTIONS		The most salient characteristic of this model is its variability of leadership, services, management and operations, which is reflected in the range of ratings given in most factors. The model generally receives an M-H rating. It is disliked by some conservative governments because they view it potentially as overly progressive or reformist, and sometimes disliked as well by private attorneys and bar associations, who view it as in competition with the traditional legal delivery system. It can be a relatively flexible delivery model that provides a comprehensive range of legal services functions.
LEGAL INFORMATION	M-H	
LEGAL ASSISTANCE	M-H	
PUBLIC ACTION REVIEW	M-H	
LAW REFORM	M-H	
ACCESS TO JUSTICE	M-H	
INCENTIVES		
REGARD BENEFITED PUBLIC AS CLIENT	M-H	
COURT SUPPORT	M-H	
PRIVATE ATTORNEY BAR SUPPORT	L-M	
PUBLIC INTEREST BAR SUPPORT	H	
GOVERNMENT SUPPORT	L-H	
COMPREHENSIVENESS	H	
EFFECTIVENESS	M-H	
STANDARDS		
EFFICIENCY	M-H	
AFFORDABILITY	M-H	
ACCESSIBILITY	L-H	
ADJUSTABILITY	M-H	
SUPPORTABILITY	M-H	

Legal Aid Models	Rating	Comments
Law School Clinic		
FUNCTIONS		The challenge of the law school clinic model is its dual role of educating law students while providing legal services, generally with some loss of effectiveness and efficiency. It tends to receive at least moderate support from most important sectors. Law school clinical services are primarily (but not exclusively) provided in the locale of law schools and where qualified supervisors can oversee student work, and are thereby generally of limited accessibility.
LEGAL INFORMATION	M	
LEGAL ASSISTANCE	M	
PUBLIC ACTION REVIEW	M	
LAW REFORM	L-M	
ACCESS TO JUSTICE	M	
INCENTIVES		
REGARD BENEFITED		
PUBLIC AS CLIENT	M	
COURT SUPPORT	M	
PRIVATE ATTORNEY BAR		
SUPPORT	M	
PUBLIC INTEREST BAR		
SUPPORT	M-H	
GOVERNMENT SUPPORT	M-H	
COMPREHENSIVENESS	M	
EFFECTIVENESS	M	
STANDARDS		
EFFICIENCY	L-M	
AFFORDABILITY	L-H	
ACCESSIBILITY	L-M	
ADJUSTABILITY	M	
SUPPORTABILITY	M-H	

Nongovernmental Public Interest Law Reform Center

	Rating	Comments
FUNCTIONS		It is sometimes difficult to draw a clear line between a staff attorney program—which primarily provides legal advice and representation to a particular client population while engaging in some deliberate law reform activities—and a public interest law reform center, which provides some basic legal assistance and representation to individual clients for their day-to-day legal problems. The distinction is that the law reform model mostly focuses on changing detrimental public policies and preserving beneficial ones on behalf of its client group, class or community. Other activities are essentially incidental to that objective. This model generally has a high regard for its intended benefited group or class client. An individual's legal needs may be assessed as to how they can best serve as a vehicle for a class action or appellate case to establish new law. The nongovernmental public interest law reform model can be very efficient and cost-effective in performing such law reform and public action review functions, while potentially generating a level of governmental opposition in some countries that can slow further effective operations. Consequently its supportability varies substantially as per time, place and circumstances. With the exception described below (the governmental public interest center), this model is normally very affordable to the state and benefited parties because it primarily functions with private funding from members, foundations and other contributors, with additional revenues from court-ordered attorney fees and low levels of client fees. The model normally enjoys a high level of independence in part because it is not dependent on public financing.
LEGAL INFORMATION	L	
LEGAL ASSISTANCE	M	
PUBLIC ACTION REVIEW	H	
LAW REFORM	H	
ACCESS TO JUSTICE	M	
INCENTIVES		
REGARD BENEFITED		
PUBLIC AS CLIENT	H	
COURT SUPPORT	L-H	
PRIVATE ATTORNEY BAR		
SUPPORT	L-H	
PUBLIC INTEREST BAR		
SUPPORT	H	
GOVERNMENT SUPPORT	L-M	
COMPREHENSIVENESS	L	
EFFECTIVENESS	H	
STANDARDS		
EFFICIENCY	H	
AFFORDABILITY	H	
ACCESSIBILITY	L-M	
ADJUSTABILITY	M-H	
SUPPORTABILITY	L-H	

Legal Aid Models	Rating	Comments
Governmental Public Interest Law Reform Center		
FUNCTIONS		This somewhat uncommon model is similar to the NGO public interest law reform center, but has been established by governmental action and receives public funding to perform certain public action review and other specified law reform functions on behalf of named constituencies. It is not as independent as its NGO counterpart, may perform a less contentious form and level of law reform, and normally enjoys a higher level of governmental support and overall supportability than its privately funded colleague. Note, however, instances when such governmentally established and funded law reform centers have been eliminated where governmental circumstances take an unfavorable turn.
LEGAL INFORMATION	L	
LEGAL ASSISTANCE	M	
PUBLIC ACTION REVIEW	H	
LAW REFORM	M-H	
ACCESS TO JUSTICE	M	
INCENTIVES		
REGARD BENEFITED PUBLIC AS CLIENT	M-H	
COURT SUPPORT	M-H	
PRIVATE ATTORNEY BAR SUPPORT	M-H	
PUBLIC INTEREST BAR SUPPORT	M-H	
GOVERNMENT SUPPORT	M-H	
COMPREHENSIVENESS	L	
EFFECTIVENESS	H	
STANDARDS		
EFFICIENCY	H	
AFFORDABILITY	H	
ACCESSIBILITY	M	
ADJUSTABILITY	M	
SUPPORTABILITY	M-H	
Ombudsmen		
FUNCTIONS		While the ombudsmen model is currently less popular than during the late 1960s and mid-1970s, what specific and limited functions it does perform—legal information and assistance in the review, oversight and remedy of public action against individuals—continue to be carried out efficiently and effectively, and with a high level of support. The model deserves consideration in countries where adequate support can be generated and sustained to establish, fund and preserve the kind of independent, respected and strong program needed of an ombudsman.
LEGAL INFORMATION	H	
LEGAL ASSISTANCE	H	
PUBLIC ACTION REVIEW	H	
LAW REFORM	L-H	
ACCESS TO JUSTICE	H	
INCENTIVES		
REGARD BENEFITED PUBLIC AS CLIENT	H	
COURT SUPPORT	M-H	
PRIVATE ATTORNEY BAR SUPPORT	M-H	
PUBLIC INTEREST BAR SUPPORT	M-H	
GOVERNMENT SUPPORT	M-H	
COMPREHENSIVENESS	L	
EFFECTIVENESS	H	
STANDARDS		
EFFICIENCY	H	
AFFORDABILITY	H	
ACCESSIBILITY	L-H	
ADJUSTABILITY	L-H	
SUPPORTABILITY	M-H	

Legal Aid Models	Rating	Comments
Simplified Dispute Resolution Center		

FUNCTIONS		In comparison with the ombudsmen, this model can perform certain func-tions—primarily helping people resolve basic disputes involving family matters, small property concerns, citizen and community conflicts, and administrative claims—in a reasonably efficient and effective fashion. But adequate attention, leadership, funding and qualified personnel must be allocated for its opera-tions. While the model has relatively high potential for helping persons resolve a fairly wide range of such disputes, in actual operation such dispute resolution centers currently perform at levels ranging from poor to acceptable.
LEGAL INFORMATION	M	
LEGAL ASSISTANCE	M	
PUBLIC ACTION REVIEW	L	
LAW REFORM	L	
ACCESS TO JUSTICE	M	
INCENTIVES		
REGARD BENEFITED		
PUBLIC AS CLIENT	L-H	
COURT SUPPORT	M-H	
PRIVATE ATTORNEY BAR		
SUPPORT	L-M	
PUBLIC INTEREST BAR		
SUPPORT	M-H	
GOVERNMENT SUPPORT	M-H	
COMPREHENSIVENESS	L	
EFFECTIVENESS	M-H	
STANDARDS		
EFFICIENCY	H	
AFFORDABILITY	H	
ACCESSIBILITY	H	
ADJUSTABILITY	L-H	
SUPPORTABILITY	M-H	

Legal Advice Center		

FUNCTIONS		While the general format of this model is not new, it currently is receiving substantial attention in a number of countries with renewed concentration on the applications of computerization and telecommunications technologies to improve operations, coordination and efficiency. It has great potential for effec-tively and efficiently performing a range of legal functions (particularly legal information, advice, and assistance in numerous legal areas, but not including law reform), while generating high levels of support from most relevant sectors. The private bar will be resistant to the introduction and expansion of this model because of concerns about economic and professional competition. But this may be counterbalanced by court, judicial and public consumer support. Where this model has recently been developed by judicial and governmental agencies, it is attracting a cadre of enthusiastic leaders, staffers and other essential re-sources, which denotes a likelihood of successful implementation, expansion and replication.
LEGAL INFORMATION	H	
LEGAL ASSISTANCE	M	
PUBLIC ACTION REVIEW	M	
LAW REFORM	L	
ACCESS TO JUSTICE	M-H	
INCENTIVES		
REGARD BENEFITED		
PUBLIC AS CLIENT	M-H	
COURT SUPPORT	H	
PRIVATE ATTORNEY BAR		
SUPPORT	L-H	
PUBLIC INTEREST BAR		
SUPPORT	MH	
GOVERNMENT SUPPORT	H	
COMPREHENSIVENESS	M	
EFFECTIVENESS	M-H	
STANDARDS		
EFFICIENCY	H	
AFFORDABILITY	H	
ACCESSIBILITY	H	
ADJUSTABILITY	M-H	
SUPPORTABILITY	H	

How large is the legal profession, and how many attorneys are in private practice? Does a substantial body of the bar routinely serve lower- to middle-income persons? What forms of compensation for services are permitted and routinely used? What are the class origins of persons who become attorneys? Does the composition of the bar reflect the racial, ethnic and gender characteristics of the population? Do members of the legal profession profess and exhibit concern for providing access to justice for the poor and other underserved groups? To what degree does the distribution of attorneys throughout the country correspond to the distribution of the population?

  • *Status of legal aid.* How have legal aid and access to justice been provided? Have various models been implemented, and if so, what factors led to the current situation? What functions and activities does the current legal aid system provide? What are its strengths and weaknesses? What are the current sources of support and opposition to modification, improvement and expansion? Who would benefit from legal aid development?

  • *Nature of the client population.* What percentage of the population is unable to obtain legal assistance and access to justice? Are such persons primarily located in areas where attorneys practice, or in rural areas and small towns without attorneys? What percentage of the population is literate? Do the people needing legal aid speak a common language, or must legal aid be provided in several languages to reach the intended service population? Is the country's population relatively homogeneous, or does it include numerous ethnic and racial groups? Does the intended service population trust the legal profession and judicial institutions? Is it involved with labor, religious, civic, human rights and other organizations?

The development of national legal aid systems or the implementation of specific service models can also be influenced by other factors, such as the level of economic development, the distribution of economic resources throughout the society, and the level of technological development.

CASE STUDIES OF SUCCESSFUL LEGAL AID AND COMMUNITY LEGAL EDUCATION PROGRAMS

This section reviews three effective legal aid programs: the national legal aid system in the Netherlands, and provincial programs in Quebec and Ontario in Canada.[2] It also looks at a legal advice and assistance model under development in Phoenix, Arizona: the Self-Service Center of the Maricopa County Superior Court.

Each of the three programs uses a mix of models with relatively high levels of

---

[2] Descriptions of the three systems are based on Legal Action Group (1992, pp. 75-90).

public funding. The Netherlands and Ontario primarily use publicly funded private attorney service models. Quebec is unique in offering a mix of staff and private attorney providers with nearly equal levels of public funding and privately funded client services. Probably because the program assures client selection of private or staff attorneys for most services, past surveys have demonstrated relatively high public satisfaction with Quebec's legal aid system.

Each of these programs has undergone public reviews and changes over the past six years, particularly that of Ontario. If changes introduced in Ontario in 1998 are successfully implemented, this program warrants careful attention for its diligent efforts to build a legal aid system using a range of models and service approaches.

The Netherlands[3]

Dutch legal aid, first established in 1957, is administered directly by the Ministry of Justice. At present, there is no intermediate body, though the establishment of regional legal aid councils is planned in pending legislation.

Total expenditure on publicly funded legal services in 1989 was 281 million guilders—the equivalent of L85 million, which represents L5.80 per capita. Private attorneys receive about 82 percent of total expenditure on legal services, reflecting a major dependence on the private sector. Most of the remaining expenditure funds a network of *Buros voor Rechtshulp*. The *buros* combine two roles: they act as a type of law center, giving initial advice, taking on welfare law cases and acting as a point of referral; and they process legal aid applications and certificates. The two functions do not always coexist easily. In 1989, these *buros* cost 40 million guilders, about 15 percent of the overall legal aid budget. A relatively small amount went to university-based law shops, training, various legal aid organizations and trade unions.

While the services provided by the *buros* are free, legal aid from private practitioners is subject to means testing. Since 1983, a charge has been levied on everyone using the civil scheme. In 1991, the minimum contribution was about $20 for advice and $120 for a court case. In practice, however, many advocates refuse to collect these charges, which have been strongly opposed by the legal profession.

Dutch advocates have maintained a tradition of professional responsibility towards legally aided work. In 1989, virtually every advocate—5,995 of a total of 6,015—undertook a legally aided case. Most of the work, however, is handled by a smaller number of specialists. In 1989, only 2,000 advocates undertook more than 50 cases. As a legacy of the radicalism of the 1970s, within the legal aid specialties

---

[3] For further information on legal aid in the Netherlands, see Bamberger (1989); Blankenburg (1992); Cousins (1993); Gorieley (1992); and Huls (1994).

there is a defined sector of "social advocates" who bring a social and political commitment to legal aid work. Their representative organization, the *Vereniging van Sociale Advocatuur Nederland,* has about 400 members and actively campaigns for better services. Dutch advocates undertake many more civil than criminal legal aid cases: 257,000 civil compared with 71,100 criminal cases in 1989. Expenditure reflects this: in 1989, civil cases brought in 157 million guilders to private practitioners, compared with 62 million guilders for criminal cases, and just under 12 million guilders for the police station duty lawyer scheme.

The relatively small expenditure on criminal legal aid may be a reflection of the Dutch inquisitorial system and low crime rates, as well as the low level of remuneration. A duty police scheme is also administered by the *buros.*

The *Buros voor Rechtshulp* developed out of the student-based law shops of the 1970s. By 1987, 332,151 clients used their services, and by 1992, 20 *buros* operated out of 57 separate offices and employed 235 legal and 160 administrative staff. The *buros* are independent foundations, each governed by a board that includes local lawyers, judges and academics. There is little community involvement in their management. The work of each *buro* is agreed to on the basis of an annual plan submitted to the ministry for funding. Although all *buros* undertake casework, some refer more cases to private practitioners in order to concentrate on education, outreach and legal reform activities. Workers in these *buros* tend to emphasize the importance of such structural legal aid.

The extent to which *buros* should be involved in law reform is a contentious issue. Although their representative organization, *Landelijke Organisatie Buros voor Rechtshulp* (LOB), campaigns for law reform, in practice much of this work is undertaken on its behalf by the larger *buros,* particularly those in Amsterdam, the Hague and Utrecht. Other workers, especially in the smaller buros, regard this approach as anachronistic.

The Amsterdam *buro* was the first to be established and is the largest in the country. It employed 62 people in 1992, including 30 legal staff in four offices, and confines its caseload to social security, employment, housing, consumer and immigration work. Its central office is open to the general public five times a week, with two morning, one afternoon and two evening sessions. There are also two counseling sessions for immigrants, one for people from Turkey and the other for Moroccans. In addition, legal staff visit the city prison to give criminal and general advice.

A member of staff acknowledged that the *buro* has a problem in meeting demand. Originally, the central *buro* had been open eight hours a day, five days a week, but this created too much work for the staff to handle. Demand has also been limited by reducing publicity about *buro* services. Consequently, its client area tends to be within a relatively small radius of its main and satellite offices.

The Netherlands also has a "Citizens Advice Bureau" network. There are 90 *raadslieden* or local information and advice centers run mostly by local authorities.

In total, the federation of *raadslieden* (FIRA) estimates that there are about 250 paid staff providing counseling. FIRA assistance often involves giving only information or advice or writing letters or filling in forms. The *raadslieden* are not seen by the Ministry of Justice as part of legal aid provision, an attitude that FIRA complains about.

Criminal legal aid is provided free to defendants in custody and to those on remand who cannot afford a lawyer. Civil legal aid eligibility levels, set by statute in 1981, are linked to statutory rates of maintenance that are, in turn, indexed to wages. This statutory and indexing scheme has been sufficient to fend off attempts by the Ministry of Justice to cut eligibility. The ministry estimates that around 70 percent of the population is currently eligible.

The four largest areas of civil legal aid work undertaken by private practice in 1989 were family (34 percent), property and contract (14 percent), social security (11 percent) and labor law (10 percent). The *buros* did most of their work in social security (18 percent), labor law (18 percent), housing (15 percent) and property/contract (13 percent), reflecting their specialist role in relation to social welfare law.

One of the most rapidly growing areas of legal aid advice for both private practitioners and *buros* concerns asylum-seekers. In 1984, there were 9,010 contacts with *buros* in this area and 10,140 cases assigned to private practitioners. By 1989, the number of contacts with *buros* had grown to 17,700 and the number of cases assigned to private practitioners had risen to 23,670. Asylum-seekers are placed in camps outside the country's main population centers. The Order of Advocates and the *buros,* which combine to provide a special advice scheme, have vigorously opposed attempts by the Ministry of Justice to deprive these people, whom it terms "illegal" immigrants, of assistance.

The Dutch legal aid scheme is demand-led. The Ministry of Justice has been concerned over the rise in expenditure, which roughly doubled from 1979 to 1992. The increased cost largely reflects an increasing caseload: civil cases rose from 219,100 in 1984 to 257,400 in 1989, and criminal cases from 46,600 to 71,100. Remuneration rates, on the other hand, did not rise; in fact, they were cut by 10 percent in relation to civil cases in 1981 and have not been increased for crime or civil work since then. The Order of Advocates estimates that, between 1981 and 1991, there was a real fall in remuneration rates of about 28 percent. Payment is by way of fixed fees, which makes the failure to increase remuneration levels a particularly effective way of holding down costs.

The Dutch legal aid system differs from the British (primarily judicare) model, notably in its use of salaried services through the *Buros voor Rechtshulp.* In some ways, however, it is similar. Though the Dutch have maintained an enviably high level of legal aid eligibility, at least in civil cases, current concern with the related questions of quality, remuneration and coverage are common to both jurisdictions.

Quebec

In the early 1970s, Quebec made a political commitment to spend a significant sum on publicly funded legal services. This initiative was influenced by developments in the United States. The name chosen for the body set up in 1972 to administer legal aid was the *Commission des Services Juridiques,* echoing that of the U.S. Legal Services Corporation. The emphasis on public education and law reform reflected the American rather than the British model. Another consideration, explicitly referred to by ministers at the time, was to have a national legal service akin to a national health service. Legal aid was, and has remained, free to recipients who meet the eligibility criteria.

The initial proposal for a fully salaried scheme with no involvement from private practitioners was fended off by the legal profession. Clients usually must go to the commission for a preliminary assessment of their case, but their right to then choose either a salaried lawyer employed by the commission or a private practitioner is a fundamental principle of the scheme. This choice marks a major difference between the Quebec scheme and those established in most other provinces and countries. Quebec does not have a completely fixed annual budget, and to this extent, its scheme is in tune with the demand-led nature of legal aid services in England and Wales.

In 1989-90, Quebec spent Can. $80 million on legal services, with 51 percent of this funding coming from the federal government and 49 percent from the provincial government. Cases were divided as follows between private practitioners (who received $23 million in legal aid expenditures), notaries (dealing with property matters) and staff lawyers:

	% of cases	Number
Private practitioners	36	87,913
Commission lawyers	61	151,175
Notaries	3	6,765
Total	100	245,853

Of the total number of cases handled by lawyers (excluding those involving notaries), 59 percent were civil and 41 percent criminal. The proportion of cases handled by private practitioners varied according to the type of law: 29 percent of them were in family law, 24 percent in nonmatrimonial civil cases, and 47 percent in criminal cases.

As in Ontario, providing legal advice is given very little priority in Quebec. A commission official explicitly stated that the policy was to concentrate on representation. But, in contrast to Ontario, this policy is not tempered by a network of legal or counseling centers. Although the legislation governing the commission allows services to be provided by legal or counseling centers, there are only two of them (in Hull and Pointe Saint Charles, Montreal). Both were set up independently, before the legal aid scheme got underway.

Legal aid work does not play a significant part in private practice. In 1989-90, only 20 percent of Quebec's advocates—2,671of 13,094—received any legal aid payment. The average payment was only $7,547. Only six advocates received more than $150,000, which was said to be possible only by concentrating on multiple criminal cases heard in the same court at the same time, and where all the pleas were guilty.

The *Commission des Services* is organized through 11 regional corporations, known as *centres communautaires juridiques* (community legal centers). Each center operates local *bureaux d'aide juridiques* (legal aid offices). The regional corporations provide for local committees "to advise…on the needs of economically underprivileged persons," but these bodies have little power. This absence of local involvement may have contributed to the commission lacking sensitivity to the needs of some communities, particularly Quebec's native peoples. A commission official admitted that a number of initiatives designed to deliver services to native peoples—none of which involved local people from the targeted communities in their management—had been discontinued for lack of use. This contrasts with the operation of Ontario's clinic system, as demonstrated by the clinic in Thunder Bay described in the next section.

In 1989-90, the commission employed 383 advocates, 536 other staff and 39 articled clerks, distributed among 114 full-time and 41 part-time offices. Sixty-two percent of the cases taken by staff advocates related to civil matters, with family law cases constituting just under half of them. Although criminal work accounted for a smaller proportion of the commission's workload than that of private practitioners, commission lawyers handled a higher number of such cases—57,000 as opposed to 41,000.

The commission maintains tight control over its staff advocates: working conditions are highly regulated and workloads carefully monitored. In 1989-90, advocates on average worked 1,060 chargeable hours, had an active caseload of 426 cases, and devoted 2.08 hours to each case. Salaries based on seniority and merit ranged from just under $30,000 to just over $70,000, and the average length of service was a creditable 13 years.

Because clients can choose between a commission advocate and a private practitioner for the same type of case, it is possible to look at the relative costs. Over 1989-90, the average cost per case undertaken by a staff advocate was $183, compared with $249 for a private practitioner. But it is difficult to know how useful this comparison is. Senior members of Quebec's Bar Association argue that like is not being compared with like, and that commission advocates can manipulate case figures in a way not open to a private practitioner who receives cases on referral.

However, the Canadian Bar Association's National Legal Aid Liaison Committee (1987), which represents private practice interests, concluded that, "having…noted some possible explanations of the discrepancies, the fact remains that the Quebec data consistently demonstrate that cost-per-case for staff lawyers is lower than for private practitioners, although the size of the cost differential may be less significant than the summary data suggest and, in many instances, negligible."

The statutory responsibilities of the commission include a commitment to "promote the development of information programs to economically underprivileged persons on their rights and obligations." One of the commission's great successes has been in the field of public legal education. A small but very effective information department has developed a number of ways to educate the public about legal rights. This includes a continuing legal information radio program that is transmitted by 110 French-language stations throughout Quebec. Such is its success that it has been used by a number of other ministries and government bodies to disseminate their own information. The department also produces a newspaper column that is published regularly in a number of daily and weekly newspapers.

For 14 years, the information department has produced *Justice pour tous,* a television series with 26 programs annually that dramatizes issues about legal rights. The series has used plot lines dealing with legal issues ranging from skiing accidents, faulty septic tanks and dangerous driving. The programs are also distributed as videos and are used in public information campaigns by lawyers' organizations to increase legal awareness.

The information department produces a range of attractive information in written form, distributing several thousand brochures and folders as part of an outreach program that includes providing legal information at fairs and trade shows. The effectiveness of the commission's information work is undoubtedly aided by the fact that its director of information is a radio personality in his own right and is sufficiently energetic to host a popular weekday morning radio show before coming to work. Nevertheless, the commission's commitment to an innovative educational approach over a sustained period of time has been impressive.

The problem with legal aid in Quebec is the low level of eligibility. The Legal Aid Act of 1972, which established the scheme, grants eligibility to those who are "economically underprivileged." Initially, the commission had the power to set eligibility levels, but this was ceded to the government in 1982. Except for one raise, which applied only to families, levels have not changed since 1981, and are now below the minimum wage.

The Ministry of Justice informally estimated eligibility at 32 percent of the population in 1982. This was disputed by the past president of the commission, who proposed 15 percent as a more accurate figure.

The future of the commission's legal reform work is uncertain, in part because the commission has survived severe cuts in its resources. Its annual report still details the education, organizing and reform work of each of its offices as a reflection of the priority given to placing casework in the context of other activities. However, staff are effectively expected to undertake much of this on their own time. The budget for information work was halved in the early 1990s to $200,000.

On the other hand, Quebec has recently renewed its commitment to legal aid. The process began with a detailed analysis by a government-appointed committee that found that the basic structure of the legal aid system was sound but short of resources. It proposed a major increase in eligibility, to be paid for largely by requiring contributions by those above minimum levels of income and capital. In 1996 eligibility was substantially increased by raising the financial limits for services and establishing a new system of sliding fee contributory payments for persons and families at the higher eligibility levels. There was also a major revision in the provision of federal funding to provincial governments for legal aid. Pursuant to the new Canada Health and Social Transfer Act of April 1, 1996, federal funding for a number of social programs including civil legal aid was provided by block grants. This allowed the provinces flexibility in their funding priorities and gave them the ability to increase or decrease portions of the federal dollars for legal aid. Quebec responded in 1996-97 by increasing its provincial contributions by 46 percent for legal aid.

Ontario

Legal aid in Ontario began as a voluntary scheme in 1951, and was put on a statutory footing in 1967. The Ontario Legal Aid Plan (OLAP), administered by the Law Society of Upper Canada, delivers services in two ways. There is a "certificated" scheme using private practitioners, derived from the model in England and Wales, and there is a network of clinics. A separate scheme provides legal services to native peoples in the remote north of the province.

Legal aid expenditure in 1989-90 was US$173.8 million. Of this, US$22 million (13 percent of the total budget, a proportion roughly similar to that paid in the Netherlands to *Buros voor Rechtshulp,* was spent on legal clinics. The sources of funds were as follows:

	US$ millions
Ontario government	68
Federal government	58
Interest on client accounts	36
Client contributions	9
Costs, awards, etc.	5
Law Society	4

The Law Society contribution comes from a compulsory $175 levy on each member of the legal profession, negotiated in 1986 between the society and the province's Attorney General. It is regarded as a contribution towards defraying the administrative costs of OLAP, which totaled $17 million in 1989-90.

The Law Society administers the certificated legal aid scheme through 47 area offices. The scheme is subject to eligibility rules (levels have not been increased since 1989), but the area director's broad discretion in determining eligibility makes it difficult to adequately estimate the population eligible for legal aid. Criminal legal aid is free for those with incomes below a certain level. In 1991, this was equivalent to about 150 percent of the long-term welfare support rate, but lower than the minimum wage. There is no mandatory free limit for civil legal aid, although the criminal limit is often followed. The upper limit for both criminal and civil cases is left explicitly to the discretion of the area director. An official explained: "There is no hard-drawn upper limit. We take into account the matrimonial home and look at both actual and normal expenditure and income."

Criminal work dominates the scheme, as shown by figures for 1989-90.

Type of assistance	Cost	Completed cases
Criminal	$71 million	64,297
Civil	$42 million	43,000
Advice only	$138,771	1,035

In the same year, private practitioners received about $131 million from legal aid (including around $21 million for various forms of duty schemes).

Comparatively fewer practitioners participate in the scheme than in England and Wales. According to the Law Society, Ontario has about 23,000 lawyers, of whom 10,000 undertake some legal aid work. Most of this, however, is concentrated in the hands of about 1,200 lawyers. The Law Society has reluctantly employed duty counsel on a salaried basis—to the tune of about $750,000 in 1989-90—to cover some of the busier provincial courts (equivalent to magistrates' courts).

The legal clinics, which numbered 67 in 1991, are formally administered under the Ontario Legal Aid Plan and, thus, the Law Society of Upper Canada. In practice, however, they achieve a measure of independence by having a separate administrative body, known as the Clinic Funding Committee (CFC). The CFC has five members: three appointed by the Law Society and two by the Attorney General. At least one representative from each must have been "associated with a clinic." It has its own staff of 10 under its own director.

The legal clinics are of three basic types. There are multi-service clinics linked to other organizations—for example, York Community Services, where legal, health and social services are all provided from one base. There are also about a dozen province-wide specialty clinics, which focus on specific areas such as the environment, landlords, the elderly and the handicapped. These clinics have different ways of working. The Advocacy Resource Center for the Handicapped, for example, is oriented towards litigation and has taken a number of cases relating to Canada's relatively new Charter of Rights. The Advocacy Center for the Elderly, on the other hand, focuses more on campaigning and education. For instance, it has worked to force the issue of abuse of the elderly into the public arena.

Most clinics are in the third category: they are community-based clinics that provide services unavailable under the certificated scheme, within a defined catchment area. The clinic funding staff has a provisional plan for a network of 90 community legal clinics to cover the whole province.

The CFC requires community legal clinics, as autonomous bodies, to have a board of directors "which includes persons belonging to the community which the clinics serve." Generally, these boards contain a large number of professional people, but an anecdote from the clinic in Thunder Bay illustrates there is flexibility in terms of representing the interests of a local community. As a clinic worker explained: "A group of native people...put in an application for a native people's clinic. They were told that it would have to be a general clinic. They said okay, thinking that it would be better to have something rather than nothing...[W]e now have a real clinic with a board that is all native. Out of a population which is around 12 percent native, most government offices get 3 to 5 percent of native people coming to them. Native people don't go to offices much. Our proportion is about 40 percent."

Main Areas of Clinic Work

The six main areas of the work of clinics set out by the Ontario Legal Aid Plan in 1990 are as follows:

Summary advice and information. Clinic staff provide information and advice in a variety of legal areas to over 100,000 people per year. This service is similar to that provided by civil duty counsel in that no financial eligibility testing of clients is generally required.

Referrals. Over 60,000 people a year are referred by clinics to other agencies or lawyers, thus ensuring that they have access to other appropriate services. Over 3,000 are direct referrals to the Legal Aid Plan's certificate program or to lawyers in private practice; the remainder are referred to a variety of social service and community agencies.

Client representation. Clinics provide traditional legal services in areas of poverty law to more than 30,000 people a year, including advocacy before the courts and administrative tribunals, such as the Workers' Compensation Appeals Tribunal and the Social Assistance Review Board. Clinic lawyers engage in appellate work at all levels of the court system.

Public legal education. Clinics have a mandate to provide legal education to the low-income communities they service. Toward this end they produce a wide variety of publications, pamphlets, video presentations and oral programs. Community Legal Education Ontario is a specialty clinic funded to produce public legal education materials for clinics and their clients.

Law reform. Clinics have a specific mandate to provide legal services "designed solely to promote the legal welfare of a community." Clinics therefore act on behalf of client groups, or the low-income community generally, to protect and promote their legal interests before a variety of public decision-making bodies, such as municipal councils, legislative committees and public commissions. Law reform is also initiated through test case litigation.

Organizing and community development. Clinics provide specialized services to help people organize themselves into groups able to protect or promote their legal interests, such as tenants' associations or self-help groups for injured workers. Clinics also provide legal assistance to groups initiating community development projects such as housing projects for low-income people, and training programs for social assistance recipients.

A few community-based clinics link with university law departments to provide training for students. The most well funded clinic, Parkdale Community Legal Services, occupies a special place in the history of the program. Established in 1971 as the first clinic in Ontario, it is linked to the Osgood Hall Law School. The specially-designed premises it now occupies, which incorporate a large area for students to work in, are situated in the rundown area of Parkdale rather than in the middle-class university area. The clinic delivers legal education to students for periods of four to eight months, at the same time providing the services expected of any community legal clinic. Its services are organized into four teams: landlord and tenant, workers' compensation, family/welfare, and immigration.

A 1978 report on the community legal clinics stated that their relationship with the private profession was harmonious: "There has been much cooperation between the two branches of legal aid and essentially no competition between the clinics and the private bar." This has continued to be largely the case. Conflict could, however, occur in the future. The Ontario government has undertaken a review of certificated legal aid to look for potential budget cuts, and the clinics may be seen as some form of alternative provision. The clinics have escaped relatively unscathed in the current recession, not least because of the strong cross-party political support they attract in the provincial parliament. They have continued to grow at roughly the rate of two or three a year. At the same time, the central role of the CFC staff is growing. For example, a resource office is being established, which will expand its training and support role, providing an incentive for greater cooperation. The clinics are required to report in detail on their work and the clinic funding staff have developed detailed mechanisms for balancing local autonomy with central accountability.

The clinics provide services in social welfare law in a way that combines casework, education and law reform. The specialty clinics function as pressure groups. The link between some of the clinics and universities has provided a solid base for legal education.

Recent Changes in Ontario's Legal Aid System[4]

Significant changes are underway in Ontario's legal aid system pursuant to the recommendations of *A Blueprint for Publicly Funded Legal Services* (Ontario Legal Aid Review, 1997) as well as other factors.

From 1990 to 1994, use of civil and criminal legal aid in Ontario and the annual costs of judicare increased substantially. In response, the Ontario provisional government in 1994 established a reduced cap on its financial support for the Ontario Legal Aid Plan until changes were introduced in operation of the system. The plan had always operated as a partnership between the provincial government, the primary funder, and the Law Society of Upper Canada, which administered the plan. The partners signed a memorandum of understanding in late 1994 to govern operation of the plan until March 1999 unless previously amended by agreement of the parties. The memorandum also called for a comprehensive review of operations of the legal aid system.

The Ontario Legal Aid Review was established by the Government of Ontario in 1996 as an independent seven-member task force. Also known as the "McCamus Commission" in reference to its chairman, John D. McCamus, the review was asked to examine all legal aid programs in the province in order to identify "aspects that should be reduced, maintained or enhanced in order that the current and future legal needs of low-income residents of Ontario can be met in the most effective and efficient way possible" (Ontario Legal Aid Review, 1997).

In conducting the study, the review members and staff met with a wide range of legal aid clients, providers and administrators, judges and community agency leaders. While the review was initially established primarily in response to a per-ceived budget crisis, its members also found that the legal aid system was failing to meet the needs for which it was designed. To correct its deficiencies and develop a program that could function within an annual capped budget, the review proposed an improved system that would:

• Assess, understand and respond to the actual legal needs of low-income Ontarians;

• Set priorities among those needs to achieve the greatest positive impact for the client group;

---

[4] In addition to the blueprint mentioned in the first paragraph, this section is based on an interview with Robert Holden, Executive Director of the Ontario Legal Aid Plan, and on Ontario Legal Aid Plan (1998).

- Use an innovative mix of delivery models and service providers to address these priorities;
- Support, coordinate and work well with other agencies serving the same clientele;
- Emphasize research and policy development to improve its own services and reduce their cost by contributing to the ongoing reform of the justice system as a whole;
- Be responsive to persons with diverse needs, including ethnic, racial, cultural and linguistic minorities, persons with disabilities, Aboriginal communities, women, children, youth and the elderly;
- Provide consistently high-quality services across the province;
- Act in a cost-effective manner that makes efficient use of modern information technology and management techniques;
- Be independent of government; and
- Have adequate and stable multiyear funding, at the current level or greater, to carry out its responsibilities.

The blueprint (Ontario Legal Aid Review, 1997) goes on to state:

In the service areas where judicare currently dominates, such as family, criminal, immigrant and refugee, and some civil matters, we are recommending a model premised on an early, sophisticated assessment of the case and the services it requires, in light of the needs of the particular client, and a provincially established framework of priorities. The model would offer degrees of assistance based on client needs, overall priorities, available resources, and the potential individual and systemic impact of the service.

Services would be provided by a mix of advice counsel, duty counsel, the private bar, staff offices (where numbers warrant), and supervised paralegals and other non-lawyer specialists. The objective would be to assess the case early, respond immediately to emergencies and obviously complex matters, deal with straightforward matters quickly, provide more extensive services where cases so demand, work well with other service providers and resources, and ensure the availability of the skills necessary to achieve the best results for the largest possible number of clients. In the area of "poverty law", we propose that services be provided by the current and possibly expanded network of community legal clinics operating under their existing mandate. Clinics should also play an important role in the overall assessment of client needs and the determination of priorities for the system as a whole.

The provision of these services will be coordinated by a new Legal Services Corporation of Ontario, independent of both the government and the Law Society of Upper Canada. Its Board would play a key role in monitoring needs, setting priorities, advocating for appropriate funding, designing and implementing service delivery options, establishing and maintaining links with other constituencies in the justice system, and maintaining quality control and public accountability. It will employ Area Managers at the local level to ensure that services meet local needs and circumstances. The Area Managers will also work to ensure coordination of services with local community clinics. (Ontario Legal Aid Review, 1997, Executive Summary, pp. 1-2)

Other key portions of the blueprint include the following:

While reforms to the legal aid system hold out some potential for realizing various efficiency gains in the utilization of legal aid resources, these gains are likely to be limited relative to the gains to be realized by improving the efficiency and efficacy of the underlying criminal, civil, and administrative justice systems, where very large potential gains can be realized through appropriate substantive and procedural reforms.

While no single issue in the history of legal aid in Ontario and elsewhere has attracted as much intensive debate as the choice of delivery models for legally aided services, much of this debate has been unproductive, and has turned on absolutist or universal claims on behalf of judicare or staff models. The empirical evidence does not point unambiguously to the superiority of either model in terms of cost, quality of service, or access to justice in a modern legal aid context where choice of models is highly context-specific, reflecting differences in the nature of legal problems, legal clients, and geographic context. In fact, a rich and eclectic range of models is required. A "one size fits all" approach to choice of delivery models is seriously misconceived, as is an "on-off switch" approach to availability of legal aid. What is needed is a graduated response that attempts to adapt to seriousness and complexity of a particular problem.

A much more mixed model of legal aid is required in Ontario than that which exists now. The new model must draw more heavily on duty counsel and staff offices, and use more non-legal specialists, if a fixed budget is to be utilized as efficiently and effectively as possible. Moreover, much more serious attention needs to be paid than has been the case in the past to issues of performance monitoring and quality assurance across the whole range of delivery models that the legal aid system employs. (Ontario Legal Aid Review, 1997, Executive Summary, p. 6)

The review also proposed an excellent set of criteria for the design of the governance of Ontario's legal aid system, including: (a) independence from government; (b) accountability for efficient use of public funds; (c) obtaining adequate resources for legal aid; (d) the ability to deliver quality service in a broad range of areas of the law; (e) the capacity to promote confidence in the legal aid system; (f) responsiveness to client needs; (g) efficient governance; (h) coordinated management of the entire legal aid system; and (i) innovation and experimentation.

To implement these criteria, it was recommended that the provincial legislature create a new Legal Services Corporation of Ontario, with an 11-person board appointed by the Lieutenant Governor-in-Council. The board would include four persons appointed on the advice of the provincial Attorney General from a list of 10 names provided by the provincial Law Society, two of whom would be lawyers with significant connections to the clinic system. The remaining seven members would be appointed based on advice from the Attorney General, with attention to ensuring that the board include persons with expertise or knowledge about providing legal services, the work of the courts and tribunals, management, and the legal needs of low-income Ontarians. The new corporation was established by the provincial legislature in October 1998 essentially as proposed by the review, with the intention that a majority of the board's members would be non-attorneys.

As the blueprint was being completed, the Ontario Legal Aid Plan established pilot projects to test alternative service delivery models to the primary judicare system. The Ontario Legal Aid Plan (1998) outlines planning and activities undertaken to date and describes the objective of the projects as follows:

To test alternative service delivery models in order to determine whether a different mix of delivery models can serve more clients with better service by answering these questions:
1. Can the plan improve access to service?
2. Can services be provided more cost efficiently?
3. Can the plan improve the quality of service? Can the plan have more control over who provides service and the qualifications they must have? Can the plan more closely monitor the services clients receive?

Some of the pilot project models underway or planned include new staff offices; law firm contracts for fixed functions or blocks of representation at fixed prices; expanded use of duty counsel; specialized criminal defense offices; specialized appeals panels; unbundled family law services; a family law information project;

and specialized immigration law offices and contracts. Many of the pilot projects are planned for three years to allow for startup and a reasonable period of full operation to facilitate a comprehensive evaluation.

Total civil and criminal legal aid expenditures for 1989-90 for Ontario was reported above as US$173.8 million, with the largest funding sources being the provincial government at $68 million and the federal government at $58 million. By 1996-97, following several years of reduced funding, total funding had increased to approximately US$265.9 million, with the largest funding sources being the provincial government at $189.7 million (reflecting the change to federal block grants to the provinces, as happened in Quebec) and federal funding of $40.8 million.

Ontario's legal aid program is one of the best funded in the world when compared on the basis of dollars per eligible person. Current activities to develop a more diverse mix of delivery systems reflect recommendations that have been on the public agenda for many years in Canada as well as other countries interested in developing excellent legal aid systems (Canadian Bar Association, 1987). The review's recommendations create an excellent general work plan for any legal aid system.

Maricopa County Superior Court Self-Service Center[5]

The Self-Service Center of the Superior Court of Maricopa County in Arizona was selected by the American Bar Association in 1997 to receive its annual Louis M. Brown Award for Legal Access. It is perhaps the most successful example in the United States of court-led activities to expand access to justice in civil areas for low- and middle-income persons. Maricopa County includes the city of Phoenix and adjacent areas, and the service systems developed by this court are being implemented throughout Arizona and considered throughout the United States.

The Self-Service Center is the result of a progressive series of steps undertaken by the court system beginning in 1994 to meet the legal needs of those who cannot afford full and traditional legal representation, as well as those not served by existing traditional public legal aid resources. The center's goal is to increase access to court services while maximizing cost-effectiveness, individual accountability, and linkages with services that already exist in the community. Its operation has resulted in the following:

• Availability of user-friendly instructions and forms that enable self-represented litigants to select and use appropriate and understandable court forms for the particular judicial action they seek;

---

[5] For additional information on this project, see Superior Court of Arizona, Maricopa County (1997); Goldschmidt (1998); and Legal Services Corporation, Office of Inspector General (1996).

• Creation of a network linkage to attorneys, community services and community dispute resolution providers, which allows litigants to obtain advice, evaluation and assistance related to matters that are the subject of court proceedings;

• Increased ability of judicial officers to devote time and attention to the judicial aspects of court services;

• Development of a higher level of self-representation, since litigants have available not only user-friendly forms and instructions, but also referrals to attorneys, social service providers and community dispute resolution providers.

The court dedicated a portion of the courthouse and staffing to the center, where court-developed self-help forms and instructions are provided. These resources are combined with "unbundled" (i.e., discrete task) assistance from area legal aid and private attorneys, and made available publicly throughout the county (and now the state) through the use of computerization and telecommunications technology. For example, a "Quick Court" computer kiosk was initially developed and tested in the Maricopa County Courthouse to provide legal information and help with the preparation, including assembly and printing, of individualized court forms and pleadings. Plans are now underway to establish 150 to 200 such self-help kiosks across the state.

The center's forms and instructions have been drafted in a user-friendly format easily understood and used by average persons. Legal services packets have been assembled in high-demand service areas such as divorce, child support and probate, with each packet including a checklist, how-to instructions and court forms. The creation of a supportive roster of attorneys was an acknowledgment that many self-represented litigants cannot afford attorneys' fees for full representation in a court proceeding, but can afford and benefit from paying for an hour or two of a lawyer's time and advice to review their matters, assure they are not overlooking important considerations, and help prepare them to represent themselves.

The center's services are provided to an average of more than 300 people per day through a variety of delivery systems. The center has two public facilities at two courthouses. People can also call a 24-hour automated telephone system with the capacity of serving up to 120 callers simultaneously. It has more than six hours of recorded information available. Clients can access Internet service available at all times. Finally, the center's services are also provided through the "Quick Court" interactive computer kiosks throughout the state.

The Self-Service Center hosts conferences for persons and organizations involved in court administration and access to justice throughout the United States, and offers technical assistance to court systems interested in implementing changes in terms of how courts can serve self-represented individuals.

CONCLUSIONS AND RECOMMENDATIONS

Each of the models reviewed in this chapter operates under differing incentives to provide legal aid and access to justice. Effective legal aid and access to justice systems use a mix of models to provide the range of functions identified as desirable by pubic policy. This chapter has briefly described and assessed the various models that might be applied in Latin America and the Caribbean to increase access to justice. The chapter initially identified implementation incentives and other factors that can influence the introduction of models of legal aid and access to justice. It then described three general legal aid systems (the Netherlands and the Canadian provinces of Quebec and Ontario) and one specialized model (the simplified court access system in Maricopa County, Arizona). All are generally acknowledged as examples of effective systems of legal aid and access to justice.

A mixed model is the most effective way to deliver legal aid and access to justice services. This was also the conclusion of the Canadian Bar Association National Legal Aid Liaison Committee (1987), which primarily focused on the private attorney judicare and staff attorney models. The committee's conclusions include the following:

> To date, the delivery models debate in Canada—as elsewhere—has focussed to an unhealthy degree upon a staff versus judicare confrontation. The initial debates took place as most jurisdictions established legal aid plans in the early 'seventies, choosing between British [judicare] and American [staff attorney] models. After legal aid matured as a program, the 'eighties have witnessed a resurgence of interest in delivery models, stimulated by the combined influences of fiscal restraint and program evaluations. The current debates have returned to the principal models of staff vs. judicare, but now with cost replacing ideology as the focus of the arguments.

> The Committee feels that cost is as bad a single benchmark for the choice of delivery models as was ideology. Issues of access, quality of service, reform and independence are too often ignored in the debate. Our study has sought to take a larger and admittedly more eclectic view of delivery models. Our review of the available data and arguments has convinced us that only a mixed model can deliver effective legal aid services in Canadian jurisdictions.

> A mixed model offers the opportunity to obtain the advantages of all of the staff, judicare and clinic models, so long as an adequate mix of all three are employed. In our view, no single model alone can meet the objectives of an effective legal aid program...

The Committee's central conclusion is that only a mixed model, with an adequate mix of staff, judicare and clinic models, can deliver effective legal aid services in Canadian jurisdictions. Once it is accepted that a mix of delivery models is necessary, much of the sterile debate of staff vs. judicare might be brought to a merciful end. Once it is accepted that each of the major delivery models has an important role to play within plans, more of our energies can be devoted to determining comparative advantages and disadvantages on a more "micro" level, e.g., rural and remote communities, different types of duty counsel services, specific kinds of casework, etc....

The mixing of models may encourage experimentation and innovation in new varieties of delivery models, encouraged by funding from the federal Department of Justice and provincial plans...The possibilities are limited only by the needs of the clients and the imagination of plans.

In conclusion, it is our hope that this study will encourage legal aid plans across the country to review and reconsider their current delivery models, with a view to creating a better mix of delivery models within the plans. Second, we hope that the federal Department of Justice will encourage plans to employ more mixed models, by a number of means: providing an adequate federal financial contribution in a single agreement covering all legal aid services, incorporating minimum standards of essential legal services, avoiding undue restrictions upon delivery models through definitions of shareable expenditures, funding more specific studies of the cost-effectiveness (i.e., both cost and quality) of different models, and offering funds for innovative models for delivery of legal services by the plans. Third, we hope that some of the data put forward in our study will encourage law societies to take a more active and interested role in the delivery of legal aid services, both through the organized channels of the profession and through their individual members. (Canadian Bar Association National Legal Aid Liaison Committee, 1987, pp. 227, 247-49)

Establishing, operating and maintaining adequate legal aid and access to justice systems requires the allocation of public funding. While the various models offer different efficiencies for various functions, the system must receive sufficient public support, combined with private contributions, to render the services needed. The development of a mixed model of legal aid can also help create the support base of various interest groups within the justice system, including private attorneys, court personnel and legal reformers. These interest groups, seeking specific personal and civic benefits, can advocate for public legal aid funding.

Cultivating a vigorous and healthy system of legal aid and access to justice can be a delicate task in countries with longstanding traditions of democracy and the rule of law, and even more difficult where such practices are more recent or fragile. Helpful to this process is conducting national legal aid development planning under the auspices of an appropriate and respected national office, such as the Supreme Court, the Department of Justice, the National Assembly, etc. This planning can help develop public consensus on the what, why and how of legal aid, and consider what timetables to establish for each subsystem and at what public and private costs. The plan should identify what national office in existence or to be established, with the requisite institutional power, will be responsible for overseeing, advocating for, and supporting implementation of the national plan for legal aid and access to justice.

When there is resistance to expanding legal aid, the sequencing of activities becomes important. Consideration should be given initially to the development of systems to provide basic information on legal rights, responsibilities and remedies to the broadest extent possible, followed by systems to efficiently provide legal assistance with common legal matters, perhaps through court-linked or similar approaches. Consideration should next be given to how to review public activities, including simplified administrative or other dispute resolution models or ombudsmen programs, insofar as meaningful opportunities exist in this area. Those developing legal services may well decide to deliberately separate less contentious legal information, advice, and basic assistance services, as well as somewhat more sensitive public review services that receive public funding, from more controversial legal reform activities provided by public interest law centers, and similar programs that require a mix of private funding, court-ordered attorney fees from successful litigation, and similar funding approaches. Which model can best attract the necessary support to provide the appropriate legal services functions in the most effective fashion will vary from country to country.

The processes of establishing, maintaining, improving and expanding systems of legal aid and access to justice are carried out around the world in many different ways and under very different circumstances. But such efforts share common goals of implementing essential human rights and protecting important public and private societal interests.

APPENDIX 2.1

The most recent effort to compile comparable data on national legal aid systems throughout the world was the *International Bar Association's International Directory of Legal Aid* (1985). A six-page IBA survey questionnaire on civil legal aid, criminal defense services and various related fee and trial practices was sent to persons or agencies in virtually every country. Completed survey responses were received from 50 countries (including each province of Australia and Canada, where there often are substantial differences across provinces). The countries responding to the IBA survey included Australia, Argentina, Austria, Bahrain, Barbados, Brazil, Brunei, Bulgaria, Canada, Chile, Colombia, Cyprus, Czechoslovakia, Denmark, Eire, England and Wales, Fiji, Finland, France, Gibraltar, Guatemala, Hong Kong, Hungary, Iceland, India, Indonesia, Israel, Japan, Malta, Mauritius, the Netherlands, Panama, Paraguay, the Philippines, Portugal, Scotland, Solomon Islands, South Africa, Spain, Sri Lanka, Sweden, Tanzania, Trinidad and Tobago, Turkey, West Germany, Zambia, and Zimbabwe.

While the IBA information is somewhat dated, relatively little seems to have changed in the ensuing period as to national authority for legal aid, types of services provided, primary legal aid models used to provide civil and criminal defense services, and permissible attorney fee arrangements. There have been some changes in eligibility criteria, gross expenditures, service contracting arrangements, and the regulation of legal practices. The following are condensed versions of responses to several survey questions that represent a reasonable sampling of national legal aid models and practices.

1. Who is responsible for the provision of legal assistance in your country? (Answers indicate some shared responsibilities in about a quarter of the responses.)

Federal government	41
Legal profession	18
Courts	4
Voluntary organizations	4
States	3
Law schools	3
Provinces	2
Trade unions	2

2. Can initial legal advice on legal problems be obtained (i.e., in instances other than litigation or before litigation)?

Yes	42
No (including Alberta, Canada, New Zealand and Turkey)	9
Unclear (France)	1

3.   How is legal assistance provided in civil cases involving litigation?

Private attorneys	33
Staffed legal aid centers	4
Mixed (private attorneys/staff centers)	14
Law school clinics	3
None	3
Civil servants	2
Nonprofit organizations	1
Law graduate trainees	1
Law students/private attorney supervisors	1
Lawyer cooperatives	1
Trade unions	1

(Attorneys in private attorney models were generally paid reduced fees with public funds, but were expected to provide service without compensation unless winning and paid by the losing party in a number of countries. Countries primarily using staffed legal aid centers included Eire, Paraguay and Zambia; mixed private attorney/staffed legal aid centers included the Canadian provinces of British Columbia and Quebec, and Indonesia, Israel, Philippines, Sweden, and Trinidad and Tobago; services provided by law students in centers under attorney supervision in Guatemala; and 15 percent of services provided by municipal public servants in Finland (see Hong Kong and Japan).

4.   Is there a fee for legal services to indigents in civil litigation?

Free	18
Fixed or proportionate contribution	10
Contribution may be required	21

(Numerous countries provide free services below certain income levels, and charge a fixed or sliding scale fee above that level up to a maximum legal aid eligibility income. In other instances, services are provided free but the client may be expected to make a contribution if the case is successful.)

5.   How is legal assistance provided in criminal trials?

Private attorneys	38
Staff public defenders	2
Mixed (private attorneys/public defenders)	12
Other	3

(Services provided in Colombia by private attorneys, law students, and nonprofit organizations' staff attorneys—private attorneys not paid; and private attorneys also not paid for services in Turkey; private attorneys in other countries paid reduced fees from public funds (see Hong Kong); "other" includes law graduate trainees in Czechoslovakia, 15 percent of services by municipal civil servants in Finland; and a mix of private attorneys and law students working at three legal aid centers in Guatemala. Legal assistance in criminal defense only provided in capital cases in four countries, or in murder, treason or other very serious charges in three countries. Zimbabwe, similar to a few other countries, requires a finding of financial eligibility and "desirable in the interest of justice.")

6.   Is there a fee for legal services to indigents in criminal trials?

Free	27
Fixed or proportionate contribution	12
Contribution may be required	10

(Services are free to persons below a certain income level in Sri Lanka and several other countries, with a fixed or sliding scale fee above that level to a certain eligibility ceiling. In Denmark, Iceland and Japan, services are initially provided free, but a fee is charged if the party is found guilty.)

7.   Is legal aid provided for appeals in criminal trials?

Yes	47
No	2

(In the two "no" countries, Fiji and Tanzania, legal aid may be provided for appeals in charges of murder or treason.)

8.   Do law centers that specialize in certain legal aid matters (i.e., welfare, housing, consumer, juvenile, elderly) exist in your country?

Yes	22
No	30

(Countries or provinces with specialty centers included Ontario, Canada, Chile, Colombia, England and Wales, New Zealand and the Philippines.)

9.   Are losing parties in civil trials liable to pay the lawyer's fees of the winning party?

Yes	40
No	14

("Yes" includes Hong Kong, where fees are waived in legal aid cases; Japan, in some cases; Norway, can be waived; Scotland, reduced in legal aid cases; Sweden, covered by legal aid plan; and Trinidad and Tobago, at the discretion of the court. Note that Canadian provinces vary in regard to this practice. "No" includes Chile, not normally in Iceland, Philippines, Spain, and Sri Lanka. In the Philippines, Spain and other countries, the court has the discretion to charge the losing party attorney's fees for the other side upon determination that the party acted in bad faith in pursuing or prolonging the litigation.)

10.   Are contingent fees permitted in civil cases?

Yes	15
No	35

(As above, note split in Canadian provinces in regard to this practice. "Yes" includes Argentina; Brazil; the Canadian provinces of British Columbia, Manitoba and Quebec; Chile; Colombia, where it is rare; India, permitted but unusual; Indonesia; Israel; Paraguay; the Philippines; and Turkey, permitted but not routine. Note that the United States did not respond in full to the IBA survey and is not included in this digest except to indicate that contingent fees are probably most used in that country in damage claims, but prohibited in family law cases. "No" includes Australia, Austria, Barbados, Canadian provinces of Alberta and Ontario, Denmark, Eire, England and Wales, Finland, Guatemala, Hong Kong, Japan, New Zealand, Norway, Panama, Portugal, Scotland, South Africa, Spain, Sweden, Trinidad and Tobago, and West Germany. Note that in Czechoslovakia, contingent fees are not permitted except in inheritance cases.)

BIBLIOGRAPHY

Abel, Richard L., and Philip S. C. Lewis, eds. 1988. *Lawyers in Society.* Vols. 1 and 2. Berkeley: University of California Press.

American Bar Association Consortium on Legal Services and the Public. 1996. *Agenda for Access—The American People and Civil Justice.* Chicago: American Bar Association.

American Bar Association Standing Committee on Legal Aid and Indigent Defendants. 1986. *Standards for Providers of Civil Legal Services to the Poor.* Chicago: American Bar Association.

Anderson, Mary H., and Anne K. Walker. 1986. *Pro Bono Hotlines: Volunteer Legal Services that Work.*

Australasian Legal Information Institute. Website. http://austlii.law.uts.edu.au/

Bamberger, Clinton. 1989. The Best Legal Aid System in the World. *Rechthulp* 10.

Blankenburg, Erhard. 1992. Comparing Legal Aid Schemes in Europe. *Civil Justice Quarterly* 11: 106.

Blankenberg, Erhard, ed. 1980. *Innovations in the Legal Services.* Cambridge, MA: Oelgeschlager, Gunn and Hain.

Bloch, Frank S., and Iqbal S. Ishar. 1990. Legal Aid, Public Service and Clinical Legal Education: Future Directions from India and the United States. *Michigan Journal of International Law* 12: 92.

Brakel, Samuel J. 1974. *Judicare: Public Funds, Private Lawyers and Poor People.* Chicago: American Bar Foundation.

Breger, Marshall J. 1982. Legal Aid for the Poor: A Conceptual Analysis. *North Carolina Law Review* 40: 282.

Caiden, Gerald E., ed. 1983. *International Handbook of the Ombudsman: Evolution and Present Function.* Westport, CT: Greenwood Press.

Canadian Bar Association National Legal Aid Liaison Committee. 1987. *Legal Aid Delivery Models: A Discussion Paper.*

Canadian Center for Justice Statistics. 1998. *Legal Aid in Canada: 1996-97.* Ottawa: Canadian Center for Justice Statistics.

_____. 1998. *Legal Aid in Canada: Description of Operations.* Ottawa: Canadian Center for Justice Statistics.

_____. 1998. *Legal Aid in Canada: Resources and Caseload Statistics.* Ottawa: Canadian Center for Justice Statistics.

Cappelletti, Mauro, and Bryant Garth, eds. 1979. *Access to Justice.* Alpen and den Rijn, The Netherlands: Sijthoff and Noordhoff; Milan: A. Giuffré.

Cappelletti, Mauro, James Gordley, and Earl Johnson, eds. 1975. *Toward Equal Justice: A Comparative Study of Legal Aid in Modern Societies.* Milan: A. Giuffré; Dobbs Ferry, NY: Duana Publications.

Center for Law and Social Policy. Website. http://www.clasp.org

Center for Law Practice Technology. Website. http://www.digital-lawyer.com

Child Support Network. Website. http://www.childsupport.org

Commissic Polak, The Hague. 1989. *Report of the Commission: Future Structure of Legal Aid.*

Committee on Legal Services to the Poor in Developing Countries. 1972. *Legal Aid and World Poverty.* New York: Praeger

Conseil D'Etat. 1990. *L'Aide Juridique: Pour Une Meilleur Access au Droit et a la Justice.*

Cooper, Jeremy. 1994. English Legal Services: A Tale of Diminishing Returns. *Maryland Journal of Contemporary Legal Issues* 5: 333.

———. 1983. *A Report on the Future of Legal Services in Australia.*

———. 1983. *Public Legal Services: A Comparative Study of Policy, Politics, and Practice.* London: Sweet and Maxwell.

———. 1981. The Delivery Systems Study: A Policy Report to Congress and the President of the United States. *Modern Law Review* 44: 308.

Council of Europe. 1995. Proceedings of the 4th Round Table with European Ombudsmen, Lisbon, 16-17 June 1994.

Cousins, M. 1993. Civil Legal Aid in France, Ireland, The Netherlands, and the United Kingdom. *Civil Justice Quarterly* 12: 154.

Dakolias, Maria. 1996. *The Judicial Sector in Latin American and the Caribbean—Elements of Reform.* Washington, D.C.: World Bank.

Desk Top Lawyer. Website. http://www.desktoplawyer.co.uk

Equal Justice Network. Website. http://www.equaljustice.org

Findlaw. Website. http://www.findlaw.com

Garth, Bryant. 1980. *Neighborhood Law Firms for the Poor: A Comparative Study of Recent Developments in Legal Aid and in the Legal Profession.* Alpen and den Rijn, The Netherlands: Sijthoff and Noordhoff.

Goldschmidt, J. 1998. How Are Courts Handling pro se Litigants. *Judicature* 82: 13.

Gorieley, Tamara. 1992. Legal Aid in the Netherlands: A View from England. *Modern Law Review* 55: 802

Gray, A. 1994. The Reform of Legal Aid. *Oxford Review of Economic Policy* 10: 51.

Huls, Nick. 1994. From Pro Deo Practice to a Subsidized Welfare State Provision: Twenty-five Years of Providing Legal Services to the Poor in the Netherlands. *Maryland Journal of Contemporary Legal Issues* 5: 333.

Human Rights Law Group. Website. http://hrlawgroup.org

International Bar Association (Judy Lane and Simon Hillyard, eds.) 1985. *International Directory of Legal Aid.*

International Human Rights Internship. 1997. *Legal Aid and Public Interest Organizations.*

International Legal Services Network. Website. http://www.ilsn.org

Johnson, Jon T. 1994. Nordic Legal Aid. *Maryland Journal of Contemporary Legal Issues* 5: 333.

_____ . 1991. The Politics of Clinical Legal Education. *Juss-Buss and Clinical Legal Education.*

Kharel, Satish K. 1996. Public Interest Litigation as a Learning Tool for Students. AALS Conference Report.

Legal Action Group. 1992. *A Strategy for Justice: Publicly Funded Legal Services in the 1990's.* London: Legal Action Group.

Legal Counsel for the Elderly, Inc., American Association of Retired Persons. 1996. *Legal Hotlines: A How To Manual.* Washington, D.C.: Legal Counsel for the Elderly, Inc.

Legal Resources Project of the International Human Rights Project. 1997. *Legal Aid and Public Interest Law Organizations.*

Legal Services Corporation. 1992. *Legal Services Corporation's Law School Civil Clinical Program.* Washington, D.C.: Legal Services Corporation.

_____ . 1980. *The Delivery Systems Study: A Policy Report to Congress and the President of the United States.* Washington, D.C.: Legal Services Corporation.

Legal Services Corporation Office of the Inspector General. 1996. *Increasing Legal Services Delivery Capacity Through Information Technology.* Washington, D.C.: Legal Services Corporation.

Lih-wu, Han, Ed. 1985. *Legal Aid in Asia and the Pacific.* Taipei, Taiwan: CAHR.

Menon, M. R. Madhava. 1996. Clinical Programs for Socially Relevant Legal Education: The National Law School Experience. Association of American Law Schools Conference on Clinical Legal Education, Expanding the Frame: Crossing the Border to other Countries and Disciplines

My Lawyer. Website. http://www.mylawyer.com

MyLegalAssistant.com. Website. http://www.mylegalassistant.com

National Equal Justice Library. Website. http://www.equaljusticeupdate.org

Nolan, Sister Michael Mary, Vera Regina Fontes, and Linnis Cook. 1994. Legal Assistance in São Paulo, Brazil. *Maryland Journal of Contemporary Legal Issues* 5: 409.

Nolo Press. Website. http://www.nolo.com

Ontario Legal Aid Plan. 1998. *Proposed Pilot Projects: Final Report.*

Ontario Legal Aid Review. 1997. *A Blueprint for Publicly Funded Legal Services.*

Ontario Ministry of Attorney General. 1997. *Report of the Ontario Legal Aid Review: A Blueprint for Publicly Funded Legal Services.*

People's Law Library of Maryland. Website. http://www.peoples-law.com

Pinetree Legal Services (international links). Website. http://www.ptla.org/international.htm

Pro-se Law Center. Website. http://www.pro-selaw.org

Reifner, Udo. 1988. Collective Legal Aid. *Recht en Kritiek* 14: 253.

Rhudy, Robert J. 1994. Comparing Legal Services to the Poor in the United States with Other Western Countries: Some Preliminary Lessons. *Maryland Journal of Contemporary Legal Issues* 5: 253.

Richardson, Mark, and Steven Reynolds. 1994. The Shrinking Public Purse: Civil Legal Aid in New South Wales, Australia. *Maryland Journal of Contemporary Legal Issues* 5: 349.

Rowat, Malcolm, Waleed H. Malik, and Maria Dakolias. 1995. Alternative Dispute Resolution Mechanisms and Access to Justice. Judicial Reform in Latin America and the Caribbean. Proceedings of a World Bank Conference.

Stacey, Frank. 1978. *Ombudsmen Compared.* Oxford: Clarendon Press.

Stephens, M. 1991. *Community Law Centers: A Critical Appraisal.*

Superior Court of Arizona, Maricopa County. 1997. *Self-Service Center: Final Report for State Justice Institute Award No. 94-12A-1325.*

Superior Court of Arizona, Maricopa County, Self-Service Center. Website. http://www.superiorcourt.maricopa.gov/ssc/sschome.html

Symposium on Legal Services to the Poor in Other Countries—A Comparative Review. University of Maryland School of Law. 1993. *Maryland Journal of Contemporary Legal Issues* 5.

Trubek, Louise G. 1994. U.S. Legal Education and Legal Services for the Indigent: A Historical and Personal Perspective. *Maryland Journal of Contemporary Legal Issues* 5: 381.

Zemans, Frederick H., ed. 1979. An International Overview on Legal Aid. *Perspectives on Legal Aid: An International Survey.* Westport, CT: Greenwood Press.

Zemans, Frederick H., and Lewis T. Smith. 1994. Can Ontario Sustain Cadillac Legal Services? *Maryland Journal of Contemporary Legal Issues* 5: 271.

CHAPTER THREE

JUDICIAL REFORM IN THE BASQUE COUNTRY: A CASE STUDY

Juan Enrique Vargas Viancos*

What makes a judicial reform successful? After 15 uninterrupted years of judicial reform effort in Latin America, there is still apparently no conclusive answer to that question.

Certainly a great number of initiatives have been undertaken with the aim of facilitating intense processes of reform. These initiatives have generally been narrowly targeted, however, and their results appear precarious. Nonetheless, they are viewed as catalysts for more radical and integral processes of change that are more likely to lead to modernization of an entire judicial system.

The most common approach to reform has been to revise the legal codes applied by the courts. This first line of reform generally involves issuing new codes of procedure that regulate the actions of lawyers and legal staff. Law reform is the type of reform most familiar to attorneys, who traditionally have held a virtual monopoly not only over the practice of law per se but also in defining the scope of legal practice, and in formulating public policy as related to the work of the justice system. One of the most prominent areas of this type of judicial reform in Latin America has been the modernization of codes of criminal procedure in order to

* The author would like to thank the staff of the vice-minister of justice for Basque Country and of the judicial branch, particularly Iñaki Sánchez, former vice-minister of justice; Antonio Guerra, director of the Judicial Documentation Center; Inmaculada de Miguel, director of relations with the administration of justice; Ricardo Olabegoya, former director of material resources; Julián Asurmendi, director of human resources; Pedro Alberto González, chief of the Judicial Computer Service; Jaime Tapia, chief judge of Bilbao; Mikel Aguirregabiria, director of the EAT of Alaba; and Manuel Garavilla, secretary to the chief judge of Bilbao. Thanks also to Cristián Riego, professor and researcher with the Universidad Diego Portales, who participated in the visit to study the Basque judicial system.

establish adversarial and oral proceedings.[1] This has been an important change, not only because it has been so widely adopted, currently extending to practically every country in Latin America, but mainly because it has a major impact on a key issue that defines the state and determines its legitimacy: how the state uses force.

A second line of reform is aimed at the system of judicial branch governance structures and at the regime of incentives for judges and court staff. In general, these reforms place emphasis on creating new institutions to lead the judiciaries, usually by establishing a judicial council *(Consejo de la Judicatura)* or by modifying structures already established to administer the courts. It is also common to seek to amend the statute regulating the labor regime of judicial staff. Some countries have even introduced profound changes in the very composition of their judicial branches.

It is common in this type of reform to assign particular importance to training, which is considered one of the most effective tools for inducing changes in the judiciary. The underlying consideration is that since judicial staff (especially judges) are critical in determining the results courts are capable of delivering, efforts should therefore be geared to ensuring the quality and conduct of the judicial staff.

Finally, a third line of reforms aims to modernize the delivery of justice services. These reforms often involve upgrading physical plant and equipment, as well as managerial capacity. Justice is considered to be one more public service that should strive to satisfy its customers. This requires efficient coverage, organization and operation. The first and most traditional of these types of reform is designed to respond to the increased demands for justice by creating new courts and increasing the number of judges.

The reforms that focus on management assume that resources are scarce, so it is not possible to increase coverage without improving efficiency and making better use of available resources. The typical changes at this level involve strengthening judicial management, reorganizing judicial offices—mainly by setting up common clerks' offices—and introducing technical support for management through professional assistance or the use of appropriate technologies.

Viewed through the lens of a typology set forth in such broad strokes,[2] the differences among the various approaches are plain to see. Especially in the first but also in the second line of reforms, one finds what could be called "rights-based" motives for the reforms, as they are required by the demands of the rule of law and individual prerogatives. Reforms based on these motives are characterized mainly by the fact that they do not pursue, as their main goal, the general well being of society, or, if you will, criteria based on an efficiency analysis. It should be possible

---

[1] This path has been followed, with varying degrees of intensity, by Argentina, Chile, Costa Rica, El Salvador, Guatemala and Venezuela.

[2] We have expressly left out changes that do not affect our framework, such as those related to diversifying petitions for protection of property or persons.

to exercise a "right" even when the majority does not approve, and even when the majority will be worse off than when the right is not exercised.[3] A judicial reform of this type will not use efficiency-based calculations for gauging its usefulness, or will accord them merely secondary importance.

The third line of reforms—and to some extent the second as well—operates within a more traditional public policy logic, whose benefits are observed mainly through an aggregational utilitarian process. What matters is to improve the well being of society as a whole: the reforms seek to improve the situation in economic, political or social terms. In contrast to a rights approach, the virtue of a policy is gauged based on whether the society is better or worse off after it is implemented. The successes and failures of the various lines of reform can be gauged by different parameters. Another difference is that as one moves from the first to the second to the third approach to reform, the law decreases in importance as leverage for change, and the direct actions of the institutions and the legal staff of the system increase.

Finally, the most significant versions of the first and second lines of reform are clearly aimed at re-establishing the foundations of the judicial system, as they are aimed at radically altering the rules of the game within the institution. The reforms that affect coverage and management, and those that rely primarily on instruments such as training, proceed from a generally incrementalist view of change. This assumes that change comes not in great leaps and bounds, but from a set of small steps, in a process that could be called "hybridization."

The advisability of one approach over the other has long been debated. Yet, none of these discussions has yielded a truly adequate formula for successful modernization of a judicial system. Perhaps the explanation for this is that in every discussion, some key aspects of public policy are forgotten. Sufficient consideration has not been given to the fact that, in general, the main problem is not inadequately choosing the content of the reforms to be attempted, but rather failing to come up with the precise strategy for achieving the change sought. From that point of view, we are especially drawn to examining the Basque experience of reforming the justice system.

One of the most prominent features of the Basque reform is that it is focused almost exclusively on changes to the management of the judicial system. In general, this reform strategy has the least followers among practitioners of judicial reform today, as it is generally seen more as a mix of actions from the other lines than as a possibility for change in its own right. This reinforces the idea that the relevance of the Basque experience lies not so much in the technocratic content of the changes proposed, but in the way in which they have been carried out and in the long-term

---

[3] Indeed, some describe the judicial branch precisely as counter-majoritarian, existing precisely to prevent majorities from imposing their will on minorities.

perspective upon which they are based. Indeed, all indications suggest that the decision to use computerization as the mechanism to affect the changes desired was based more on an analysis of the factors that conditioned the reform, rather than on a deliberate decision that computerization was in itself key. Had the situation been different, no doubt other approaches would have been chosen.

Among those conditioning factors was the very impossibility of intervening from the standpoint of the other two traditional lines of reform discussed above. The Basque government did not have the power to change the legal framework that defines the organization of the judiciary as well as the other bodies of law which the judges must apply,[4] or to amend the status of judicial employees.[5]

The key to the successes in the Basque Country can be found more in the overall reform strategy than in its content. Therefore, on analyzing it as a case study, special emphasis must be placed on the lessons this experience has to offer in terms of defining a successful reform. Prominent among these are being clear on the long-term objectives; persistently developing policies over long periods of time; properly situating the impetus of reform at the appropriate institutional level; taking advantage of opportunities as they arise; acting flexibly without renouncing one's objectives; involving judges in the reform process (getting them to become committed to it without co-opting it to their own interests); efficiently administering the "carrots" and "sticks"; producing tangible results in the short term; and constantly incorporating new actors and sources of support into the changes.

Although the Spanish judiciary has some problems similar to those found in Latin America, they are on a smaller scale and overall the situation is quite different from that of most Latin American judicial systems. The *Libro Blanco de la Justicia,* published by the *Consejo General del Poder Judicial* (1997) clearly identifies problems in Spain familiar to Latin America, such as excessive formality and slow and inefficient practices. It notes in particular "a widespread opinion in society that reflects profound dissatisfaction with the operation of the administration of justice, and which affects, or may affect very negatively, the confidence of the Spanish people" (p. 17). Even so, the suitability of the procedures, the level of judges' training, the degree of corruption, and the coverage of the judicial system is markedly better in Spain than in most of Latin America.

This chapter aims to clarify and isolate the factors that define these differences and to draw out what are the most important and useful lessons of this

---

[4] As will be seen, legal changes have been made in connection with these reforms, as in the case of common services, but they have been more consequences than causes.

[5] It was not until 1996 that the authority to administer judicial personnel was transferred to the Basque government, but this authority applies only to judicial administrative staff, not judges or clerks, and has encountered some difficulties, as will be seen further on.

reform process for Latin America. The chapter provides a general description of the process whereby judicial changes were brought about in the Basque Country and the context in which the changes unfolded. The content of these changes is then examined and evaluated in greater detail.

ORIGINS AND STRATEGY OF THE REFORM PROCESS

Autonomy Statute for the Basque Country

The autonomy process spurred the reforms to the justice system in the Basque Country and is the key to understanding them. The Autonomy Statute for the Basque Country, also known as the Statute of Gernika, was approved on November 18, 1979 by Organic Law 3/79.[6] Under this law, Spain recognized a broad set of powers of self-government, including the judicial function, vested in the Basque people. The *Comunidad Autónoma del País Vasco* (Autonomous Community of the Basque Country) was created under the 1978 Constitution.[7] The most significant provisions are:

> Article 13-1. As regards the administration of justice, except for the military jurisdiction, the *Comunidad Autonómica del País Vasco* shall exercise, in its territory, the powers that the Organic Laws of the Judicial Branch and of the General Council of the Judiciary recognize, reserve, or attribute to the [Spanish] Government.

> Article 35-3. It shall be up to the autonomous community, within its territory, to provide for the personnel of the administration of justice and the material and economic resources needed for its operation, in the same terms in which that power is reserved to the Executive in the Organic Law on the Judiciary, and preference should be given, in the personnel systems, to knowledge of Basque Civil Law *(Derecho Foral Vasco)* and the Basque language.

---

[6] The Basque Country historically had an autonomous regime, but it was lost as a consequence of the civil war in 1936.
[7] "The autonomy statutes take the place of what in a federal system would be the constitution of each state or province, and at least in theory, state or provincial constitutions are approved without external intervention and the review for federal constitutionality is done a posteriori, whereas the statutes must be approved by the Spanish legislature" (Elorza and Guerra, 1996).

Article 35-3 is particularly important for understanding the judicial reform process in the Basque Country; there is no equivalent provision in any other autonomy statute. This statute set off a process unprecedented in Spanish history, since the Ministry of Justice of Spain was the only ministry in the entire public administration that had not delegated any of its powers to the regions. The autonomy statute for the Basque Country adds new complexities to an already intricate system of jurisdiction in which various government organs and offices impact on the judiciary:

(a) As regards the legal framework—both that which regulates the judiciary and that which the courts must apply in settling disputes—the general rule is that the scope of jurisdiction is national. In other words, both the organic laws regulating the judiciary and judicial procedures and the substantive law are adopted by the *cortes nacionales* (i.e., the legislature),[8] and they are not matters over which the autonomous government has any authority.[9] However, there are some minor powers vested in the autonomous government, such as conserving, modifying and developing Basque civil law *(derecho foral vasco)* (Article 10-5).

(b) In the strictly judicial sphere, there is a Superior Court of the Basque Country, under which one finds the appellate courts *(audiencias provinciales)* and the entry-level courts *(tribunales de instancia)*.[10] All are integrated into a national judicial structure,[11] at the head of which sits the Supreme Court of Spain *(Tribunal Supremo de España)*, which has jurisdiction to hear motions for cassation.[12] At the same time there is a *Tribunal Constitucional* (Constitutional Court) whose rulings apply to the courts of the Basque Country just as they apply to all other courts and institutions of the Spanish state.

(c) The administration of material and economic resources is handled in Spain by the executive, which exercises this power through the Ministry of Justice. This distinguishes Spain from most Latin American countries, where this power is vested either directly in the judiciary or in a judicial council (usually the *Consejo de la Judicatura* or *Consejo de la Magistratura*).

---

[8] The establishment of new courts is also the subject of a national statute.

[9] Notwithstanding the lawmaking powers of the European Union, which must be directly applied by member countries, one of which is Spain. The coexistence of external political integration and the creation of autonomous domestic regions gives Spain a unique polity not without its conflicts.

[10] Spain also has *tribunales de paz* entrusted to lay judges organized under the respective municipalities. These courts are found in all municipalities that do not have a *juzgado de primera instancia* or a *juzgado de instrucción*. Their jurisdiction, which is limited, varies depending on whether they are located in municipalities with more or less than 7,000 inhabitants. In the latter case, they may hold proceedings with respect to lesser infractions *(faltas)* and provide specific judicial assistance.

[11] However, regular appeals generally proceed through the judicial entities within the autonomous community. "Judicial activity constitutes a system of relatively closed flows within each Autonomous Community" (Elorza and Guerra, 1996).

[12] In the case of applying civil law particular to the Basque Country, jurisdiction to hear motions for cassation is held by its Superior Court.

This power was the first that the autonomy statute allowed to be transferred to the government of the Basque Country, as provided for in Royal Decree 1,684 of 1987, which entered into force on January 1, 1988, making official the agreement reached in the committee created for that purpose.[13] The minutes of the committee specify that the administration of these resources in the Basque Country encompasses:

• Planning, programming and administrative control of the material resources required for the activities of the courts of justice;

• Acquisition of buildings, furnishings and office equipment and supplies for the use of the courts;

• Preparation, design and implementation of programs for the construction, repair and conservation of the judicial buildings and for their inspection;

• Subsidies for attorney's fees, where appropriate, for the defense by a lawyer and representation by a public defender before Basque judicial entities, and for the legal counsel for detainees or prisoners when the place of custody is within the autonomous community;

• Examination, verification and payment of the accounts of operating expenses, and compensation for judicial procedures outside the judge's office, autopsies, judicial procedures, and for witnesses and experts before the courts.[14]

The transfer of these powers comes together with the economic resources earmarked by the Spanish state for that purpose.[15] The Basque autonomy statute is exceptional in that it gives the Basque government its own treasury, i.e., the power to collect taxes and administer its own budget (Article 40).

(d) There are three distinct classes of personnel in Spain. First are the judges and magistrates, whose professional service is under the General Council of the Judiciary (CGPJ), based in Madrid. In addition, there are the clerks (*secretarios*) and judicial administrative staff (*empleados*), both of whom are subordinate to the Ministry of Justice. The rules regulating their professional service are not identical.

These three classes of officers—judges, clerks and administrative staff—constitute what are known in Spain as *cuerpos nacionales* (national corps), i.e., classes of

---

[13] This was the first transfer of judicial powers to an autonomous community, followed by transfers to Catalonia on July 20, 1990 (supplemented by the transfers of July 8 and September 23, 1994, and March 1, 1996); to Galicia on November 4, 1994 (supplemented on January 26 and November 22, 1996); to Valencia on March 24, 1995 (supplemented on August 23, 1996 and April 14, 1997); to the Canary Islands on December 2, 1996; and to Andalusia on January 31, 1997.

[14] In the next transfer, in 1996, the Basque government also assumed the administration of the material and economic resources of the Public Prosecution Service (*Fiscalía*). It is expected that it will also have authority over penitentiaries, for which the government is already preparing.

[15] Economically, the transfer operates by discounting the amount of resources equivalent to expenditures on the powers transferred from the quota that the autonomous community must pay to the national government.

personnel not circumscribed to a particular part of the national territory (as might be the case of an autonomous community). Rather, their professional service covers all of Spain, and in the performance of their functions they can move from region to region. Therefore, they are subject to a common set of regulations. The notion of the national corps emanates from the principle of the unity of the Spanish judicial branch, provided for by Article 117(5) of the Constitution. It aims to institute a homogeneous regime in all the autonomous communities to govern the exercise of citizen rights in their relationships with the administration of justice (Lamarca, 1994).[16] This attempt at homogeneity, as will be seen further on, has led to clashes with the national government in the process whereby the Basque government has assumed the new powers.[17]

The autonomy statute covers only the transfer of judicial administrative staff, not of judges and clerks. The transfer to the Basque Country of medical examiners, court officials and auxiliary personnel,[18] as well as other judicial staff,[19] was made in April 1996.

Assuming Authority over the Justice System

The Basque Country has unique characteristics. Its territory is relatively small (7,234.8 km^2), with a population of nearly 2.1 million and a population density of 290 inhabitants/km^2. The standard of living is high, with per capita income at $17,904,[20] even though the region has just begun to recover from an economic crisis that saw unemployment at 21.1 percent as late as 1997.

The Basque Country is made up of three provinces: Alava, Guipúzcoa, and Vizcaya. Vizcaya has the largest population, and its capital, Bilbao, is home to about half the population of the Basque Country. The capital of the Basque Country is Vitoria-Gasteiz. Communication and transportation are excellent, even though several mountain ranges crisscross the country.

---

[16] The Organic Law on the Judiciary, Article 454, provides that judicial clerks, medical examiners, and auxiliary personnel (oficiales, auxiliares and agentes) constitute cuerpos nacionales. Article 455 stipulates that in consideration thereof, the Ministry of Justice should assume responsibility for their selection, training, assignment, promotion, discipline, and related administrative matters (Lamarca, 1994). The constitutionality of creating cuerpos nacionales has been challenged and affirmed in Judgments 25/1983 and 56/1990 of the Constitutional Court. Judgment 56/1990 expressly addressed this rule of the Organic Law on the Judiciary.

[17] Another category of judiciary personnel who are not part of the national corps are called personal laboral, and include psychologists, expert witnesses, translators, and cleaning personnel. The transfer also gives control over such personnel to the autonomous community.

[18] They number 1,700 in all.

[19] In 1988, some 107 personal laboral who cleaned the courts were transferred. The 1997 transfer covered the remaining 80 staff members.

[20] The purchasing power of a Basque worker is 112 percent of the average in comparison with the rest of the European Union.

At the time of the first transfer of authority to the Basque Country, there were 90 judicial entities with a total of 104 judges and magistrates. This yields a ratio of 4.96 judges and magistrates per 100,000 population.[21] At the time of the transfer, a new law on judicial demarcation and plant was under consideration to improve the ratio throughout Spain from 1.96 courts per 100,000 population to a goal of 5.26.

The Basque Country has crime rates substantially lower—by some 20 percent—than the rest of Spain (see Table 3.1). This trend has not changed since the transfer. Year-to-year growth of crime has increased at the same rate as for the rest of Spain, about 15 percent over four years.

The Basque Country has a solid legal culture and tradition based on the performance of professionals with solid training and a rule of law that enshrines respect for individual rights. There have been significant advances with regard to these rights since Spain's return to democracy. The advances have come both in terms of legislation and in the case law of the Constitutional Court. In repeated and significant rulings, the court has profoundly modified the way in which power is exercised in Spain as well as the work of the judicial system as a whole. The most urgent problems with respect to procedural guarantees were already resolved in Spain before the transfer of authority took place.

As favorable as they might be for development in general, and especially for the proper performance of judicial functions, these advances occurred in the context of a society torn asunder by a particularly violent pro-independence group, ETA (*Euskadi ta Askatasuna,* or Basque Homeland and Liberty). Terrorism was clearly an important issue when the Basques themselves assumed the task of directing their justice system. But not all ETA violence has been carried out in the Basque Country, and not all persons tried in connection with these acts were tried within the territory, since jurisdiction in these cases is vested in the *Audiencia Nacional* in Madrid. ETA members held in prisons are not incarcerated in the Basque territory, but rather dispersed across Spain. Despite these issues, the problems faced by the new Basque government with regard to the justice system appear to be manageable and have given rise to policies based on continuity rather than disruption. As stated by the President (*Lehendakari*) of the Basque Government:

> We could have opted to improve what we received within a policy framework in line with that followed by the Ministry of Justice. We would have provided new locales and installed small computers, one per entity, following the logic of the Inforius Project; and we would

---

[21] This does not include justices of the peace.

Table 3.1. Offenses per 1,000 Inhabitants, Spain, 1992-96

	1992	1993	1994	1995	1996
Alava	38.91	36.78	41.70	42.31	59.78
Vizcaya	39.57	46.37	39.84	49.54	56.83
Guipúzcoa	37.04	38.97	42.70	47.02	49.73
All of Spain	57.37	60.97	63.72	67.54	73.69
Barcelona	61.08	59.21	62.08	64.84	68.89
Madrid	55.25	72.80	67.17	78.08	87.12
Seville	90.18	85.73	82.05	88.07	99.19
Valencia	83.02	83.52	94.18	80.70	82.76

have limited ourselves to facilitating more fungible resources for judicial staff. In short, we would have made things excessively complex for ourselves, and even so, the effects would have been limited yet positive (Basque Government, 1991).

The new authorities instead proposed a different policy, entailing deeper changes than their powers allowed. The effects of terrorism may have contributed to this approach, but they do not appear to be the most compelling factor. Rather, there are other interrelated reasons behind the decision, such as:

• A widespread perception that justice was not working well, that it did not provide quality service to users.

• Training for the new authorities was different from what had traditionally been done. Because the government in the Basque Country is autonomous, it is made up mainly of persons from business or the private sector.

• A profound sense that the legitimacy of the new autonomous government cannot be based solely on cultural or political factors, but that it would be judged instead on the efficiency and effectiveness with which it performs its functions.

As stated by the president of Basque Country, "...autonomy is not only a right and a political claim, but also a synonym of effectiveness. My government's initiative in this area has been strong in budgetary terms and clear in political terms: to completely modernize this administration" (Basque Government, 1991).

This vision of the role that the justice system should play within the Basque government has been surprisingly stable over time. The very stability of the Basque government has helped, as the same person has been at its head through all these years. Yet this alone does not suffice to explain judicial stability, for in the 11 years since the first transfer, the government has been supported by very diverse political pacts, and the authorities entrusted with the justice sector have been identified with very different political movements.[22] The absolute coherence and consistency of the justice system over time shows that policy for the sector was based not on short-term choices or the preferences of a given sector of Basque society, but rather reflects a deep-seated consensus and concept regarding this sector.

The consistency in the policies and the tendency to seek support from the society at large for initiatives that have led to modernization of the justice system have not come about by chance. They have had an important impact on the low degree of conflict involved in the process of adopting a reform strategy, on the energy and initiative with which the reforms were undertaken, and on the technical content of the reforms themselves.

Defining the Reform Strategy

Changes to the structure of the Basque government that permit it to assume the functions transferred to it have included the creation in 1988 of the Department of the Presidency, Justice, and Autonomous Development. This includes the Vice-Ministry of Justice, entrusted with government functions with respect to the justice system. Over time, the entity entrusted with exercising the judicial authority of the autonomous community would undergo several changes, both rising and falling in rank.[23] The current structure is shown in the organizational chart in Figure 3.1.[24]

The Basque government did not have a well-defined plan of action when the new powers in the area of justice were first transferred to it. Its initial actions were basically exploratory, since this was an area entirely unfamiliar to the authorities. These included measures as basic as taking inventory and keeping a record of what was received and in what condition. Basque officials visited courts to ask judges and magistrates directly about their situation and their main needs.

The nature of the transferred powers, and the clear needs of the judicial offices—particularly demands related to the establishment of new courts—convinced the authorities that the first priority was infrastructure. "The courthouses were old, not very functional, small, and in many cases did not meet the minimum requirements of dignity" (Basque Government, 1998b, p. 3).

---

[22] The vice-minister of justice at the time this chapter was being prepared noted that even though his post is a political appointment, he has had to work with six different ministers from three different political parties. Yet he said this has neither posed significant problems nor provoked policy changes.

[23] At one time justice was a *consejería*, and it later became a *viceconsejería*.

[24] Some 2,000 people work in the Vice-Ministry of Justice, including some personnel who have been transferred from the national government. There are 64 judicial staff directly involved in the central administration of the system, distributed as follows: eight in Relations with the Administration of Justice; 10 in Material Resources and Planning; 10 in Human Rights and Cooperation with Justice; and 13 in Human Resources Management. A total of 26 staff work in the administrative offices, including six in Alava, nine in Guipúzcoa, and 11 in Vizcaya.

Figure 3.1. Organizational Chart of the Vice-Ministry of Justice

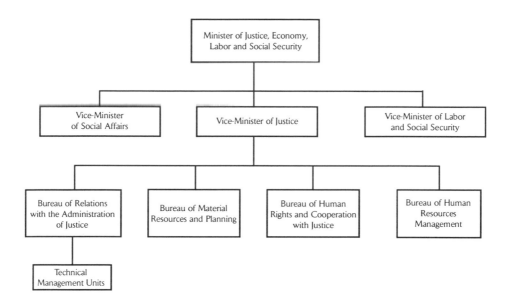

Visits were organized to France, Germany, Belgium and Canada to explore the latest in judicial architecture. From those visits evolved not only architectural ideas but also the deep-seated belief that it was necessary to introduce even more changes in the organization of the courts, particularly "as the organizational aspects, centered on the new judicial office, came together with the information technology needs, with the architectural considerations as a physical base for the entire effort" (Basque Government, 1991, p. 36).

Improving physical work spaces may have had a positive impact on forms of work and work routines, but it was not enough to solve the problems besetting the system. An assessment of the operations and productivity of the judicial office was critical. General at first, the assessment evolved into a more comprehensive vision of what the judicial function was and what it could be.

What was most striking at that stage about the operation of the judiciary? A later document (Basque Government, 1998b, p. 3) outlined the following observations:

• The organizational model was very dispersed, with each judicial entity, whether a single person or a collegial body, making do however it could and in its own way to develop methods to carry out the full array

of tasks[25] (paperwork, keeping accounts, sending out notices, sending out summons, filing, managing material resources, etc.).[26]
• The economic and material resources provided by the executive were insufficient and inadequate.
• The particular criterion of the judge or clerk determined how a task was performed, which meant there were as many models for how to run a judicial office as there were judges or clerks.
• There were no overall pre-established criteria of efficiency or productivity.
• The particular circumstance of each entity with respect to its staff was a determining factor in the performance of its work.
• The system impeded the retraining and continuing education of staff, as it was not possible to draw personnel away from the courts for such activities.
• The use of computers and the like was practically unheard of.
• The work methods were artisanal, as there were no general criteria for the judiciary as a whole.
• The office of the clerk was the meeting ground for judicial staff, attorneys and the public, resulting in continuous interruptions in the work of the judicial entities.
• The changes in the assignments of judges and judicial personnel was absurd.
• There was a confused mix of administrative and judicial activities.

The key to this first stage of judicial reform was to renounce easy solutions. This opened the way to take on the challenge of making more profound changes to the system. Carrying on business as usual and simply increasing the resources available to judicial institutions would have had a limited impact on the productivity of the system. More importantly, it would not have been perceived by the users of the judicial system as a change that would benefit them.[27]

There had not at that point been a complete assessment of the problems in the judiciary. Many ingredients would be added as the reforms progressed. Nor was there any comprehensive plan for long-term reforms. The initial stage involved shaping a

---

[25] It was also striking how the courts were organized, which made the buildings seem like "beehives…in the sense that there was an accumulation of self-reliant entities disconnected from one another" (Sánchez, 1998).
[26] At that time each court administered its own operative resources, so each made purchases on its own.
[27] This has been a common problem in Spain. Ramón Alloza Arasa, representative of the justice section of the *Federación Sindical de la Administración Pública* (public employees' union) of Catalonia said: "First, there are those who thought in their day that the ills of Spanish justice came fundamentally from the survival of various forms of corruption, from the insufficient number of judges and their insufficient salaries, and, finally, from

vision for the direction of the changes that had as a first consideration to satisfy the users, while also taking into account the interests of judges in order to win their support.

There was also an awareness of the constraints within which the new authorities had to operate in order to address judicial reform. These constraints included the following:

• The limitations on the powers of those undertaking the reforms, which at that point covered only material resources.

• The need to act fast to assume responsibility for management of an institution already operating and faced with ongoing daily needs. The new government of the autonomous community had to be in a position to address those needs in the short term in order to demonstrate its capacity to take charge of the judiciary.

• The fact that the new authorities were not familiar with the milieu in which they had to operate. They had to turn quickly to members of the judiciary (judges and clerks) to serve as their advisers. A complex learning process was required to take stock of the situation and make the personal ties necessary to win support for measures to modernize the judiciary.

• The importance of not provoking distrust or confrontations with the other institutions at the national level—the Ministry of Justice and the General Council of the Judiciary—that continued to have authority over key aspects of judicial work.

In this context, the specifics were developed for the reform process for judicial modernization. Priority was accorded to infrastructure, but different aspects of information technologies were also added because they were regarded as a major tool to implement a new model for how to run a judicial office.

Full responsibility for implementing the changes in infrastructure and information technologies lay with the Basque government. The reforms to the judicial offices went beyond the government's exclusive powers. This set off a national debate, but the search continued for different approaches that did not involve waiting for changes in the law.

The first step toward consolidating these ideas into a plan was to prepare an initial design for the overall modernization of the administration of justice. This model was validated in several internal meetings within the autonomous community that included the judicial governing bodies, magistrates, prosecutors, staff, and

---

the chronic lack of human and material resources assigned to the administration of justice. Those who so stated find themselves without arguments today to justify the stubborn failure of the administration of justice to respond to social demands.

"Even though widespread corruption was eradicated, even though the number of judges multiplied in just a few years (at the cost of everything, including the minimum level of training that should be required), and even though judicial salaries were set at levels that represented a fivefold and sixfold increase even for the *agentes judiciales*, nothing substantial appears to have changed. For although the total number of staff and the number of courts have been increased, none of this appears to be sufficient. Repeatedly, opinion polls and reports by qualified observers point to the administration of justice as one of the institutions with the worst performance and the one most in need of in-depth reform" (Alloza, 1994).

legal professionals, and also with members of the General Council of the Judiciary, judges' associations, and the Ministry of Justice.

The next step was for the Ministry of Justice, together with the Basque government, to contract a private firm to come up with a new design for the judicial office based on complete computerization. The design was ready by June 1989. It was submitted to the Ceneral Council of the Judiciary, which "considered the work to be very positive, and encouraged the Basque government to continue along that line of action" (Basque Government, 1991).

The plan evolved over time. An initial computerization plan led to a second version in 1996 that was to be concluded in the year 2000. The services common to the judicial institutions have been growing in number and depth. The new areas of transferred authority have represented new challenges and actions. In summary, the plan has had a clear long-term vision, but it has focused on attaining short- and medium-term objectives that have led to new and more significant steps.

CONTENT OF THE REFORMS

Infrastructure

The first actions of the Basque government with respect to the justice system focused on supplies. It soon became clear, however, that infrastructure was in need of attention.

The infrastructure plan was the original framework for the more complex reform of the justice system designed by the government of Basque Country. Infrastructure was the issue that generated the most demands for change, and that change was most accepted by lawyers and other legal staff. Offering more comfortable and adequate workplaces was a good first step for winning the trust and acceptance of judges, judicial staff, and attorneys. That became the starting point from which to figure out what else had to be done and to move to more in-depth reforms.[28] In order to show tangible short-term results that would both meet pressing needs and win the confidence of lawyers and other legal staff, two distinct infrastructure programs were defined: provisional and definitive programs.

The provisional program sought immediate solutions to the most urgent infrastructure problems, since the definitive program, which entailed the construction of new buildings, would take several years. The program involved renovating offices

---

[28] It subsequently became apparent that the changes in infrastructure did not always represent gains for judicial staff, for the physical changes required organizational transformations not always to their liking. Compartmentalizing physical space in the court system addresses not only infrastructure needs, but also oversight issues.

that had been transferred to the Basque government as well as renting and even purchasing and renovating provisional locales when necessary. The demands for infrastructure stemmed not only from deficiencies at the time of the transfer, but also from the creation of many new courts mandated by the new law on demarcation and facilities.

As of 1997, a total of 35,283 m^2 had been renovated, accounting for 74.2 percent of the total area transferred in 1988 (47,569 m^2). This included new provisional locales and construction done on buildings that had been transferred over. Despite the magnitude of these figures, execution of the provisional plan accounted for no more than 8 percent of the total resources invested in infrastructure during that period (5 percent, purchase and leasing, and 3 percent, renovation).

The definitive program was designed to establish courthouses that reflected an architectural concept in line with current and future judicial needs. It included construction of 13 new courthouses (two in Bilbao) and the remodeling of two more. All but two (San Sebastián and Eibar) have been completed. The program entails providing an additional 168,819 m^2 of new facilities.[29] Together with the buildings transferred at Azpeitia and Bergara, this brings the total renovated or constructed building space to 172,372 m^2, practically quadrupling the amount of space transferred in 1988.

The number of judicial entities that the new palaces of justice could house is 187, i.e., 20 percent more than the existing ones. This was done to anticipate and provide for future growth of judicial infrastructure.[30]

---

[29] The buildings are as follows:
- Palace of Justice at Vitoria-Gasteiz (all jurisdictions)
- Building with four courtrooms in Amurrio (plant for two, according to the LDPJ)
- Superior Court of Justice and Palace of Justice in Bilbao (all jurisdictions, except the Audiencia Provincial and the Juzgados de Instrucción)
- Annex building on Calle Buenos Aires, Bilbao (Audiencia Provincial and Juzgados de Instrucción)
- Palace of Justice at Barakaldo, with 19 judicial organs (plant for 15)
- Building with six courtrooms at Gernika-Lumo (plant for four)
- Building with six courtrooms at Getxo (plant for four)
- Building with six courtrooms at Durango (plant for four)
- Building with two courtrooms at Balmaseda (plant for one)
- Palace of Justice at Donostia-San Sebastián (all jurisdictions)
- Building with six courtrooms at Eibar (plant for four)
- Building with six courtrooms at Tolosa (plant for four)
- Building with six courtrooms at Irún (plant for four)

[30] In the case of the Palace of Justice at Vitoria-Gasteiz, the sixth floor is unoccupied, as it was left unfinished but ready for completion. Some are of the view that these plans have been too generous and, therefore, too costly. They could have been smaller, or the lots could have been larger, to allow for the possibility of future expansion, but without incurring the expenses now, when it is not known when or to what extent the additional space will be used.

The following are the main guidelines for the infrastructure program:

(a) To the extent possible, judicial entities and related services should be consolidated into a single building (the palace of justice). This encourages economies of scale in the work of both judges and other professionals, and facilitates the incorporation of more sophisticated management models, such as common services.

(b) The courts should be accessible to the public. This serves to balance the previous guideline, since there are instances when difficulties in communications or transportation could make it ill-advised to group together all of the courts of a given metropolitan area.

(c) The palace of justice should reflect the image of the judiciary and therefore be integrated into the urban structure and centrally located, if possible. Special attention should be given to certain particularly symbolic spaces, such as the main lobby and the hearing rooms.

(d) Functionality and efficacy are paramount. This means considering not only the strictly administrative needs of judicial personnel (from judges to judicial police), but a whole series of auxiliary and judicial support services, including libraries, meeting rooms, medical clinics and morgues.[31] The most modern computer and communications equipment should be used, and optimal use made of such facilities as electricity, air conditioning, sprinklers and fire extinguishers. Functionality and efficacy require making the best use of physical space, which means establishing shared hearing rooms[32] and creating multi-purpose rooms for taking statements and performing similar judicial tasks in each court.

(e) Practical and economical building maintenance should be taken into consideration throughout the design process.

(f) Security should be paramount in judicial buildings, especially if they are to house criminal courts. Previously, it was common for judges, the public and detainees to share the same entries and even the same elevators. The public often mingled with witnesses and experts. To respond adequately to security requirements, the new buildings were divided into the following areas:

Open access: Areas where the public can pass through without major restrictions,[33] including the main entrance, the information office, the civil registry, the

---

[31] In the Basque Country, the morgues are also located within the Palaces of Justice. In the building at Vitoria-Gasteiz, it is in the basement, with separate access.

[32] In principle, each court has its hearing room, but shares it with another court, with each using it every other day. There are also larger hearing rooms administered by the chief judge and allocated based on the requirements of any given case. Also included are "institutional" rooms for official ceremonies. Further, hearing rooms for collegial bodies are different from those for courts having only a single judge. Special hearing rooms have been set aside for jury trials, and there are spaces designed to be used by members of the jury during the trial and for their deliberations, including a room for deliberations, a lounge, a kitchenette and a bathroom.

[33] People must go through metal detectors to gain access to some of these areas.

Forensic Anatomy Institute (*Instituto Anatómico Forense*), the *Juzgado de Guardia*,[34] (the court that remains on duty after hours), and the hearing rooms.

Controlled access: Areas to which access is limited to judicial personnel and visitors who have been checked in. Each staff member must use an identification card to gain access. This system records his or her entry, and keeps general control of all persons.[35] These areas include the waiting rooms for courts and judicial offices; the offices where people are processed; the waiting room for the prosecutors' offices; the offices of the *Colegio de Abogados* and *Colegio de Procuradores* (equivalent to bar associations); trade union offices; classrooms used for training; the technical unit entrusted with managing building maintenance; general communication centers; services for notifications and attachment of embargoes; the internal communications service; the electoral board; and the copy center.

Judicial personnel work together in large spaces, without dividers, that accommodate the staff of more than one court. There are minimal divisions between the spaces for the staff of different courts, as they are all located contiguously in these open spaces.[36]

Restricted access: Areas to which access is limited to specially authorized staff, including the offices of judges, clerks, prosecutors and medical examiners, meeting rooms and the library, rooms for meetings of judges, judicial police, offices of the chief judges, the garage, and rooms housing building facilities.

Prohibited access: Areas with special security measures that are reserved exclusively for the personnel assigned to them. These include building security and control, archives, deposit areas for safekeeping of evidence, the telephone switchboard, the area for prisoners (for unloading from prison vehicles, holding cells, and for prisoners in the hearing rooms), the area for building police and custody, and the computer room.

Special rooms have been provided in the basement, alongside the holding cells, for examining prisoners and for line-ups, so as to avoid having to transport suspects within the building. There is direct access from the holding cells to the *Juzgado de Guardia*, located on the second floor, where there are other rooms for taking statements. It is the judges who must move about in the building; prisoners rarely leave the strict security area. The physical location of the various areas is closely related to their security status and accessibility. For example, the freely-accessible areas are on the first floor.

---

[34] *Juzgados de Guardia*, or courts open round-the-clock, exist only where there are more than 10 investigative courts, which is not the case in all of the palaces of justice.

[35] The entrances have infrared detectors that indicate when someone is present.

[36] This placement is designed to facilitate more ambitious steps in the future towards common secretariats.

(g) The buildings must have a flexible design so they can be adapted to changes in judicial organization and the concomitant space requirements.[37] This is achieved by building in open spaces and using partitions to divide the various aras.[38]

Along these same lines, special mention should be made of the process of defining a generic program, which was later adapted to the specific requirements of each Palace of Justice. Model spaces were defined for the various functions of each judicial organ, then the requirements for each were spelled out. The exact determination as to how to organize these physical spaces in precise architectural terms was left to the private companies awarded the construction contracts. In other words, the authorities set standard requirements that the contractors had to respect. The job of the respective government agency was to design the model spaces, make the tenders, and oversee construction.[39]

Computers/Information Technology

Computerization was formally introduced into the Spanish justice system by the Ministry of Justice in 1982 through the Inforius Project. The objective was to automate judicial procedures as they were at that time without making any change to them. The project did not integrate the various judicial offices. This rather modest approach was basically limited to making use of word processing in the courts.

At the time of the first transfer, even this limited project had not yet started in the Basque Country.[40] This explains how it is that the Basque government promoted a radically different computerization project when the time came to introduce computer tools into its judicial system.[41] That project was designed based on work contracted out by the Basque government to the consultancy company Seintex, S.A. The Basque government and the Ministry of Justice had previously hired Seintex to reorganize the judicial offices. New guidelines were proposed for judicial organization in order to establish common services for the different judicial entities, and these shaped computer needs.

---

[37] This was an especially important need addressed in the reform plan, as it was accompanied by suggestions for changes in the judicial office that would have affected physical space requirements in the future.

[38] While this solution is practical, it does not adequately insulate noise, which can pose major problems for some of the work of a court.

[39] Only minor remodeling was done directly by the Office of Material Resources and Planning.

[40] With the exception of the Public Prosecution Service.

[41] Even so, "and as an initial shock measure," terminals were placed in certain courts for word processing, until a more complete computer program could be installed (Basque Government, 1991). In addition, personal computers were put in the provincial courts (*audiencias provinciales*) and in the Contentious-Administrative Chamber. This first effort came prior to even determining an overall strategy in the sector. It received poor marks, for it could not be integrated into the more complete computerization process that followed.

The government described its approach at that time to introduce computerization as follows:

> The idea of the Inforius Project, of computerizing the courts individually and based on autonomous computer equipment for each court, was abandoned in favor of horizontal computerization of services and common offices, using computer equipment that serves many courts. (Basque Government, 1991, p. 91)

With this background, an initial computerization plan designed for the 1990-95 period defined the introduction of technology:

> From a comprehensive perspective, consistent with the philosophy of common services and offices, and based on a network of compatible and powerful computer equipment, making available to each user the computer tools suitable for his work (for judicial procedures, management of common services, word processing, consulting documentary data bases, etc.), establishing the necessary mechanisms of security, integrity, and privacy of information, and with the elements of intercommunication essential for making consultations, obtaining statistics, transferring files to other entities, etc. (Basque Government, 1998b, p. 9)

The principal characteristics of this computerization plan can be described as follows:

(a) The plan is universal and covers all the institutions for the administration of justice of the autonomous community as well as all offices directly linked to it. Therefore, the plan encompasses the appellate and various other courts and common services for them, the Clinic of the Office of the Medical Examiner, the central file system, the Public Prosecution Service, and the public information service. Both the active users (magistrates, judges, clerks and administrative staff), who can consult and update the information, and the passive users (lawyers, solicitors and the general public), who can only consult, have access to the same system.

(b) There are specialized modules for computerizing tasks specific to the various services. For example, there is a special module for the notification office that makes it possible to classify all notices geographically.

(c) To keep information organized, each matter is individually identified by a code that it keeps throughout its life, independent of the entity before which it is pending, or the stage of the proceedings.

(d) The system is physically integrated. The basic cell from which it has been built is the *partido judicial*, or judicial district. Consequently, all of the judicial district entities are served by a single computer or by a single network when a single computer is not possible due to the size of the district. An intranet or judicial communications network has been set up for communication between districts.[42]

While the Basque government has assumed major responsibility in executing the information technology plan, committees of magistrates and judges played a key role in its development. Most important has been the Mixed Committee for Follow-up of the Information Technology Plan, established in 1992 and made up of the former presidents of the three provincial courts, the chief judges of the three provincial capitals, one magistrate from the administrative chamber of the *Tribunal Superior de Justicia* of the autonomous community, the vice-minister of justice, the director of relations with the administration of justice, and the person in charge of the computer service. The importance of this commission goes far beyond computerization, as we will see in due course. In addition, specific committees have been created to assist in the development of certain components of the plan.

The areas that make up the computer system are procedure; the documentary data bases; the judicial work station *(puesto de trabajo del juez–PTJ)*, a software package; and personnel management.

Procedure

The architecture of the system's processes, which of course requires the necessary integration of information, provides for two major sets of computer applications. One is for handling trials and proceedings, which in turn is subdivided into proceedings in the following areas: civil, criminal, contentious administrative, labor, juveniles, and supervision of the prisons. The other is for common services, which are subdivided into recording the entry and distribution of matters (by jurisdiction), official communication, judicial assistance, auctions, general files, deposit of property, public information, forensic clinic, statistics, and the judicial cashier.

The computer system supports the processing of judicial proceedings by delivering to users predefined models for each of the distinct types of proceedings or resolutions that must be carried out to move on to each subsequent stage in the procedure. In other words, a complete collection of standard documents has been designed covering all possibilities that could arise in a judicial proceeding from beginning to end. In the civil area, for example, this collection includes more than 3,000 model documents, including resolutions such as orders to organize the file *(diligencias de ordenación)*, judicial orders on substantive issues *(autos)*, judicial orders on minor questions *(providencias)*, acts of communication, and acts of judicial assistance.

---

[42] The system also provides for connecting with other entities outside of the autonomous community, such as the General Council of the Judiciary (for statistical purposes and to facilitate the inspection function), and the Supreme Court, in connection with appeals of decisions by the Basque judiciary.

These documents have been prepared by a Committee on Standardization of Documents and Procedures, made up of a large group of prestigious judges and judicial staff and directed by a former president of the territorial court. It also has a secretariat for technical support that prepares the documents based on the committee's guidelines. This committee not only takes charge of preparing new documents, but also reviews and improves the old ones.

The documents are not imposed on the magistrates and judicial staff. Once prepared, the documents are presented to them, and within a reasonable time they may make observations on them. Even when documents are in the system, the person who issues a resolution may depart from the suggested text and substitute his or her own. Of course this new resolution is not entered permanently in the system as a new model, so that whenever the same matter is posed, only the original model format will appear. This is an indirect way of forcing all staff to use the documents proposed. The discussions within the Committee on Standardization of Documents and Procedures have represented an important stride toward uniform judicial criteria that involves the use of predictable and clear language.

At each moment during its operation, the computer system proposes the alternative procedures that a judicial staff member may follow, and the content of the actions he or she must take. These are duly codified to facilitate their processing. This standardization effort is common across the various procedures, so that the information can be integrated. Even though the actions are different for each procedure, the categories into which they are grouped have been defined uniformly.

The system also facilitates the work of judicial staff by automatically providing and entering the standard information on the matter that should be incorporated into each resolution (such as the case number or the names of the parties). In addition, the computers help—in this case as mere word processors—in taking statements and for carrying out similar tasks. The system does not eliminate written records. In fact, a file is still kept and the lawyers continue submitting printouts of their briefs. The system only supports and records the production of documents for those procedural steps that are the court's responsibility.

Later versions of the system, developed in the Second Information Technology Plan, link the computer system more closely with case processing, impeding the issuing of resolutions that correspond to a phase of processing different from that recorded for a given matter in the computer. To the extent that progress is made in that direction, the system becomes a more effective instrument for automatically generating judicial statistics.

Documentary Databases

An application has been developed in a Windows environment that includes many simple search alternatives,[43] viewing formats, possibilities for connections between documents, and facilities for editing and importing search results. The following sources of information can be accessed through this system:

Basque case law made up of all resolutions handed down by the collegiate courts of the Basque Country and certain important resolutions from the single-judge courts.[44] The text of the resolution and the votes cast are included and can be automatically retrieved from the judiciary's computer system. Analytical data is added, corresponding to descriptors adjusted to the thesaurus.

Institutional case law that contains the judgments of the Supreme Court and the Constitutional Court of Spain. Judgments of the Court of Justice of the European Union and of the European Court of Human Rights at Strasbourg will be included in the near future.

Legislation that contains the legal provisions of Spain and of the autonomous community. European legislation is expected to be included in the future.

Bibliography that provides access to the data bases, the Basque judiciary's own books and documents, and outside databases of bibliographic references.

All the judges and magistrates can access this system from their own computers by connecting to the central computer in Bilbao.

Mention should also be made here of the national Judicial Documentation Center *(Centro de Documentación Judicial, CENDOJ)*. Organized not under the Basque government but under the General Council of the Judiciary (CGPJ), the center was established through an agreement between the government of the autonomous community and the CGPJ. It is located in San Sebastián.

The CENDOJ was created in 1997 in order to:

• Meet the need for documentary legal information (case-law, legislation and doctrine) to assist judges and magistrates in deciding cases, facilitating access to the CGPJ and other libraries;

---

[43] The alternatives being considered for search systems are simple search (which has an assisted search mode), search by index, search by thesaurus, and search by table.

[44] All resolutions since January 1, 1997 are included, and resolutions dating back to January 1, 1994 are in the process of being incorporated. The resolutions include those that express the "constant case-law" of the court; set forth a novel argument, interpretation or application; address the violation of fundamental rights; address jurisdiction; look at evaluation of penalties, damages, compensation, pensions and the like; and address problems with special social repercussions because of their economic importance or their impact on public debate.

• Electronically compile and disseminate all the case law of the Supreme Court as well as selected case law of other courts;

• Provide statistical, sociological and economic information regarding judicial activity.

• Put out all CGPJ publications.

The CENDOJ is still in a start-up phase. Its main actions have included supplying computers to the courts, publishing a CD-ROM with case law (which is updated periodically), rationalizing the judicial publications policy insofar as an automated system of legal consultation is in the process of being developed (today consultations are by telephone), and producing a CD-ROM containing CGPJ publications.

The commitment of the Basque government to create the CENDOJ (which represents a major investment) reflects its interest not only in justice-related issues, but also in extending its outlook on them beyond the borders of the autonomous community. In this stage of development, the full potential of the synergies that could result from this process has yet to realized.[45]

Judges' Work Stations

Work stations for judges (*puesto de trabajo del juez*) is a natural evolution of the procedural system, which was initially designed to support the work of the clerk of the court, which does not have a direct impact on the work done by the judge. The judge's needs are covered by the work stations, which the judge can use to gain access to the documentary information and procedural management systems.

The work stations are designed for use in a personal computer in a Windows environment. This distinguishes them from the procedural system, which operates using asynchronic alphanumeric computers. This makes it easy for the judge to exchange information with his or her personal computer.

Personnel Management

These are the general management systems used by the Basque administration for personnel management in terms of new staff, resignations, leave, etc.

The Information Technology Plan for 1996-99

Once the initial goals proposed in the area of information technology were met, a new plan for investment in the sector had to be designed and implemented that

---

[45] Indeed, the databases and programs for accessing them are different.

largely entailed deepening and extending the original plan. The main innovations were as follows:

• For judicial offices, the most important innovation was to include the Public Prosecution Service (*Ministerio Fiscal*) in the computerization process by adapting the previous system to features particular to this institution.[46] Specific projects are also being considered for forensic medicine, implementation of a new jury system, and adoption of bilingual administration of justice. In addition, the computer program has been updated several times, grouped in a 5.0 version of the same program, which is the current application.

• For documentary information, an effort is being made to improve the quality and quantity of available information, integrate properly catalogued bibliographic information, and facilitate remote consultation.

• In terms of technological renewal, an effort is under way to standardize and adapt the current working environments to technological advances, with a tendency towards client-server schemes such as that already in place in the judges' work stations. The plan also aims to replace the equipment initially acquired with faster computers and PCs.

• The plan will regulate judicial communications appropriately in order to facilitate more sophisticated applications, such as the Model for Electronic Data Exchange, which are replacing written communications. This includes completing the interconnection between the trial courts and the appellate courts, between the appellate courts and the Supreme Court, and between the Supreme Court and the national courts. Interpersonal electronic mail will also be implemented.

• To better provide information services to professionals, the plan is facilitating access to judicial information by establishing points of information in the style of an automatic teller machine to which previously-identified persons can have access,[47] or by providing access via Internet to a system Web page (see Figure 3.2).

• The plan will extend computerization to other areas under the responsibility of the Basque government that have not been entirely covered, such as civil registries, justices of the peace, the prison system,[48] some management or administrative procedures, and free legal assistance.[49]

---

[46] This stage coincides with the transfer of material resources to the Public Prosecution Service, so it involves applying a policy that was successful with the courts to the prosecutors' offices.

[47] Such a pilot project is being carried out in Vitoria-Gasteiz.

[48] It is anticipated that these areas will be transferred at a future date.

[49] Law 1/1996 amended the existing system of free legal services, placing the administration of the new system in the hands of the Basque government.

Figure 3.2. Information Service Scheme

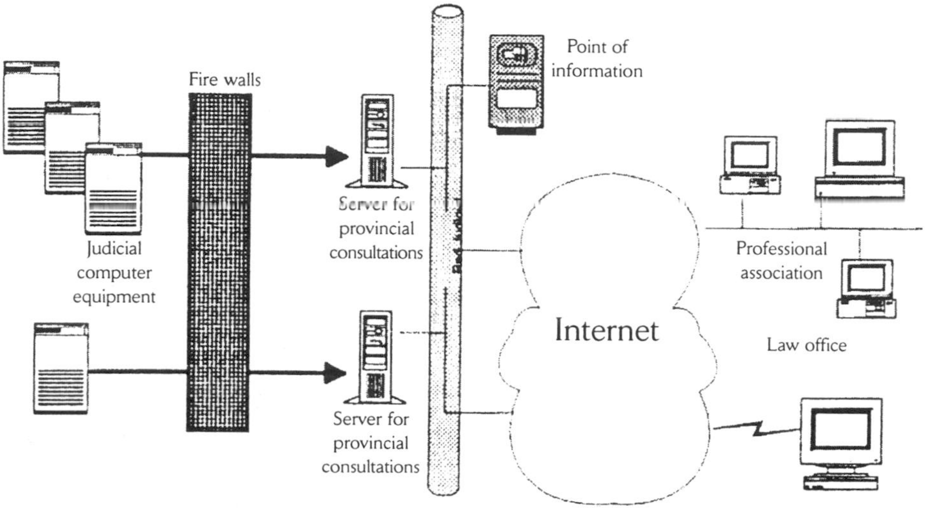

Managing the Computerization Plan

A key factor in the process of developing and maintaining the computer systems has been the structure of the relationship between the administration and the firms providing services. The studies and initial development of the computer systems were entrusted to Seintex. Subsequently, the Basque government introduced a policy of diversifying its contracts in this area, as a result of which it has also begun to work with a second firm, Ibermática.[50]

The role of these firms has evolved over time. While they have always been responsible for development of the systems, the weight of their voice with the administration in defining the functional system and the guidelines for technical design has gradually increased. On the other hand, management of the systems, which initially was entirely in the hands of the companies, is today assumed directly and entirely by the administration. Finally, user services, also contracted out initially, are today provided both by outsourcing and by the judiciary itself.

Personnel from the contractor are assigned specific functions as required by the Computer Department. To the outside observer, there is no difference between staff placed by the consulting firms and staff contracted directly by the administra-

---

[50] The advantages of this decision, in addition to generating more competition in the sector, include having a company that is physically closer, for Ibermática has its offices in San Sebastián, whereas Seintex is in Barcelona.

tion. This approach offers the administration greater flexibility, since these contracts are of limited duration and the administration is thus not as burdened by contractual rigidities on longer term contracts imposed by public law. So this mixed mode is more economical and ensures an adequate transfer of know-how and continuity of the services provided.

To ensure stability, contracts for developing the systems are more or less long term. Specifically, the contract with Seintex calls for the firm to designate a project director, two full-time senior experts who cannot participate in any other project, [51] and a variable number of programmers who participate on a revolving basis.

This arrangement makes it possible to keep a small team in the administration, though in the opinion of the project director that team should play a larger direct role overseeing the system. The ideal is to internalize all the critical functions, such as supporting and developing all system standards and the reusable infrastructure. The other system components would be purchased on the market. But to make this happen, the administration would require more technical resources. In other words, an effort would have to be made to develop capacity for total control over the process, so as to enable the administration to interact more freely, even with the outside consultants.

It is vital that the intellectual property rights in the programs be vested solely with the administration. [52]

The progress report on the First Information Technology Plan for 1990-95 sets forth figures on the work that was carried out (Basque Government, 1998b). Table 3.2 describes the central units (CPUs) set up to support the information systems and how they have evolved since 1990. The progress report indicates that the configuration originally considered, with three central processing units for the main cities servicing only 450 users, has increased to 12 CPUs serving more than 1,000 users in the same localities and new ones as well. In 1995, the computer stock was partially updated and replenished, as reflected in parentheses in Table 3.2.

The stock of computer terminals also evolved continuously during the course of the plan, as new judicial entities and information systems started operations. Table 3.3 presents the approximate annual increments in number of computerized workstations. Most of these workstations were non-intelligent terminals (asynchronic and alphanumeric), while approximately 200 were personal computers running on Windows.

---

[51] For a time, one of these experts was located in the Basque Country, but this arrangement was abandoned after a few months. Since then, the work is done from a distance, with periodic meetings in the Basque Country.

[52] In the specific case of the Basque government, the program in use is exclusively its own. The program that Seintex markets today is another product that was developed based on the company's experience with the Basque system.

Table 3.2. Number of Central Units Supporting the Information Systems Created in the Basque Country since 1990

Services for:	1990	1991	1992	1993	1994	1995	Current number
Courts of Bilbao	1		3	3		(4)	7
Courts of Donostia	1		1	1		(2)	3
Courts of Vitoria	1			1		(1)	2
Courts of Barakaldo			1	1		(1)	2
10 smaller localities		10					10
Library, documentation, other				1	2		3
Technical support and training			4			1	5
Total	3	10	9	7		(8) + 1	32

Table 3.3. Increase in Computerized Work Stations in Basque Country since 1990

Central units providing services to:	1990	1991	1992	1993	1994	1995	Current number
Courts of Bilbao	230	130	200		40		600
Courts of Donostia	110	30	100		35		275
Courts of Vitoria	90	20	50		40		200
Courts of Barakaldo			140		10		150
10 smaller localities			300	30	20		350
Library, documentation, other				80	50	30	160
Technical support and training				15	15	10	40
Total	430	180	790	125	210	40	1,775

This ambitious process of computerization also required an all-out effort to train staff in the use of the new systems. Most of the courses have been geared to training in the use of computerized support for individual procedures, followed by courses in document management. The turnover of judicial staff has meant that training has been provided to many staffers who later resign or go on to another job within the system. So the total number of people trained is larger than the number currently working in the Basque judicial system.

Centralization of Functions

Common Services

Of the changes proposed in the new model of judicial offices designed by the Basque government in 1991, creating common services has advanced the most. These gradual strides toward creating common services have accompanied the computerization effort.

The philosophy behind the common services is to take advantage of the benefits of economies of scale for tasks that each of the courts need not replicate.[53] This process favors specialization of functions, standardization of services, making optimal use of resources, learning from best practices, and facilitating oversight of functions. Much of the work of a court, except for that which involves the judge most directly, seemingly could be centralized. However, legal constraints on the Basque reform process have limited this process to establishing such services only in the areas most indirectly related to the processing of cases. The evolution toward centralization in areas closer to the active processing of cases has been more complex and slow.

Establishing these services has sparked strong resistance among lawyers and other legal staff. There has been an ongoing effort to persuade and negotiate with this staff, as well as instances where changes have been imposed without full endorsement of staff.

Figure 3.3 describes the already-existing common services for Vitoria-Gasteiz according to the courts under which they are organized, as well as those being planned.

The first of the services created, and the most representative, is the common services for notice and communication (*servicios comunes de actos de comunicación–SCAC*) in the judicial headquarters. A specialized firm was contracted to develop the service, in particular to measure the frequency and location of delivery of no-

---

[53] The most typical example was service of process, which each court had hitherto done with its own staff. Such was the level of redundancy that it was common for servers to run into one another delivering notices that could easily have been delivered by the same person.

Figure 3.3. Existing and Programmed Common Services in Vitoria-Gasteiz

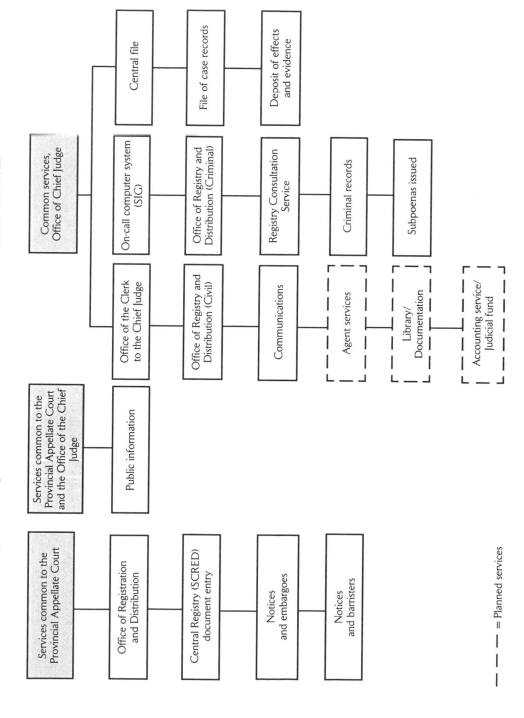

- - - - = Planned services

tices and writs or subpoenas. Each municipality was then divided into zones, and the number of staff each would need to perform the judicial procedures was determined. At the same time, a computerized system was developed to enter data on judicial procedures to be performed, making it possible to quickly organize and classify them.

A clerk was put in charge of each of these services,[54] which were implemented gradually. At first, a limited number of matters were allowed per court; the remaining notifications still had to be made by the court itself. Once there was sufficient experience on a limited scale, the services were fully implemented, which meant taking from each court the staff who had been delivering notices until then. An additional economic incentive was offered to encourage staff to make the switch.

In Bilbao, the creation of the SCAC resulted in taking away two administrative staff *(oficiales)* from each of the 13 courts of first instance there.[55] The new service, however, has a larger number of employees than the number previously assigned to such tasks, as it includes 17 court officials, six auxiliary personnel, and 16 court agents, plus the clerk, who is in charge (Guerra, 1994).

Agreements were negotiated with taxi companies to provide the transportation to perform those judicial procedures that require considerable travel. The cost of the service of process is currently one of the key issues drawing the attention of the authorities, since each notice costs from 700 to 900 pesetas (between $5 and $6.50).[56]

The efficiency of the service is based on cutting the time it takes to perform judicial tasks, increasing the effectiveness of process service,[57] widening the range of the service (as it includes notice in places where authority used to be delegated to the justice of the peace courts),[58] and improving processing.

Service of process was a critical bottleneck in the Spanish judicial system, since it had not considered the possibility of notice by decree. Therefore, to facilitate notification of barristers *(procuradores)*,[59] an office was established specially for this purpose, in which a barrister designated by the Barristers' Bar *(Colegio de Procuradores)* receives all notices and distributes them among his or her peers. It is sufficient to direct a communication to the barrister so designated to ensure that he receives it. Figure 3.4 shows the numbers of notices served through this system.

---

[54] The rules that govern the service were applied by the Board of Judges (after a hearing with the judicial clerks), and then communicated to the Administrative Chamber of the Superior Court of Justice.

[55] The staff of a court the size of those in Bilbao normally includes five court officials, five auxiliary personnel, and one court agent.

[56] One cause of the high cost is the excessive use of taxis.

[57] The number of cases in which it was not possible to serve the notice reportedly has declined significantly.

[58] The service covers the entire judicial district *(partido judicial)*, which in the case of Bilbao includes another 20 municipalities.

[59] The barristers represent the parties at trial. In Spain, it is a profession unto itself, with its own professional association.

Figure 3.4. Number of Notices Served by the Barristers' Bar in the Basque Country, 1991-95 (Courts of first instance)

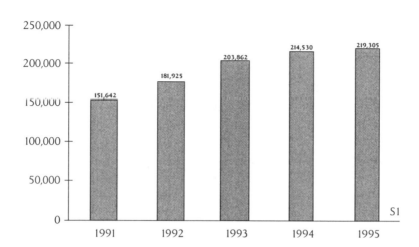

The remaining common services include the following:

• The *General Registry for the Submission of Briefs,* which receives and distributes the briefs from the parties for all of the courts that share the same space in the Palace of Justice. The entry of each document is registered so the court can immediately and officially recognize it, and the registry then takes charge of distributing it. The registry is at the entrance to the buildings, limiting the flow of persons going in and out.

• The *Public Information Service,* which guides users through their judicial and administrative procedures, which saves them from being sent from office to office.

• The *distribution of new cases,* which provides analysis based on the nature of the issue. New cases are then distributed randomly among the courts, guaranteeing a more even workload.[60]

• The *Registry Information Service,* which makes it possible to jointly and more expeditiously process all requests for information on ownership prior to attaching writs. Uniform treatment of these requests has made it possible to reduce the response time and increase the number of positive responses.

Plans are also in place to establish common internal and external messenger, fax, accounting, and library services. In addition, efforts are under way to bring together the judicial agents from the various towns in order to strengthen the offices of the chief judge, and to provide services from the large courts to the smaller ones.

---

[60] This new system brought an end to certain abuses that made it possible to choose the court in which one wanted to litigate.

Common Offices

Much less progress has been made in establishing common offices, as their creation more directly affects the processing of trials. Resistance is strongest to this change, and the powers of the Basque Country in this area appear to be weakest.

Nevertheless, experiences in this area to date include the following:

• In the Appellate Court of Vitoria, a new secretariat was to have been created when a second section (a chamber with three magistrates) was established. However, a single secretariat was maintained with common functions.

• In San Sebastián, a pilot experience is under way for processing final judgments, which is a major problem in criminal proceedings. This pilot office is entrusted to a type of "common judge" and has its own staff. Its work load and response capacity have increased considerably, from 1,000 to 5,000 procedures.

• In Bilbao, a pilot experience with the regular processing of criminal appeals is being tested.

In general, the process of centralizing functions has speeded up, which is attributed to the common services and offices winning a degree of legitimacy based on their results, as well as on the agreement reached with the unions, discussed below.

In addition to creating these common services or offices, the Office of Relations with the Judiciary has implemented a system of process audits handled by judicial staff contracted by the administration. The aim is to provide managerial support to courts with special problems such as delays, and to propose alternative actions (without legal reform) to solve problems besetting the courts in general. These audits clearly have been important when it comes to establishing the common services.

Judicial Management

The central administration of the judiciary is completely decentralized in each of the provinces of the autonomous community and is entrusted to Technical Management Units (known as EATs, the Basque language acronym). The EATs report directly to the Basque executive branch, notwithstanding their functional link to the judicial branch. The reporting to the government is done informally, however, through the president of the provincial appellate court or the respective chief judge. The Vice-Ministry of Justice *(Vice-Consejería de Justicia)* for the Basque government defines general policies on the administration of justice and oversees their implementation. All operational work is entrusted to the EATs.

The general function of the EATs is to oversee spending to cover the needs of the various judicial entities, providing them the supplies and services they need to operate properly. Before the creation of the EATs, each court administered its own

Figure 3.5. Organizational Chart of the Technical Unit for Management (EAT) at Alava

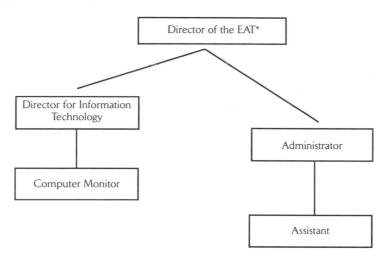

* On rare occasions, the EAT director at Alava takes charge of procurement of furniture and furnishings for all the EATs of the Basque Country.

budget and therefore did its own procurement. The courts did not have trained professionals to assume these functions, and so failed to take advantage of possible economies of scale. Giving this function to the EATs meant taking away a significant part of the powers of the courts, which resented the decision.

One example of how an EAT operates can be seen in Alava. The EAT provides services to all the courts of the province[61] and is located in the Palace of Justice of Vitoria-Gasteiz. It has five workers organized as indicated in Figure 3.5.

In addition, the janitorial staff of the Palaces of Justice are under the EAT; seven are employees of the administration and eight from a contracting firm. Service workers in the administration of justice (psychologists, experts, translators, medical examiners, and autopsy assistants) are soon expected to become part of the EAT as well.

Among the various tasks assumed by the EATs directly or through contracts, special mention should be made of procurement of equipment and supplies, maintenance of equipment and infrastructure, translation and interpretation services,

---

[61] These are made up of one appellate court with two sections, two courts of first instance and investigation, four investigative courts, five courts of first instance, one juvenile court, three criminal courts, and three labor courts. There are also the following agencies: the Institute of Forensic Anatomy; the Public Prosecution Service; the Institute of Social Reinsertion (IRSE); the Victim Assistance Service; the Judicial Police; and the maintenance staff of the Vitoria courthouse. In all, the EAT at Alava serves 278 staff.

mail and telegraph services, taxi service for process servers, payment of compensation for the cost of transporting witnesses, and administration of the jury system.

Personnel Management

Responsibilities for judicial personnel were assumed by the Basque government in 1996. As already noted, this is limited to administrative personnel.[62] Excluded, therefore, are judges and magistrates, who are under the General Council of the Judiciary, and the clerks, who are under the Ministry of Justice.

The functions of the judicial administrative staff are only described in generic terms in the law, which indicates that the *oficiales* do the technical work of the clerk and act in his place, and participate in proceedings by drafting resolutions, minutes and paperwork for judicial procedures; the *auxiliares* play a more administrative role, such as record-keeping and procedural communications; and at the lowest level, the *agentes* do not have functions in processing matters, but serve as messengers and in other lesser capacities (Cremades, 1994). The vagueness of this description of functions does not suggest a precise ranking among the levels of officials, and in practice these roles become confused with one another and juxtaposed.[63]

The transfer of staffing authority, which had been tenaciously sought by the Basque government, gave the autonomous community a more powerful tool for impacting the judiciary and consolidating the judicial office model proposed by authorities. Yet by no means did this confer complete powers to change the status of staff functions, especially with respect to the staff that continue to belong to the national corps of civil servants. As was to be expected, the transfer also brought pressures to bring salaries paid these staff into line with those of the rest of the Basque public administration, since Basque salaries are considerably higher than judicial salaries in the rest of Spain.

The challenge to the Basque government, then, was to respond to those pressures and at the same time turn the judicial staff into real agents of change in the system. This process was not without its ups and downs. Negotiations with unions began shortly after the transfer and dragged on until mid-1997, including a six-week judicial strike. Finally, an agreement was reached, entering into force on July 31, 1997 and running until January 1, 2000. The agreement was entitled "On Modernizing the Provision of the Public Service of Justice and its Repercussions on the Working Conditions of the Personnel at the Service of the Administration of Justice." The very title describes its meaning and scope, and the preamble sets forth the commitments that the parties agree to respect in the exercise of their functions:

---

[62] Notwithstanding the existing responsibilities that were reinforced with that year's transfer.

[63] "... this is the daily reality of most of the Courts of First Instance and Investigation of the Spanish State; one can definitely say that they all do everything..." (Del Valle, 1994, p. 221).

- That citizens of the autonomous community who come into contact with the administration of justice should receive the attention one can demand of a modern, developed society respectful of the individual and collective rights reflected in fundamental laws.
- To seek means of providing information about the justice system that facilitates an adequate understanding and brings about:
  – Greater familiarity with and understanding of the justice system on the part of citizens.
  – Greater participation in the issues specific to the justice system, making suggestions and proposals, holding citizen fora, and taking complaints from all parties or potential parties.
  – Adequate dissemination of constitutionally protected values and principles, in an effort to include the participation of social, educational, and political actors, among others.
- To guarantee that the policy of two official languages is carried out.
- That personnel management in the administration of justice become more in line with the main characteristics of the other areas of the public administration in our autonomous community.
- Through negotiations with the signers of the agreement, to achieve flexible mechanisms for making personnel changes to adapt staff assignments to actual needs.
- To make optimal use of existing material resources, mainly those that have to do with plans to computerize the administration of justice and bring it into line with the new situation.
- To carry out specialized training and professionalism of personnel.
- That compensation paid to all permanent and temporary personnel at the service of the administration of justice should be similar to that of the rest of the Basque civil service, with parity of conditions, enhancing the quality of the function they carry out and ensuring real accountability in the performance of their duties.

In Chapter 5, agreements were adopted in even more specific terms regarding judicial offices and common services:

The administration and the unions, aware of the failure of the current organizational structure to adapt to the needs of society, understand that common services facilitate the implementation of more up-to-date work systems and an agile organizational infrastructure. Consequently, during the period this agreement is in force, several common services will be developed, with the participation and impetus of the parties who sign this agreement.

The parties also agreed to advance the process of clarifying the functions within the judicial sphere. They negotiated a list of job posts in an effort to adequately define the ranks and specify the special knowledge required for each post.

In 1996, the Basque government had resolved to freeze the judicial payroll, a decision that was validated in the agreement, which stated "...the creation of new positions, where necessary, must be financed by making the corresponding adjustments elsewhere." Further on, the criteria with which the new positions must be filled are spelled out, and certain orders of preference are established to benefit the staff with greater seniority.

With respect to computers, Chapter 7 "reiterates that it is compulsory for all staff at the service of the administration of justice to use computers in performing their functions. In some cases, computers are used for management, whereas in other cases merely to perform a specific task."

To balance these obligations, which are mainly shouldered by the administrative staff, the government committed to paying a bonus to bring salaries into line with those of all other Basque civil servants,[64] which means wage increases of 25 to 40 percent.[65]

This bonus is explicitly contingent on each staff member following his or her work schedule and accepting the mechanical means for monitoring them.[66] It also depends on the proper use of computers and on putting the following concepts into practice:

• Helping out in the work of colleagues when they are absent from the workplace.

• Following the measures included in the Charter of Services.[67]

• Following the instructions or indications given by the members of the improvement team.

---

[64] The increases were phased in gradually according to be following schedule: 1997 (January, signing of the agreement),10 percent; 1997 (December, signing of the agreement), 15 percent; 1998, 25 percent; 1999, 25 percent; January 2000, 25 percent.

[65] With the salary increases in place, court officials will receive gross annual compensation of approximately $20,290; auxiliary personnel, $18,158; and judicial agents, $16,000.

[66] Disciplining judicial staff to abide by their schedules is one of the most complex dilemmas in the administration of justice in Spain.

[67] Included in the Charter of Services are the following:

• "The service extended to all parties will also be provided with the utmost respect for each party, independent of the capacity in which he or she comes before the administration of justice.

• "To the extent that they depend on the judicial staff covered by this agreement, the scheduling of oral hearings, presentation of evidence, appearances before the court, etc....shall be planned so as to reduce waiting time.

• "The information that needs to be conveyed to the party shall be clear and easy to understand, it being desirable, to this end, to simplify the legal language and make it more concrete."

In addition, the letter stipulates mechanisms for gauging "quality in services to the public," such as user surveys, examination of complaints, and working groups to suggest improvements.

- Carrying out measures as may be agreed upon for standardizing the use of the Basque language.

The agreement, which calls for forming a Parity Committee as a follow-up mechanism, made allies of employees who opposed or were reluctant about reforms that not only put their personal situation at stake, but also provided them a key role in the reform process.

Not all sectors have looked favorably on the results of this negotiation, since some fear the demonstration effect it might have in the rest of Spain. The Ministry of Justice filed a motion before the Constitutional Court on July 31, 1998 challenging the constitutionality of the agreement. As a result, on August 12, the Constitutional Court suspended the application of the agreement until the matter is resolved.[68]

As noted above, the principal argument of the Ministry of Justice is that the judicial employees constitute a national body of staff for whom basic and supplementary compensation should be common. The Basque government argues that the supplemental compensation is not fixed, but is an incentive for productivity that the Constitutional Court has expressly accepted in similar cases. Underlying these issues is the question of the degree of freedom or autonomy the Basque government should have to carry out further reforms and manage its human resources in the sector. It goes without saying that administrative staff have aligned with the Basque government in this dispute.

Training

In 1991, an agreement was signed between the CGPJ and the Department of Justice of the Basque government, under which the latter formally assumed the tasks of training judges and magistrates. In 1993, it was agreed that the Law and Sociology Institute of Oñati should be the base for ongoing training activities. The agreement defined the objectives of training as being "to foster debate, study, and professional exchange among the persons in attendance, with a practical and participatory approach," and to determine the priority subjects that should be taught, including Basque civil law and the law of the autonomous community, European Community law, human rights, specialized training, and the Basque language. It was also decided that there should be parity participation by the management entities and shared financing.

A similar agreement was signed with the Ministry of Justice in 1997 with respect to the clerks and prosecutors. Training had already begun with other judicial staff based on agreements signed with their unions. As of the transfer of personnel in 1996, the Basque government assumed complete responsibility for their training. At that time, the following guidelines were defined:

---

[68] As a result of the suspension, the bonus has not been paid since October 1998.

- Initial training on general matters, geared to newly-incorporated staff or those seeking to move to a new jurisdiction through internal promotion.
- Specific training and professional advancement on specific procedural or substantive subject areas.
- Training and general advancement on subjects of general interest in communications, citizen services, organization of work, etc.
- Language training that involves making assistance available for attending Basque language classes, both during working hours and after hours, and for attending full-time over the summer.
- Computer training involving implementation of the Plan to Computerize the Administration of Justice, which has entailed a special effort to train and retrain the staff in the use of computer hardware and software.

From 1988 to 1995, 49 courses were organized for judges and magistrates, with 1,661 participants in the courses on justice of the peace, Basque civil law (*derecho foral*), law of the autonomous community, European Community law, civil law, criminal law, forensic issues and other matters. Regarding other staff, and not counting computer workshops, there have been 273 courses attended by 4,819 persons. Fellowships have also been set up to prepare for competitive exams for positions as judge, prosecutor and clerk, and for the technical corps and administrative staff of prisons. The Basque government has financed visits by judges from other parts of Spain to learn how the Basque justice system operates, and it has also provided law school scholarships.

Other Actions

The reforms undertaken by the Basque government have not been limited strictly to the judicial sphere. They have also extended to various collateral elements of the system, some closely bound with the system's effectiveness. For example, the government has implemented plans to support the justices of the peace through subsidies or by consolidating court secretariats, even though this is not the government's direct responsibility.

In the area of human rights, three service centers for crime victims have been set up to provide psychological and health care as well as advice on police and judicial procedures. Four centers were also established to provide services and counseling to detainees. They receive initial assistance and are informed of programs available to them, such as drug rehabilitation, that have been implemented by the Basque government.[69] In addition, agreements have been signed to work in pris-

---

[69] Treatment involves the use of drugs (Naltrexone and Methadone) and psychological support. In addition, a pilot needle exchange program has been implemented. There is another program for creating and maintaining facilities to transfer drug addicts and chronically ill patients.

ons to provide legal aid, health care, counseling and training.[70] The Basque government finances and administers free legal aid services[71] and family mediation services. In the youth justice area, alternative (nonjudicial) dispute resolution mechanisms have been developed such as mediation, conciliation, reparation, probation and parole systems, treatment with release, and residential educational centers.

In the area of gathering and disseminating information, there have been polls (1997) and media campaigns (1997-98) on the subject of justice, and a basic justice guide was prepared for the general public in 1998. In addition, information on advances in the Basque justice system has been provided to representatives of the judiciary from a number of countries outside Spain.[72]

EVALUATING THE REFORMS

Costs

A reform that relies so much on technology and infrastructure will naturally be expensive. This was understood from the outset by the Basque government, which anticipated that taking charge of the judiciary would require more money than the government would receive as a result of the transfer.

After an initial year set aside for "study and planning," judicial expenditures began to climb sharply from 1990 on. The judicial sector budget more than doubled from $34 million to $79 million from 1990 to 1997. This increase is large not only in absolute terms—although this could represent an appropriation of new resources to which the autonomous community has access—but also in relative terms, which could mean that other sectors are ceding part of their budget share.

Personnel expenditures for the judiciary were not taken on by the Basque government until 1996, and then only for administrative staff, not judges, magistrates or clerks. Considering that personnel costs generally account for more than 80 percent of judicial budgets, one can appreciate the magnitude of the budget effort entailed.

The increase in the judicial sector's share is not only in terms of the government budget, but also with respect to the GDP for the Basque Country, which rose from 0.14 percent in 1995 to 0.21 percent in 1997. It is not surprising, then, that

---

[70] These agreements also cover the Basque Institute of Criminology, the Law and Sociology Institute of Oñati, and the Gernika Gogoratuz Foundation, which carry out dispute resolution programs.

[71] Free legal aid is provided by lawyers and barristers, who later charge the state for these services at predetermined rates.

[72] From 1996 to 1998, visitors were received from the Supreme Courts of Bolivia, Colombia, Costa Rica, El Salvador, Guatemala, Morocco, Panama, Paraguay, Ukraine, Uruguay and Venezuela.

Figure 3.6. Evolution of Justice System Expenditures

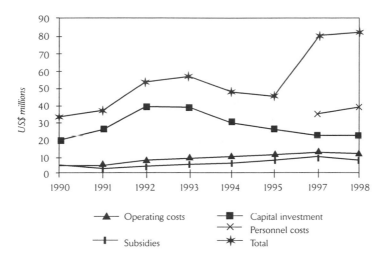

Figure 3.7. Breakdown of Investment

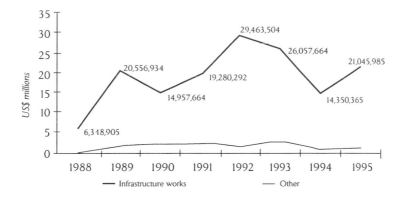

actual capital investment is the main force driving this increase. Figure 3.6 reflects the importance of this item as a share of total expenditure, especially up until 1993, when the costliest infrastructure works were concluded. This spending category then began to diminish, yet continued to remain at levels significantly higher than the initial ones. Figure 3.7 details how the investments have been earmarked.

The same data, now expressed as per capita spending, give a more precise idea of the magnitude of the economic effort for a region as small as the Basque

Table 3.4. Per Capita Investment in Justice in the Basque Country
(In US$)

	1990	1991	1992	1993	1994	1995	1997
Operating costs	3.08	2.88	4.18	4.60	4.61	4.99	5.69
Subsidies	3.04	2.42	2.39	3.39	3.36	4.01	4.74
Capital investment	9.82	12.51	18.77	18.54	14.45	12.47	10.73
Personnel costs							16.45
Total	**15.95**	**17.80**	**25.34**	**26.53**	**22.42**	**21.47**	**37.61**

Figure 3.8. Percentage Distribution of Judicial Spending, 1997

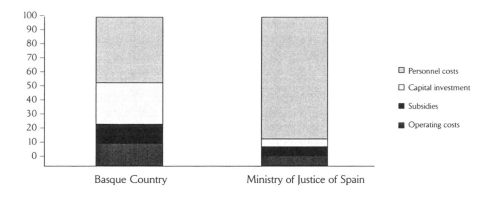

Country (Table 3.4). There are notable differences between the status of the judicial sector in the Basque Country and that of the rest of Spain, which is under the administration of the Ministry of Justice. Personnel costs are by far the most significant expenditure for the ministry, accounting for almost 82 percent of the total. With respect to capital investments, the Ministry of Justice invests in all of Spain as much as the Basque government spends in the Basque Country alone. Per capita spending of the Ministry of Justice on personnel, however, is greater than per capita spending of the Basque Country ($46 compared to $38) (Figure 3-8).[73]

---

[73] Personnel expenditures include the salaries of judges, magistrates and clerks who work in the autonomous communities.

Substantial growth of the judicial budget has not meant relaxation of controls on spending; rather, the opposite has been the case.[74] There have been drastic cuts in some items in order to ensure that the budget adds up. The most serious problem occurred during 1995-96, when budget restrictions led to the implementation of savings policies that meant, for example, cutting total phone bills of the judiciary by 40 percent.

There were also cuts in subsidies paid to attorneys for free legal assistance. Rationalization was achieved here mainly through greater control over disbursements. Salaries are another item where there has been significant economic pressure. The union agreement signed after the 1996 transfer entailed a major salary increase. To be able to cover it, payrolls were frozen, which made it possible to finance the higher salaries out of the money that would have been spent to fully staff the new courts created in the meantime. Compared to the Ministry of Justice, the Basque Country invests 3.8 times more on the judiciary while spending only 1.6 times more on operations, which indicates greater efficiency in the administration of resources by the Basque Country.

Results

It is difficult to evaluate changes in the operations and productivity of the judicial system with certainty, in part because baseline information at the outset of the reform process was incomplete and unreliable. Judicial statistics were plagued by major definitional problems (what is to be measured) and operational problems (how does one measure).

Form the outset and since the initial transfer of personnel and resources to the Basque government, the focus has been on implementing changes rather than on evaluating them. Evaluation would have required slowing down the process and diverting professional staff and resources to validate something that was considered obvious: the need for and advisability of the changes. Today, however, this perception is changing, and officials responsible for carrying out the reform process feel an increasing need for more precise information on the impact of the reforms.

The computerized system clearly provides information on system operations more expeditiously than before. Yet this system is not designed exactly as a management control tool. There is no set of pre-established indicators that, when quantified, enable authorities to make the decisions within their purview. The computer system mainly provides support for the substantive work of the organization, that

---

[74] The Vice-Minister of Justice said in this regard that "even though the number of judicial entities is growing, and the number of square meters has quadrupled, spending has been brought under control" (Sánchez, 1998, p. 6).

Table 3.5. Management Factor in Basque Country Judicial Offices, 1990-94

	1990	1991	1992	1993	1994
Courts of First Instance for Civil Matters	1.09	1.18	1.06	1.03	0.94
Investigative Courts	0.94	0.95	0.96	0.98	0.99
Labor Courts	1.14	1.31	0.90	1.04	0.88
Juvenile Courts	1.07	0.90	0.79	1.07	1.03
Criminal Courts	1.69	1.27	1.48	1.05	0.96
Average	**0.99**	**1.03**	**0.99**	**0.99**	**0.97**

Note: The management factor is the ratio between the number of matters initiated and the number concluded in a give period. If this ratio is greater than one, it means that the system is not capable of processing the whole workload that comes in. If it is less than one, it means that the cumulative caseload is diminishing.

is, the processing of cases and the organization of certain activities such as common services.[75]

The productivity of the judicial system has remained at highly satisfactory levels in recent years. Calculating the management factor for 1990 to 1994—that is, the ratio between the number of cases initiated and the number concluded—the system has processed more cases than came into the system in every year except for 1991. There was significant improvement in the management factor toward the end of the period, as seen in Table 3.5.

Though the backlog of cases is now being reduced each year, there is still a high number of backlogged cases pending. In 1990, 177,743 cases were initiated, and at the end of the year 66,449 remained (i.e., 37 percent of those that came in), despite the fact that 179,404 cases were completed (0.9 percent more than came in). Even though in almost all years more cases were completed than initiated, at the end of the period 61,000 cases remained pending. Figure 3.9 shows the trends in the number of cases pending.

It is not easy to attribute these increases in productivity to the reforms in judicial management, since they may also stem from the increased number of judges in the period, as illustrated in Table 3.6.

It should also be noted that the increase in the payroll has been much greater for judges (29 percent) than for administrative staff (growth in the number of court officers, auxiliary personnel and judicial agents was only 0.07 percent). Nonethe-

---

[75] Manuel Garavilla (1997) argues that "to date, computer technology is used only for word processing. It has not been possible to effectively control the general procedure, or the execution phase, or the statistics..."

Figure 3.9. Trend in Total Number of Cases Pending (includes Criminal Courts)

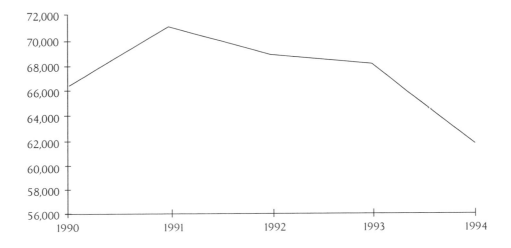

Table 3.6. Total Judicial Personnel in the Basque Country, 1990-98

	1990	1991	1992	1993	1994	1998
Judges and magistrates	128	143	162	163	165	173
Prosecutors	56	58	60	60	62	72
Clerks	94	108	124	124	124	137
Court officials	451	459	406	461	461	442
Auxiliary personnel	673	711	706	670	670	758
Court agents	313	308	315	307	307	365
Other	68	85	155	169	186	31*
Total	**1,783**	**1,872**	**1,928**	**1,954**	**1,975**	**1,978**

Note: There are 319 barristers and 4,671 lawyers registered in the Basque Country.
*The information for 1998 is for medical examiners only.

Table 3.7. Personnel per 100,000 Population in Basque Country and Spain

	1990	1991	1992	1993	1994
Judges per 100,000 population					
Basque Country	6.08	6.80	7.70	7.75	7.84
Spain	na	na	8.57	8.59	8.62
Judicial staff per 100,000 population					
Basque Country	84.74	88.97	91.63	92.87	93.87
Spain	na	na	104.00	103.47	103.09

less, this growth in personnel was also experienced by the rest of Spain, which, despite having a larger number of judges per capita than Basque Country, resolves a smaller percentage of disputes (see Table 3.7).

In qualitative terms, the reforms have no doubt changed the face of Basque justice. The new buildings are impressive and the technological support base for the work of the judiciary gives it an air of modernity that it had clearly lacked. However, in some respects, this modernity appears to be limited by what the judicial culture is capable of assimilating. In terms of infrastructure, for example, it is of little use to have "smart buildings" that can control passage from one sector to the next if objects are constantly placed in the doorways to keep them from closing, thus making it possible to move around without having to use a security card. In practice, areas to which access is restricted have been disappearing.

In the words of the director of material resources, it doesn't make sense to build buildings without changing the management or the processes that take place within them. The buildings may be functional to change, and may be one of the most attractive "carrots" for change, but once built, they are not forces for change at all. If inserted into a managerial context that is antiquated, the buildings are simply modern structures whose potential remains untapped—and all this is in the context of an investment that, in economic terms, has a significant impact.

In the Basque case, infrastructure policy was linked to changes in the organization and operation of the judicial office. Changes in organization and operation proved difficult to implement, in large part because organizational changes had to be developed within a narrow framework of potential change, since the Basque government was not free to completely overhaul court organization. The government applied maximum pressure for change during the window of opportunity when management changes could be made, but the results were not as optimal as they were with infrastructure, where it was possible to obtain almost everything modern technology had to offer. The result today is that there is a gap between suboptimal management and optimal infrastructure, which makes expenditure on investment less efficient than it might otherwise be. In terms of computer technology, in the opinion of the lawyers and legal staff, the new systems facilitate, provide security for and accelerate the processing of cases. Calculations by the Basque government indicate that before the introduction of computers, judicial staff spent 80 percent of their time searching (for files, items of evidence, or other information) rather than processing. This poor use of time, and the consequent delays, have been drastically reduced with computers.

Nonetheless, the process of computerization is taking place in a culture of written documents. Thus much of the potential of the magnetic media is reduced, as parallel records have to be kept. In addition, it is taking place amidst excessively formal judicial procedures more concerned about not failing to foresee any exceptional situation than about adequately responding to the typical situations that account for more than 80 percent of cases. Thus, the great effort to standardize judicial rulings has resulted in an extremely long list of resolutions or proceedings that can only be understood as reflecting the best of intentions to change the procedures so as to reduce or eliminate unnecessary procedures.

Furthermore, it is difficult for a judicial culture so resistant to change to take quickly to radically different systems, even where there are powerful incentives to do so. In the Basque experience, tangible incentives were only possible after the transfer of material resources in 1996 and the signing of the agreement with the unions that linked salary increases to adequate use of the computer system. Even under the agreement, computer usage continues to be far from optimal.[76] Services such as automatically generated case reports (alardes)[77] are rarely used, even though they allow for reducing the days it takes to do this task by hand to a matter of minutes.[78]

In the Basque case, once it was decided to make profound reforms to the judicial system, there were not many alternative paths that could have been taken. In other words, the key question was not whether there were more effective or

---

[76] This also raises another question: it is one thing to agree on a criterion for withholding the bonus, and quite another to require that the bonus be paid. This is as valid for computers as for the other areas, such as work schedules. Indeed, it was not until September 1998 that warnings began to be issued to employees who had not worked their scheduled hours. To date, their pay has not been discounted accordingly. The problem is due in part to the way in which the bonus has been defined, since it is included in staff salaries, and only taken away if any of the negative conditions provided for come to pass. An alternative system would have been to give the bonus only if certain positive conditions were met (for example, meeting certain productivity indicators). This would have been easier to administer politically.

[77] Alardes are reports that each judge is to prepare on the status of each case before him or her.

[78] This may be due to a certain distrust of the computer system, or because staff are not sure that they adequately entered all the information about the cases they are handling.

profitable possibilities for making changes in the sector, but how to minimize the costs and make these policies more effective and profitable.

In any event, the Basque reform correctly chose computerization as one of the lines of action. As opposed to infrastructure changes, introducing computers has the virtue of unleashing incremental changes. Computers are an effective tool for forcing order and standardization in a sector where staff are accustomed to doing things their own way.[79] Computerization has changed deep-seated perceptions of the judicial system and the role of lawyers and other legal staff. Thus, unlike other reforms, computerization is seen not as an end unto itself but as a useful instrument for improving the everyday functioning of the judicial system. Of even greater interest, it can spark other more substantive changes.

It has traditionally been thought that judicial independence covers not only tasks associated with judicial work, but also those that are purely administrative. It was thought that issues such as defining internal working procedures or assigning tasks to staff and monitoring their performance were best determined by each judge. The Basque experience has shown that it is possible to change this concept and gradually remove many of these decisions from the exclusive province of judges, without limiting or affecting their capacity to judge impartially. It is that capacity to judge impartially that is precisely the purpose of judicial independence.[80]

In all merely administrative matters, which are simple inputs to judicial work, it is feasible and advisable to introduce and then professionalize more modern management techniques. Creating common services reflects this logic, and profoundly calls into question the judicial office model in place. The central process service facility (SCAC) today takes less than two days to perform tasks that used to take over a week (Figure 3.10).

The most complex judicial procedures are those where one judge must ask another to perform some task—such as the attachment of writs. Such procedures require the assistance of the police, which explains why they are more time consuming.[81] The reduced time frames achieved under the reforms have held up and even improved over time, even as the demand for notifications has increased significantly, as shown in Figure 3.11.

---

[79] It is paradoxical that a sector as heavily regulated as the judiciary—for in no other does the law spell out in such detail what must be done and how—has such a mix of practices and procedures in its day-to-day operations.

[80] Throughout Spain this same vision has begun to become more widespread: "It is necessary for judges and magistrates to admit that their constitutional role begins and ends with administering justice with all the necessary guarantees, and to let go of the temptation to "administrate justice," i.e., to take the initiative in and shape the administrative organization of the judicial system" (Alloza, 1994).

[81] The increase in the delay for this last type of judicial procedure (from 7.47 days in 1994 to 7.7 days in 1995) is due, we were told, to petitions from the lawyers and barristers in the respective cases, since the speedier process didn't give them enough time to adequately indicate the assets to be attached, as they are allowed by Spanish law.

Figure 3.10. Average Response Time (in days) of Notices Delivered via SCAC

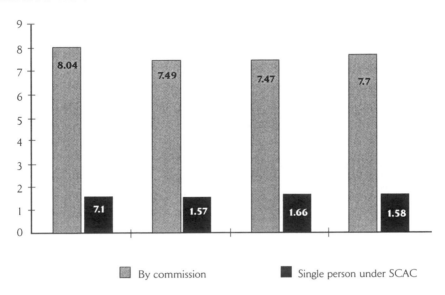

No doubt such a process requires that certain actors relinquish powers—mainly judges who, even though they have been relieved of difficult administrative burdens, perceive that they have lost a part of their power, and therefore react negatively to the change. The only way to take on this perception is by quickly showing positive results from the new system that provide improvements in supporting the work of the very judges who are unhappy.

Nor should one think of implementation of common services as a panacea. Indeed, there has been much criticism.[82] Consequently, an initiative is being taken by Spain's Ministry of Justice to derogate the provision of the Organic Law on the Judiciary that allows for the establishment of such services.

The problems associated with the common services stem largely from the judicial culture, from which they cannot be separated during the transition phase. The problems are related to the lack of well-defined hierarchies, effective systems to control the work, delegation of responsibilities, and experience with teamwork. These have made Basque authorities reluctant to create large services, which are considered too unwieldy. Thus the services have been limited to 20 staff.

---

[82] The professional association of judges said that "the proliferation of common services is worrisome, when, however enthusiastic the intent of the persons responsible for implementing them, the already-existing ones are having very negative results, further distancing each judicial organ from the matters before it, and causing grave dysfunctions" (cited by Guerra, 1994).

Figure 3.11. Number of Notices via SCAC

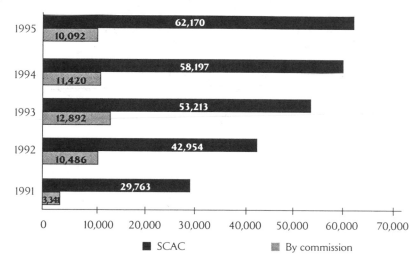

Another problem besetting the common services is that judges tend to distance themselves from the issues that common services address and are not committed to success or failure. This often leads judges to make demands that are
impossible or difficult for common services to meet. Judges often prefer to do their
work "a la carte," i.e., as they please and when they please, even when this cannot
be reconciled with normal operations of the judiciary. The argument for not submitting to the standard operation once again was based on an interpretation of
judicial independence, which would allow judges to do their work as they see fit.

In any event, the process of standardization and centralization of administrative tasks in the Basque Country was limited by the very characteristics of the
Spanish procedural system, which is highly reliant on written procedure, especially
in the initial stages. In practice, this reliance gives administrative staff great power;
their merely bureaucratic tasks can easily become confused with others related to
the substance of the matter in dispute. This lack of a clear-cut distinction between
what is administrative and what is judicial explains why the centralization of functions has not been extended with full force. Technically, more centralization would
be desirable in the judicial office, but instead it has reached only those tasks more
indirectly linked to the processing of the cases rather than to the process itself,
which is at the core of the problem.

In this context, the fact that common offices have not been set up as originally anticipated would appear to be an appropriate policy given the circumstances.
If the common services are inserted in a context of defectively-established functions, they may well lead to more delegation of functions, or to a similar degree of
delegation, but with more tenuous control.

Another major shortcoming in the establishment of common services is that they have had to be headed up by clerks. The clerks are lawyers who have the special function of attesting to the authenticity of documents *(dar fé pública)* in judicial proceedings, without any special training in or vocation for management issues. Legal training in this area is generally a liability rather than an asset. Once again, the limits placed on the reform process have kept it from entrusting these new responsibilities to real administrators, who clearly could have assumed their roles with greater efficiency. The mere example of what the EATs do shows how helpful it is to have experts in charge of these matters.

One very positive move has been to build a close relationship between the judges and these services, through the chief judge *(juez decano)*.[83] The role of the chief judges is not only key to centralizing functions, but to the reform process. The chief judge can articulate the interests, needs and fears of judges to the reformers, at first, and subsequently to the persons responsible for implementing the reforms. Many chief judges in the Basque Country are young and committed to the reforms, and enjoy broad legitimacy in the eyes of their peers. The post has not been seen as honorific, and the tradition of electing the senior judge is now a thing of the past. It is important that judges see that the success or failure of the chief judge's work will determine their own working conditions and professional development. Otherwise they will not be motivated to elect someone who is capable and in whom they can place their full trust.

A second positive step is related to the management scheme chosen to administer priority investments in the judiciary. The flexible system that was chosen draws on the alternatives available in the market. In no way does it mean relaxing the state's powers in these areas; rather, it involves redirecting and reinforcing them. It is no longer a question of the government producing the services required, but of having sufficient technical capacity to define the policies, set the bases, conduct the bidding processes, and then adequately monitor performance of the contracts. The Basque experience identifies each of these abilities as critical. The worst thing that can happen to a judicial system is for it to be in the hands of a contractor, without the authorities having the technical skills to remain engaged. When that happens, the system soon becomes dependent on the contractor's services.

It is also fundamental to create competition in each of these areas, even though that may mean losing part of the benefit of having fully stable suppliers. And there must be a certain physical proximity between the supplier companies and the beneficiaries, especially if the relationship is going to be a long-term one. Finally, special care should be given to ensuring the transparency of the whole outsourcing process.

---

[83] Or the presiding judge, in the case of the common services, of the appellate courts.

Relationship with Lawyers and Legal Staff

In examining the strategy adopted to implement judicial reforms in Basque Country, special mention should be made of the close relationship between the judges—and especially the judicial governing bodies—and the officials of the Basque government. Mixed Committees formed in 1992 to follow up on the most sensitive issues, such as computerization, were the result in part of the need to further involve judges in the reform process. One of the criticisms of the reform process was simply that these committees were not formed earlier.

However, these committees should not be understood to be fora for discussion of the bases or scope of the plan, for which authority lies exclusively in the political departments. These plans should precede the dialogue, as the committees' role is merely to determine the most appropriate and participatory way to implement the plans. The roles are plainly demarcated: the reform initiative comes from the executive, from which all proposals and plans emanate. The executive sets the agenda for the meetings of the Mixed Committees and conducts the sessions. The role of the judicial branch is more passive, legitimizing each of the steps taken and cooperating to help make those steps happen. Clarity in the respective roles of both the committees and the executive has been essential for developing a good relationship. Minister Juan Ramón Guevara of the Basque government's Department of the Presidency, Justice, and Autonomous Development said in 1991:

> These three years of intense and complex work have made it clear, contrary to what is constantly conveyed to the public, that the executive and judicial branches can "get along." In effect, many of the actions by my department at this time would have been, simply put, unthinkable in the climate of confrontation and tension that one often finds between different parts of the state.

Elorza and Guerra (1996) report that "...both the Council and the Administrative Chamber of the Superior Court of Justice of Basque Country had more conflicts with the judges than did the Department of Justice."

What has helped this good relationship along is the fact that the compensation of judges and clerks does not depend on decisions of the Basque administration, and there is, consequently, no conflict over this compensation.

The main instrument of change used by the Basque government has been persuasion. That same strategy was also applied by the Basque government in its dealings with the national authorities, such as the Ministry of Justice and the CGPJ, with whom good working relationships were also key to the success of the reforms. In general, despite normal tensions associated with such a process, the strategy has yielded positive results, at least until the filing of the current motion challenging the

Figure 3.12. Opinion of Basque Citizens on How the Justice System Operates

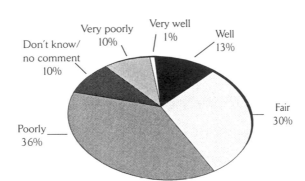

constitutionality of the reform. This has made it possible for national authorities to comprehend the philosophy behind the changes the Basque government is pursuing.

Perceptions of Users

In 1997, a survey was undertaken in the Basque Country to study the perceptions of users of services of the justice system. The survey found a negative public opinion about operation of the justice system, although the view was more favorable in the Basque Country than in the rest of Spain. Approximately 46 percent of respondents said the justice system worked poorly or very poorly, whereas 30 percent perceived it as fair (Figure 3.12). The opinion among Basque legal professionals was slightly better, with 34 percent viewing the system as poor or very poor (Figure 3.13). In comparison, for Spain overall, 52 percent of the general public saw the justice system as operating poorly or very poorly (Figure 3.14).

This negative opinion of the system carried over to those in charge of imparting justice: 63 percent of Basques don't trust judges, 76 percent do not consider them impartial, and 69 percent believe that there is discrimination based on social status. This opinion of the justice officials was slightly better than that found in Spain overall (Figure 3.15).

Most citizens believed that the justice system had the material and human resources it needs, with only 23 percent saying that resources were lacking. Some 69 percent of legal professionals thought that judicial buildings were adequate or very adequate.

Over half of all Basque citizens believed that the justice system continued to be the same as it had been four or five years earlier: 21 percent said it had im-

Figure 3.13. Opinion of Basque Legal Professionals on How the Justice System Operates

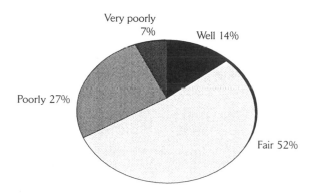

Figure 3.14. Opinion of the Justice System: Spain vs. the Basque Country

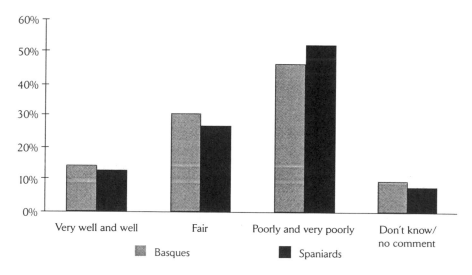

proved, and 18 percent said it was worse. In contrast, 42 percent of the legal professionals of Basque Country thought that the justice system had improved (Figure 3.16). When attorneys and barristers are asked about the reasons behind that improvement, most pointed to the computerization of judicial procedures (85.7 percent). Even so, nine of every ten professionals believed there should be more judges.

Figure 3.15. Trust in Judges in Spain and the Basque Country

70%
60%
50%
40%
30%
20%
10%
0%
Much/quite a bit
Little/none
Don't know/
no comment
Basques
Spaniards

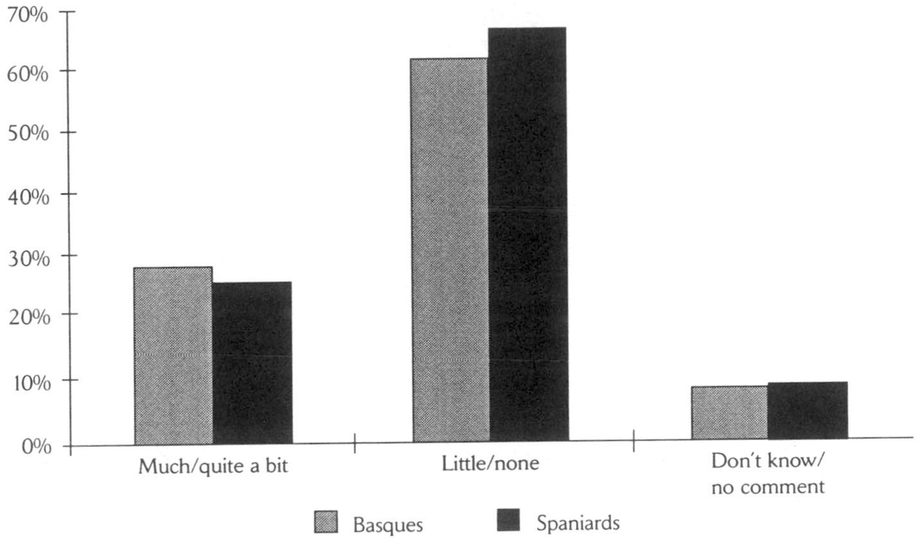

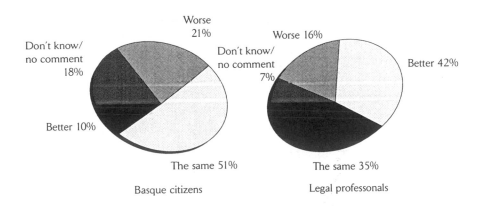

Figure 3.16. Has the Justice System Improved? Views of Basque Citizens and Legal Professionals

Worse
21%
Don't know/
no comment
18%
Better 10%
The same 51%
Basque citizens
Worse 16%
Don't know/
no comment
7%
Better 42%
The same 35%
Legal professonals

Those who have or have had regular contact with the justice system had a more positive assessment of it. While this is positive, it also is testimony to the failure to better publicize the changes that have been made. So the average citizen, unaware of the reforms that have taken place in recent years, still has a highly stereotypical view of judicial work. This is the main reason why the Basque government has organized public information campaigns in recent years.

LESSONS LEARNED

This section looks at some of the reasons behind the success of the judicial reform process in the Basque Country, giving priority to those aspects of reform that might prove useful in Latin America. Clearly, the particular conditions in each country should be the determining factor when it comes to designing public policy, especially in areas as sensitive as justice. Yet beyond this caveat, experience also shows that many assessments and solutions are generally quite similar. In such a globalized world, it is difficult to conceive of absolutely original solutions applicable only in a particular country, especially when there is so much accumulated experience in a field such as the administration of justice.

The possibility of extending conclusions from the Basque experience to Latin America is particularly attractive because the legal and organizational framework for justice in Spain and Latin America is essentially similar. The summary assessment of the ills that beset Basque justice at the outset of the reform process could be applied, practically unchanged, to any country of Latin America. Perhaps even more important is that the background and culture of the judges, lawyers and legal staff—the most critical factor for reform—are practically identical.

Political Commitment

The first factor of success that can be clearly discerned is the political will at the highest level to carry out the changes. For some, the inspiration for justice reform may originate in the search for greater respect for individual rights, while in others it may stem from the need for greater security and more effective law enforcement. The various sectors that have supported the changes in the Basque Country represent just such a variety of perspectives. Most important has been the basic agreement on the need to make changes and on the principal guidelines in terms of how to go about it. In other words, although each sector might attribute special importance to a particular aspect of the plan, this has not been tantamount to rejecting the rest of it.

A key motivation behind the Basque reforms was to have a justice system that supports economic development, rather than constituting an obstacle to doing business. The background of the new justice authorities furthers this perception. In addition, the link between the justice system and healthy social relations is important, particularly in the Basque Country because of the threat of terrorism. These two rationales are not mutually exclusive. For the Basques, it was clear that terrorism contributed to shaping the justice system, considering that for the terrorists the "...main economic problem does not have economic roots" (Elorza and Guerra, 1996).

The importance of the issues at stake and the overall perspective with which they were addressed made it possible for the reform to be taken on in a truly nonpartisan spirit. It was clear that what was at stake was the success or failure of a reform that was in the interests of everyone.

An essential condition for this cohesive vision to become a reality was to set aside any fear that reforms might be used to benefit a given sector. Thus it was important to incorporate all sectors in the process of decision-making on judicial reform. Perhaps what is most needed to make judicial reform more than just a short-term policy issue is to view it as an eminently technical process, selecting work teams carefully and ensuring that the reform always stays on a technical level.[84]

The main indicator of broad support from the various political forces for the Basque judicial reforms was the success of the budget debate and ultimately approval of the budget. Elorza and Guerra (1996) reported that "...throughout the period in which the costliest reforms were undertaken, the justice budget was subject to the fewest amendments in the parliamentary debate, and practically all of the few amendments that were offered were resolved by compromise among groups."

This agreement also points to another important factor in the judicial reforms. The mere request for more resources for the sector on the basis of its social importance clearly never has a significant impact. Expanding the sector's budget share is only possible when the requests for additional resources are accompanied by well-designed plans that show, in technical terms, why it is more effective to invest in the judicial sector than in other sectors. The persons responsible for public finance must constantly deal with requests from all sectors, each, in its own view, more important than the others. How can one distinguish where to invest, be it in education, health, housing or justice, if all are important? If this is decided based on the political dividends that the investments may bring, justice will generally lose out. The only way for it to win is if the discussion takes place at a technical level based on specific projects. This is the challenge that must be addressed—and one that was explicitly taken up by the Basque government in its plans for judicial reform.

Persistence over Time

That judicial reforms can be to some extent protected from the contingencies of changing policy, and supported by the society at large, does not mean that the

---

[84] Other reform experiences that have overcome political uncertainties have pulled together many studies on the operation of the current system, especially empirical ones, in order to consolidate a shared assessment. Also critical has been creating fora for dialogue that bring together representatives from all the sectors and political forces involved. Finally, the presence in projects of international cooperation agencies or multilateral lending institutions is often an endorsement of technical and apolitical work.

justice sector can ever be completely isolated from the important political issues of the day. The judicial sector is, after all, part of a society's political system. The decisions that affect the courts are inevitably political to some degree. Thus, however one may try to influence a reform process, it will always be vulnerable to a political process that is not wholly predictable. This uncertainty counsels against adopting rigid plans or ones with a more prolonged time horizon than can reasonably be anticipated or managed. In judicial reform as in politics, skill is measured in large part by the ability to influence various scenarios, turning events to your favor and capitalizing on opportunities that arise.

As the Basque experience shows, such opportunities often emerge from two types of sources. First, they may be external to the process, having a merely tangential influence, as in the case of legal reforms that affect the terms of the debate. Thus, in 1994, the Organic Law of the Judiciary was amended so as to expand the modern management of the judicial office by establishing common services and introducing computerization. Another milestone was the institution of a chief judge (*juez decano*) elected democratically by his or her peers to coordinate the interests of all of the judges with respect to the administration of judicial services. The chief judges have turned out to be an essential link between the judges and Basque authorities. They have become important agents of change, and have taken on direct responsibilities in some of the most significant reforms, as for example in certain common services. One change with enormous implications for this process was the transfer of new powers to the Basque Country in 1996.

Yet, opportunities may also arise internally. The very dynamic of change, particularly if it is perceived as successful, generates new possibilities not contemplated in the initial forecasts. Demands by users and even lawyers and legal staff who work in the system may lead to more profound changes. This is a key factor in innovation that is often overlooked when there is an overly messianic vision of an omniscient planner, as if one could, ex ante, map out with precision exactly where this sort of program will lead, especially in an area as political as justice reform.

This certainly doesn't mean that reform programs need necessarily go adrift. The vision should remain clear and the actions consistently directed toward it. The specific steps to achieve that end may well and indeed *should* vary, depending on the circumstances, and on the successes and failures, as opportunities arise. Before taking the next step it is necessary to strengthen each accomplishment and measure the resources, equipment and support available to continue. Successful reforms such as those in Basque Country, however profound they may be in their ultimate objectives, are incremental in their development—something the people responsible for carrying them out recognize quite clearly. As stated in Elorza and Guerra (1996): "Judicial reform, probably like any other important reform, is largely a process of accumulation of forces. As it advances and is better defined, it wins more support and is eventually considered inevitable, even by those who don't support it."

For any such reform to be fruitful, *persistence over time* is decisive. Without it, no change has any possibility of succeeding. In view of the deep-rooted cultures and characteristics particular to the legal milieu, it may take a long time to win the trust of the actors involved, design the changes, and, most importantly, implement them. Only consistency over time ensures the ability to successfully take on counter-reform efforts that inevitably come up in matters such as these, and, as experience shows, often prevail.[85] In the Basque case, there have been 10 uninterrupted years of reforms that have just recently begun to bear fruit, and which still need a few more years to mature.

Leadership

Leadership is extremely important to the reform process. In the Basque case, leadership has clearly come from the executive. The advantages of leadership from the executive instead of the judiciary are clear. The purpose of the executive is to develop public policy to benefit the general public, to which end it has (or should have) two essential assets: popular legitimacy and technical capacity. In addition, the executive is sufficiently distanced from the object of the reform to be in a position to decide on the best options without compromising its own interests. In this regard, the executive can best represent the *user*'s interest, which should be the guidepost for the reform.

It is more difficult for that to happen from within the judiciary, since it does not have the popular legitimacy needed to carry out changes that require large investments, and it generally lacks sufficient technical capacity to undertake the most radical reforms. When the initiative for change is placed in the judiciary, the Supreme Court usually plays the leading role. Unfortunately, circumstances often dictate that these courts themselves should be targeted for change. It is difficult to assume the role of both judge and party. For the same reason, it is difficult for the judiciary to properly administer both the carrots and the sticks, which is fundamental for a reform process. Often they give out the carrots without ever recurring to the sticks. What judiciary, for example, is able to withstand an internal strike to impose a modernization program on judicial personnel?

The possible disadvantage of the executive assuming leadership is that decisions become politicized and there can be undue intervention in what are properly judicial matters. Despite problems from time to time in this respect that are typical to any democracy, this kind of politicization has not occurred in Spain. In Latin America, however, the situation is quite different in many countries, an important

---

[85] If one were to draw up a list of failed justice reforms in Latin America and seek a common cause for all of them, no doubt it would be the lack of consistency over time.

consideration when determining who should have what powers. Nonetheless, the limitation on internal interference implicit in giving the Supreme Court reform powers reinforces the preeminence of these courts over all other courts, structuring the judiciary vertically in matters not related to judicial concerns. This approach, as the Latin American experience also indicates, has drawbacks related to internal rather than external independence.[86]

In any event, if leadership by the executive involves interference in the work of the judiciary, the reform process will not meet preconditions for success, particularly in terms of moving beyond political parties and persisting over time.

Participation

The fact that the initiative for reform comes from outside the judiciary must not involve distancing the judges, judicial staff and other relevant actors from the reform process. Moreover, getting them actively involved in the change should be one of the reform leaders' essential objectives. In the Basque experience, care has been taken to separate out the roles appropriately, but having done this, an ongoing effort has been made to work together with all the actors. On the one hand, the judges have been accorded a political and social role that should be respected in the changes. On the other, it has been considered that the particulars of judicial work are fully known only by those who do that work. Thus, once the issue of leadership was cleared up, an effort was made to generate a dialogue through the use of the Mixed Committees, and to take advantage of opportunities for working together.

In order for such participation to be efficient, it is essential to find common ground with the judiciary, which the Basque government attained by including in its teams judicial staff who shared its vision of the changes. In addition, it is fundamental that the formal links between the institutions be well defined and placed in the hands of persons who have sufficient powers and legitimacy. We have already described the importance of the chief judges in this regard.

To avoid friction, it is important to reduce to a minimum the number of protagonists, and even to give up some of the medals achieved through successful reforms. A shared sense of initiative, responsibility and credit for the reform is crucial. Finally, in order to win over all the actors to the reform, it is essential to adequately administer the benefits the reforms may produce. There should be dividends, but always in exchange for taking a new step along the path of modern-

---

[86] One alternative is that these powers be held by the judicial councils, as is common in Latin America. However, executive intervention in these councils can be a problem. Meanwhile, this approach precludes the reform process from benefiting from the advantages of executive involvement, such as popular legitimacy and technical capacity.

ization. In the Basque case, some of these benefits may not appear to be very profitable from a narrow perspective on the effectiveness of a reform, but in the long run they have proven essential to making it happen. And so general or partial salary increases have been negotiated, or subsidies have been provided for the purchase of housing, etc.

Besides judges and judicial officers, lawyers have also been directly affected by the reforms, particularly the one involving provision of free legal services. This reform was aimed at clamping down on the payment of subsidies in order to reduce fraud. An estimated 30 percent of the total amount paid out for such services was believed to be fraudulent. The reform to the judicial office also affected lawyers, who lost much of the direct contact they generally had with judicial staff. This change eliminated corrupt schemes in which some lawyers had participated. All this was resented by the lawyers. Consequently, rather than assuming the role of agents of change as they might have, the lawyers became just one more sector that had to be persuaded to go along with the reform process.

Finally, special efforts also had to be made to include the national entities—the Ministry of Justice and the CGPJ—in the process of change. The Basque government was convinced that many of the solutions it came up with were best not only for the Basque Country, but for all of Spain as well.

Technical Work

Both leadership and rigorous technical work demand a solid and competent professional team that can bring reforms to fruition. In the Basque experience, the team is made up of professionals from a variety of disciplines and backgrounds, which gives it special strength and shows that multidisciplinary work is the only way to overcome the problems associated with longstanding modes of operation of the justice system. The composition of this team has varied over time, but it has maintained a consistent character that in part helps explain the stability of the policies implemented.[87] In general, there is a highly flexible work methodology with clear leadership, but also with ample room for maneuver for the persons with responsibility.

Of course, the direction of the changes answers not only to the capacity of this team. It is also fundamental that the judicial reform process be able to draw on all the knowledge available. The Basques achieved this through a careful study of certain comparative experiences and by contracting specialized business services for the areas where specific technical developments were needed. To avoid becom-

---

[87] A key factor here is also the basic structure of the Spanish bureaucracy, which brings together demanding systems of selection, job security and reasonably competitive remuneration.

ing trapped by the contractors, the leadership of the reform process must itself have sufficient technical capacity to negotiate on equal footing.

In the Basque experience, no other actors, such as universities or civil society organizations, have put forth ideas or proposals for the reform process. This is not surprising with regard to universities, for rarely have they played an active role in this area.[88] The lack of participation by the Basque Country's generally active civil society organizations is more disconcerting.

Short-term Results

It is essential to consider how to best make a quick and clear impact in order to sustain the reform. Long-term changes are costly and can generate resistance, which has the potential to doom them to failure. Having to come up with quick results is not always consistent with long-term objectives, but it is a compromise that involves gains in its own right. One needs to adequately gauge how much emphasis to place on short-term results without mortgaging the ultimate goals of the reform process. Such an analysis was carried out in the Basque Country:

> The transfer suggested two distinct levels of intervention, which in my opinion are present in any judicial reform, independent of time and place: the short term, dominated by reforms that are immediately plain to see, and the long-term, which, freed from that need, looks to make use of the increase in resources and the already-existing resources in a different way, so as to make more efficient use of them. Of course, these two levels of intervention may be contradictory. (Elorza and Guerra, 1996)

The Basques put infrastructure in place that could quickly help lawyers and legal staff overcome some of their most pressing problems. In addition, immediate steps were taken regarding information technology, though these did not receive as positive an evaluation as the infrastructure works. Both actions showed that the new authorities were committed to the sector and made it possible to consolidate an appropriate relationship with the representatives of the judiciary. Clearly less controversial than the more in-depth and definitive changes, these measures helped the various actors in the reform process get to know one another and gain the experience that would enable them to address more complex challenges in the future.

---

[88] There was been some cooperation from the Law and Sociology Institute of Oñati, but none from the Institutes of Criminal Procedure and Criminology.

The Role of Law Reform

Law reform is traditionally the main tool for introducing changes in the judicial sector. Consistent with the characteristics of the Spanish autonomy process, however, this was not among the powers devolved to autonomous communities, which consequently had to develop their own strategies for change.

How have they done it? From the outset, they recognized that there is considerable room to make changes to a judicial system without changing the law. This explains how it is that working with the same laws, some courts work reasonably well and others work poorly. There are judges who act with procedural immediacy and others who do not. Furthermore, the laws are not so rigid as to allow for a single interpretation. Interpreted with a progressive view, they can address situations that could not possibly have been foreseen when they were adopted.[89]

This does this mean that there have not been changes in laws during the reform process. At the initiative of the Basque government, changes to the national Organic Law on the Judiciary were approved in 1994 to formally incorporate computer resources and common services into the judicial organization.[90] Nonetheless, this strategy, even in the Spanish context where many of the most basic definitions are adequately incorporated in the law, poses serious problems:

> I believe there are constitutional deficiencies, not in the definition of the judicial branch or in its independence, but in the support services for the judiciary, and from the perspective of providing a public service to citizens. There has been a major failure to define powers that in the medium and long term, if not in the short term, are going to lead to problems that the citizens are not going to understand. I believe there needs to be a new Organic Law on the Judiciary. (Sánchez, 1998)

These shortcomings were especially evident so long as the autonomous community didn't have any authority over judicial employees:

> In order for the action of the community to effectively impact the reality of the justice system, it needs to have authority over the real agent of change in any organization: human resources. As our autonomous community lacks authority over fundamental aspects of human resource management—understanding management to mean the selection and assignment of personnel, training and development—our ideas on modernization of the judicial office will have little or no meaning, and it will

---

[89] The Basques recognize that they have stretched certain rules to some extent.
[90] Organic Law 16/1994, of November 8. The Ministry of Justice now wants to derogate this very provision.

be difficult to effectively plan. Such planning—in terms of determining the dimensions of the spaces that are to house the judicial organs, and in terms of designing computerized work stations, to cite just some examples—is entrusted to the Department of Justice. (García, 1994)

Even more important than defining institutional powers in the leadership of the judiciary is having to intervene in systems plagued by deficiencies in the definition of functions and how they are carried out, without being able to change them. No doubt many efforts in the form of infrastructure buttress a system in need of even more profound changes.

One of the clearest examples of this is to create common services and place them under the responsibility of the clerks. No one can question that the clerks are not administrators and that it would be difficult for them to be so even if they were given training in administration, since their function is defined in radically different terms.[91] In addition, few people believe that the function of "ensuring the public faith" *(velar por la fé pública)* in judicial proceedings adds any value. Writes Cao (1994, p. 173): "The outmoded and anachronistic practice of attesting to authenticity today has become a mere ritual formula and ultimately an ambiguous assignment of responsibilities to the directors of the judicial offices."

Nonetheless, the reforms have not been capable of radically redefining this role. What has been said of the clerks also applies to the other staff. The categories of court administrative personnel, for example, have little to do with what one should find in a modern court. The same can be said of judicial procedures that could undergo reforms in key areas that would yield great benefits for procedural immediacy and speedy process, which would go a long way to adapting them to the new guidelines for the judicial office.

From the Latin American perspective, it is difficult to conceive of a reform that would renounce the drafting of new legislation as a mechanism for improving the workings of the judiciary. Without it, the scope of change would be limited, and legislative reform of the judiciary might fall into the hands of counter-reformers.[92] Changes at the management level inserted into highly deficient systems may legitimize and strengthen such systems, as it may make little sense to change them once major investments have been made.

Even more important is the argument that a reform aimed at redesigning a country's judicial system must include mechanisms to ensure expression of the popular will. In Latin America, that mechanism is no more than the process of adopting a

---

[91] Some clerks indeed have special administrative skills, which should be put to good use. But they should not always be guaranteed the jobs and should have to compete with professional administrators for them.
[92] Something similar may be happening in Spain with the initiative to amend the Organic Law on the Judiciary.

law. An alternative position would accept that technocratic criteria suffice for dealing with those other issues, there being no need to hear the voice of the citizens.

What has been said should not be interpreted as meaning that legal changes are a precondition for initiating any reform in the sector. The very experience of the Basque Country certainly indicates otherwise. It shows that such changes, sooner or later, should draw on legislative reforms in order to be as effective as possible and achieve a radical transformation of a sector that is regulated to the smallest detail.

Judicial reform entails many changes in law that are certainly important. Yet legislation is but one of several tools that should be used in the process, as on its own it tends not to solve problems. Judicial reform implies a change that is no doubt much more complex than the mere adoption of a law. When one speaks of implementing reforms, reference is being made to human and financial resources, to managing and organizing them rationally, and, in large measure, to a cultural change in the thinking, habits and work styles of lawyers and legal staff.

The main tool for addressing these elements of reform is human resource training, including education and training of lawyers, legal staff, and the general public. Activities are needed to incorporate those who should carry out the changes into their design, financing and implementation. The effort will meet with success only to the extent that the people involved internalize the virtues entailed in changes that, in judicial affairs, are usually traumatic, particularly in organizational structures traditionally resistant to change.

The Costs of Reform

The economic factor is extremely important in a judicial reform process. The sector has generally been so abandoned by public policy that the investments needed are relatively large. Changes in management are especially costly, although other approaches to reform can be expensive as well, since implementation of whatever approach is used will necessarily involve management issues. In other words, all the changes in this sector somehow touch on such issues as infrastructure, information technology, and organization of judicial offices.

As occurs in any sector, budget allotments are the best indicator for assessing whether there is political will to carry out change, and to accord it greater prominence. This is particularly important in an area such as the justice system, where, unfortunately, reforms are often more rhetorical than real, and as such lack the resources necessary to go from initiative to reality.

The great challenge in obtaining those resources is to design well structured and socially and politically attractive reform programs. They must be accompanied by instruments that make it possible to show the social profitability of such investments. Only in this way will the justice sector successfully compete with the other social areas for the same scarce resources.

BIBLIOGRAPHY

Alloza Arasa, Ramón. 1994. Funciones de los Diferentes Cuerpos y Carreras. In *La Oficina judicial*. Vitoria-Gasteiz: Servicio Central de Publicaciones del Gobierno Vasco.

Basque Government. Undated (a). Resumen de Actividades de la EAT de Álava. Unpublished.

————. Undated (b). Guía Técnica para el Tratamiento Documental y Recuperación de Resoluciones. Unpublished.

————. Undated (c). Guía Información para el Candidato a Jurado. Unpublished.

————. 1998a. Planes de Actuación con Adolescentes y Jóvenes Infractores en la Comunidad Autónoma del País Vasco. Unpublished.

————. 1998b. La Administración de Justicia en el País Vasco: Una Década de Gestión en Justicia. Unpublished.

————. 1998c. Actuaciones de la Viceconsejería de Justicia en la Legislatura 1994-98. Unpublished.

————. 1998d. *Estatuto de Autonomía del País Vasco*. Vitoria-Gasteiz: Servicio Central de Publicaciones del Gobierno Vasco.

————. 1998e. *Programa de Formación para Jueces y Magistrados de la Comunidad Autónoma del País Vasco*. Vitoria-Gasteiz: Servicio Central de Publicaciones del Gobierno Vasco.

————. 1998f. *Programa de Formación y Euskaldunización para el Personal al Servicio de la Administración de Justicia*. Vitoria-Gasteiz: Servicio Central de Publicaciones del Gobierno Vasco.

————. 1998g. *Guía Básica de la Justicia*. Vitoria-Gasteiz: Servicio Central de Publicaciones del Gobierno Vasco.

————. 1998h. *Servicio de Mediación Familiar*. Vitoria-Gasteiz: Servicio Central de Publicaciones del Gobierno Vasco.

————. 1997a. *Servicios de Asistencia y Orientación Social al Detenido en la C.A.P.V. (años 1991-1996)*. Vitoria-Gasteiz: Servicio Central de Publicaciones del Gobierno Vasco.

————. 1997b. *Servicios de Asistencia a las Víctimas en el País Vasco (años 1991-1996)*. Vitoria-Gasteiz: Servicio Central de Publicaciones del Gobierno Vasco.

————. 1997c. *Acuerdo sobre la Modernización en la Prestación del Servicio Público de la Justicia y su Repercusión en las Condiciones de Trabajo del Personal al Servicio de la Administración de Justicia del País Vasco*. Vitoria-Gasteiz: Artes Gráficas Elkar.

————. 1997d. Los Vascos y la Administración de Justicia en la CAPV. Unpublished.

_____ . 1991. *Propuesta de Modernización de la Administración de Justicia*. Vitoria-Gasteiz: Servicio Central de Publicaciones del Gobierno Vasco.

Cao Barredo, María Antonia. 1994. Organización, Estructura y Diseño de las Oficinas Judiciales. In *La Oficina judicial*. Vitoria-Gasteiz: Servicio Central de Publicaciones del Gobierno Vasco.

Centro de Documentación Judicial. 1997. *Boletín Informativo Nº 0*.

Consejo General del Poder Judicial. 1997. *Libro Blanco de la Justicia*. Madrid: Consejo General del Poder Judicial.

Cremades Morant, Juan Bautista. 1994. Corrupción, Disfunciones y Atención al Ciudadano. In *La Oficina judicial*. Vitoria-Gasteiz: Servicio Central de Publicaciones del Gobierno Vasco.

Del Valle Carriles, Eduardo. 1994. Funciones de Diferentes Cuerpos y Carreras. In *La Oficina judicial*. Vitoria-Gasteiz: Servicio Central de Publicaciones del Gobierno Vasco.

Dóvalo Taboada, José. 1994. Organización, Estructura y Diseño de las Oficinas Judiciales. In *La Oficina judicial*. Vitoria-Gasteiz: Servicio Central de Publicaciones del Gobierno Vasco.

Elorza, Mikel y Guerra, Antonio. 1996. Enseñanzas de la Experiencia de la Reforma Judicial en el País Vasco. Unpublished.

Garavilla, Manuel. 1998. Servicio Común de Notificaciones. Unpublished.

_____ . 1997. Optimización de la Oficina judicial. Unpublished.

García Hidalgo, Víctor. 1994. Competencias en Materia de Administración de Justicia. Colaboración. Transferencias. In *La Oficina judicial*. Vitoria-Gasteiz: Servicio Central de Publicaciones del Gobierno Vasco.

Guerra Gimeno, Antonio. 1994. Organización, Estructura y Diseño de las Oficinas Judiciales. In *La Oficina judicial*. Vitoria-Gasteiz: Servicio Central de Publicaciones del Gobierno Vasco.

Jiménez Asensio, Rafael. 1994. Funciones de los Diferentes Cuerpos y Carreras. In *La Oficina Judicial*. Vitoria-Gasteiz: Servicio Central de Publicaciones del Gobierno Vasco.

Sánchez Guiu, Iñaki. Undated. La Informática Judicial en la Comunidad Autónoma del País Vasco. Unpublished.

_____ . 1998. Costo y Efectividad de la Justicia. Conferencia en la Universidad Carlos III. Unpublished.

Xiol Ríos, Juan Antonio. 1994. Reforma a la Oficina judicial. In *La Oficina judicial*. Vitoria-Gasteiz: Servicio Central de Publicaciones del Gobierno Vasco.